WHAT PEOPLE ARE SAYING ABOUT
THE LOST ART OF LINGERING

Mention "spiritual mentoring" and most people think of a one-directional relationship in which an experienced person imparts information to one who knows less. Yet most people want mentors who will pass on something deeper than content: wisdom. And they want it in the context of give-and-take "mutual fascination" that recognizes both people as having something to offer. In his book, *The Lost Art of Lingering: Mutual Mentoring for Life Transformation*, Rowland Forman speaks to those seeking such a listen-and-learn model of discipleship. Taking the pressure off mentors to know it all and mentees to hold back, he provides a clear, accessible guide for ordinary people wishing to meet and share their lives in a way that leads to transformation. Forman includes primary practices, such as prayer, reflecting and multiplying, in a book that guides, rather than dictates meaningful conversations.

Sandra Glahn, Author, Coffee Cup Bible series,
Editor-in-Chief, Kindred Spirit

Someone once said that the kingdom of God advances through spiritual friendship. In *The Lost Art of Lingering*, Rowland Forman sketches a beautiful portrait of spiritual friendships and provides an actionable blueprint for how to build them. Rooted in mature reflection on Scripture seasoned with years of personal experience, and steeped in the good news of the gospel of grace, here is a book that can change your church, your relationships and your life.

Brian Hedges, Pastor, and author of Christ Formed in You

Rowland Forman has awakened the nerve that has long been dulled. In this seminal book, Forman ushers us back to Jesus' design of how life and love were to be transferred: through thoughtful, intentional, even time-consuming mentoring. In a world of convenient sound bytes and insta-everything, The Lost Art of Lingering is a refreshing reminder that the true transfer of life only happens up close and personal.

Dr. Wayne Cordeiro, Senior Pastor,
New Hope Christian Fellowship, Honolulu, Hawaii,
and author of Leading on Empty

The Lost Art of Lingering will be my #1 go-to resource on mentoring and life transformation. I highly recommend it for the mentoring novice and for experienced mentors alike. Comprehensive, filled with Scriptural applications, practical mentoring habits, mentoring commentaries and additional mentoring resources, it will undoubtedly become one of the best mentoring handbooks ever written.

Linda Stanley, Team Leader,
Leadership Community Director, Leadership Network

This is not a textbook. It is not a "How-to" manual. It reads as if you were sitting with a master mentor over a cup of coffee and learning to live life as Jesus intended. With real-life stories, crisp examples and rich biblical reflection, Rowland helps us discover that the greatest life transformation comes when we learn to linger, share our heart and encounter the Holy Spirit who meets with us.

Rev. Dr. Kevin G. Harney, Pastor,
Shoreline Community Church, Monterey, California,
and author of Reckless Faith.

The message of this book is greatly needed in the contemporary church. In conforming to the cultural pattern of incessant busyness, we have tended to neglect the importance of spending time with a few others in meaningful, purposeful, transformative and spiritual relationships. Rowland gently makes a compelling case that we need to consider re-prioritizing our time in a way that elevates mutual mentoring to a top priority. I am grateful for the many practical insights and ideas he provides that guide us into making the most of these regular times with others.

Dr. Clinton E. Arnold, Dean and Professor of New Testament,
Talbot School of Theology

If you're hungry for a life of discipleship in the company of others, Forman's book is a smorgasbord of the finest fare. With a generous spirit, he embraces a wide range of approaches and distills the essence of "one-anothering" into insightful teaching, engaging reflections and a host of practical tools and resources. This is a book you'll return to over and over again in the years ahead, such is the wealth of wisdom it contains. This is the most useful and encouraging book on mentoring that I've read for many years.

Dr. Rick Lewis, Mentoring Coordinator,
New South Wales, Australia, and author of Mentoring Matters

If you hunger for deep friendships with mutual spiritual encouragement, Rowland's book will help show you a path that leads to the rich relational world you long to experience. This is not a program, a complex system or a quick fix for relationships. Rowland offers a biblical vision for mutual encouragement and learning in spiritual friendships. If you long to have richer relationships where Christ is in the center and growth in godliness is the natural outgrowth, this book will help you walk this path with friends who also long for more in their relational world.

Sherry Harney, Author, Speaker and
Director of Women's Ministry at
Shoreline Community Church, Monterey, California

This book is a catalytic call for a multiplying movement. Rowland is the "Picasso" of mentoring. His art strokes can be seen at significant milestones and seasons in my own life. Simple conversations over good coffee have served as powerful catalysts. I encourage you to brew a good coffee and savour this book.

Jonathan Dove, Lead Pastor, Mount Albert Baptist Church,
Auckland, New Zealand

Reading *The Lost Art of Lingering* is like sitting in an easy chair reading a good novel, and ending up learning that new language you wanted to learn but always found the task too daunting. *The Lost Art of Lingering* is a well told story that is enjoyable to read. The topic is one that every leader wants to do well but the learning curve seems overwhelming and the success rate dismal. Rowland Forman makes mentoring practical, accessible and natural. It is a book of profound wisdom dispensed in simple strokes. I highly recommend this book for leaders at every stage of life.

Brad Smith, President, Bakke Graduate University

The Lost Art of Lingering is a book that will touch the life of every Christ follower. It's both intensely biblical and practical. Honesty and vulnerability flows throughout. It's both structural and fluid. It demonstrates, however, how every member of the body of Christ should and can function. Furthermore, it reflects the life of a man who "walks his talk," which I have observed "up close and personal."

Dr. Gene A. Getz, President, Center for Church Renewal,
and author of *The Measure of a Man*

Life is exceedingly busy for most of us. Taking time to slow down, to reflect and to spiritually grow in the context of the Christian community is something we all desperately need to do, but where does one start? In *The Lost Art of Lingering*, Rowland Forman with pastoral wisdom, personal candour and rich biblical insight, provides us a compelling place to begin. In this book he invites the reader on a journey to consider the significance of mutual mentoring as he traverses through the why, what and how of spiritual leadership. Each chapter provides deep food for thought for both the mind and the soul, and at the same time puts one on the trajectory to application and practice. In our media-saturated and time-deprived culture, we urgently need to hear the message of this book.

Dr. Malcolm Gill, Lecturer New Testament, and Preaching,
Sydney Missionary & Bible College, Sydney, Australia

Almost every pastor I know values mentoring enormously but struggles over how to make it a consistent part of their life, let alone a part of their ministry. What makes it all the more frustrating has been the lack of any solid resource on mentoring—until now. *The Lost Art of Lingering* is more than just a book on mentoring; it is a guide, a tool box and a starting point for anyone looking to leave a legacy with their life. You will go back to this book often.

Drew Leaver, Lead Pastor, Northeast Bible Church,
San Antonio, Texas

We live in a world of constant activity and overwhelming access to information. Yet this frenzied world seems to have lost the inestimable richness of true relationship. This book is convicting for busy people like me, but also profoundly stirring. I feel stirred not to greater activity, but to slow down and linger for the sake of genuine life-giving relationship. Let this book nudge you back into the Bible with eyes to see the relational hues on every page. When we see the kind of God revealed to us in the Bible, what could be more important than genuine life-giving relationship?

Dr. Peter Mead, Director and Co-Mentor of Cor Deo,
a UK-based mentored training program

Are mutually impactful relationships as described in this book too good to be true? Do relationships like this really exist? As one of many who have been profoundly impacted by hours lingering with the author, I can assure you that the approach to transformational mentoring outlined in this vitally important book really works.

Jason Williams, Legacy Campus Pastor,
Chase Oaks Church, Plano, Texas

The Lost Art of Lingering is a book written by a man who knows and lives what he's talking about. It is well written, comprehensive and applied, filled with practical examples and useful exercises. It is a resourceful practitioner guide for the experienced mentor as well as for the emerging leader.

Dr. Ditmar Pauck,
International CCBT Catalyst, Coach, Mentor and Pastor,
Sao Paulo, Brazil

It often said, "Those who can, do. Those who can't, teach." As someone who has benefited immeasurably from Rowland Forman's "lingering" in my life, I am thrilled to report that he is able to both do *and* teach. If you long to be a part of relationships that imprint the soul but wonder how to help them emerge, you will want to have this book within reach. I am thrilled to recommend it to you.

Chris Freeland, Senior Pastor,
McKinney Church, Fort Worth, Texas

Many people think about being a mentor to others, but don't know how or even where to start. Well, Rowland Forman is a man that has God's heart for mentoring! Read this book and be prepared to watch lives change—including yours.

Norm Miller, Chairman of the Board, Interstate Batteries

Forman braids biblical truth, the wisdom of many counsellors and personal experience into a practical, effective guide to mentoring. This book is a refreshing mix of personal stories and sage advice for those of us who seek to catalyze positive transformation in the lives of others. Its 10 "practices that may become habits" are relevant to many forms of mentoring and speak to my educator's heart. I am particularly impressed with Forman's ability to integrate the best advice from so many other sources. As an exceptional mentor, he clearly "lives in this space."

Michael Higgs,
Professor and Chair of Math and Computer Science,
Austin College

The Lost Art of Lingering

Mutual Mentoring for Life Transformation

by Rowland Forman

Entrust Source Publishers is committed to partnering with local churches by providing biblically based, culturally relevant and highly practical resources to help individuals and groups in the local church to mature in Christ. For more information please go to www.entrustsource.com or call 520-885-9278.

The Lost Art of Lingering. All rights reserved. No part of this publication may be reproduced, stored in a retrieval system, or transmitted in any form by any means—electronic, mechanical, photocopy, recording, or any other—except for brief quotations in printer reviews, without the prior permission of the publisher, except as follows: Individuals may make copies of the Resources for personal use or for classroom or seminar use, not to exceed one copy per attendee.

ISBN-13: 978-1-942308-57-7

© Copyright 2025 Entrust Source LLC
. *All rights reserved.*

Cover illustration by Greg Holmes.

Printed in the United States of America

Unless otherwise noted, Scripture taken from the HOLY BIBLE, NEW INTERNATIONAL VERSION. Copyright © 1973, 1978, 1984 International Bible Society.
Used by permission of Zondervan Publishing House.

Scripture quotations marked (ESV) are taken from the HOLY BIBLE, English Standard Version®.
Copyright © 2001 by Crossway, a publishing ministry of Good News Publishers.
All rights reserved.
ESV Text Edition: 2007

Scripture quotations marked (NLT) are taken from the Holy Bible,
New Living Translation.
Copyright © 1996, 2004, 2007 by Tyndale House Foundation. Used by permission of Tyndale House Publishers, Inc., Carol Stream, Illinois 60188. All rights reserved.

Scripture quotations marked J. B. Phillips version are taken from *"The New Testament in Modern English,"* published by HarperCollins, 1962 edition.

Entrust Source Publishers
281 Camino la Pasida
Rio Rico, AZ 85648

To Elaine
my loving wife, God-given mutual mentor and sacred companion
on this amazing spiritual adventure.

And to her soul-friend Barbara Debenport,
without whose encouragement and prayers
this book may never have been written.

TABLE OF CONTENTS

Foreword i
Preface v
Introduction xi

PART ONE: MORE THAN JUST A GOOD IDEA

Chapter One:	Linger to Mentor	3
Chapter Two:	Linger for Life Change	19
Chapter Three:	Linger with the Trinity	37
Chapter Four:	Linger in Community	49
Chapter Five:	Linger with One Another	61

PART TWO: PRACTICES THAT MAY BECOME HABITS

Chapter Six:	Praying	77
Chapter Seven:	Meeting	89
Chapter Eight:	Listening	101
Chapter Nine:	Asking	113
Chapter Ten:	Affirming	125
Chapter Eleven:	Admonishing	137
Chapter Twelve:	Learning	149
Chapter Thirteen:	Reflecting	163
Chapter Fourteen:	Multiplying	175
Chapter Fifteen:	Releasing	185

PART THREE: MENTORING RESOURCES

Resource One:	20 Warning Lights for Highly Vulnerable Leaders (Matthew 5-7)	199
Resource Two:	Lingering on the Emmaus Road (Luke 24:13-35)	241
Resource Three:	Holy Discontent (2 Peter 1:3-11)	251
Resource Four:	The Art and Craft of Great Questions	259
Resource Five:	Mentoring and Discipleship Books to Linger Over	271
Resource Six:	The Biblical One-Anothers	283
Resource Seven:	Lingering Together Wisely: The WISDOM Process™	289
Gratitudes		293
Notes		297

FOREWORD

Having read many books on mentoring, it's easy to think, "Not one more?" But what *The Lost Art of Lingering* gives us is deeper and richer than anything available on the topic. Beyond clichés and formulas, it gently paints a compelling picture of mentoring, one that makes you want to be part of it.

Virtually every leader we know values mentoring as a concept, but very few do it well. From our own experience, and the examples of leadership development in the Bible, we know that mentoring is by far the most effective way to build leaders. We all, therefore, really do want to be great mentors. Yet, most of us just aren't. Only a small percentage of leaders are naturally gifted mentors, for whom mentoring seems as easy as breathing. Rowland is one of those gifted mentors who doesn't just value mentoring, or speak about it, or write books about it. He actually does mentoring, and does it well.

We should know, because we are recipients of his mentoring friendship in our own lives and have seen him interact with hundreds of leaders over the years. When something we value is not natural to us, we need some structure and systems to help guide us. That's the gift *The Lost Art of Lingering* offers us.

For nearly 20 years we've benefited from Rowland's lingering with us, sometimes on a regular basis and at times more periodically. He lives what he writes, so each chapter drips with reality in story after story of real people. With appealing transparency he does not shy away from success or failure in his mutual mentoring. This book comes not from the deadline of a publisher asking for a book on a hot topic, but from the overflow of a lifetime living and reflecting on mentoring.

Reading *The Lost Art of Lingering* gives you a gallery of the best quotes from the best books on mentoring. As an avid reader and quote collector, the author treats us with richly colored quotes from the best writers on the topic, which gives you a sense of having read a library on mentoring.

As a deeply spiritual man who has walked closely with Jesus for a long time, Rowland takes us on a spiritual journey. This book offers far more than a manual on how to mentor; although it does give great practical help. It sculpts spiritually deep truths in a way that convicts and inspires.

If you are looking for the "guru-on-a-hill" type mentoring book, where the mentee climbs up the mountain to be enlightened by the all-knowing sage, this is not it. Healthy mentoring doesn't work that way. Healthy mentoring takes into account mutuality, that mentoring is an ongoing reciprocal interaction that combines intentionality, relationship and time.

Most people do not feel qualified to mentor anyone. If you ask people to sign up for mentoring in your church, nearly everyone wants to be mentored, not to mentor. Rowland understands that dynamic and his approach cuts through it. He shows how any Christian can mentor another Christian in practical and yet powerful ways. At once, he demystifies mentoring and fills it with spiritual depth.

As pastors we would love every person in our church to benefit from reading this book. Read thoughtfully, it's the kind of book that spurs spiritual growth, and more than that, motivates a person to help someone else grow as well. The author understands the reality of the local church and shows how mentoring can be threaded into the fabric of relationships without creating yet another program.

Sometimes people in our churches fall into simply going to lunch or "hanging out" with a mentoring label attached. We might call it organic discipleship. And yet not that much of spiritual value happens. On the other end of the spectrum are folks who define mentoring as going through the latest course with very specific guidelines. That can become rote, legalistic and lifeless. This book gives us very practical approaches to such transforming relationships, so that we aren't just "hanging out" or simply following a program. We are lingering in a mutually life-transforming way. The ten practices shared in the book help us spiritually impact each other.

Rowland asks great questions; ones that make you pause; ones that take you deeper into your walk with the Lord. After each chapter, he offers us tools to help us grow personally or with another person or with a group—questions and quotes that provoke thought and conversation on the Scriptures and the truths drawn from the Word of God. This is one of those great books to read with another person or a group.

The author's gentle, humble approach draws you in and convinces you that God could use even you to mutually mentor another person so that you are both transformed by the Spirit for the glory of God. If you read one book on mentoring, this is it.

Thankful for the life-transforming friendship we share,

Jeff Jones and Bruce Miller

PREFACE

*"And he said to them,
'Follow me, and I will make you fishers of men.'"*
—Matthew 4:19 (ESV)

*"As with the journey Abraham was asked to undertake, it is
impossible to specify precisely the route that has to be followed
in a soul's journey of transformation. This is because rather than
following a map, in this journey we follow a person—Jesus. …
Spiritual friends help us most when they make clear their job is to
point the way, not to lead the way.
And the Way to which they should point is Jesus."*[1]
—David Benner

This book is written for ordinary Christ-followers who long to experience whole-life transformation through a mentoring friendship but find the concept a bit daunting. How do you start the relationship? Whom should you approach? You've tried for months to locate a mentor—a sage, someone wiser and more mature—but all the people you have approached are unavailable and somewhat intimidated by the prospect. You hesitate to ask the most suitable and talented person because he or she seems so busy and is already in a mentoring relationship with several others.

The Lost Art of Lingering is also written for church leaders who dream about a day when mentoring friendships will become the norm in their church, folded into every aspect of church life, rather than the domain of a few very dedicated people. They dream about a day when every person in their church has a spiritual friend that nudges them toward greater likeness to Jesus. They long for a day when all of their leadership meetings and all of their small groups become opportunities to experience Spirit-orchestrated transformational friendships.

Another reason for writing this book relates to my stage of life. In his book *A Resilient Life,* Gordon MacDonald describes how he asked God to give him a fresh sense of calling at age 67. That got my attention as I'm in the same age bracket. After his prayer, Gordon spoke at two leadership gatherings, one in Germany and one in the United States. The leaders who thanked him at the conclusion on both occasions said something like, "Gordon, you speak like a father and so many of us are spiritually fatherless." In that moment, he felt God whisper, *You've got your call. Be a father to a younger generation. Speak like a father; talk to younger men and women like one; write like one.*[2]

I wept when I read that as it captured this stage of my journey. God has graced me with many spiritual friends who look to me as a mentor-father of sorts. This book is in part a response to their request for help in how to become a mentor in a way that is more like what Lois Zachary calls a "guide on the side," than a "sage on the stage."[3]

More Mature to Less Mature Phase

God has blessed me greatly through my mentors—spiritual mothers and fathers who invested in my life. As you will hear throughout this book, my very private Scottish grandmother, Bella-Jane Miller, was one of those. When I was a young boy, she sat me on her knee and told me countless Bible stories, always with passion, sometimes with tears. She mentored me until I was 25. I was also blessed to have input from wise men like Eric Wilson of The Navigators. He faithfully met with me every Monday morning for six years! He passed on his passion for Christ and for Scripture memory, and I'm eternally grateful.

This more mature to less mature model of mentoring has great biblical warrant. In Titus 2:3-4, Paul tells his understudy to teach older women so that they can train the younger women. And it is an approach implied in many of the "mentoring" stories in Scripture for example, Moses to Joshua, Naomi to Ruth (or is it the other way round?), Elijah to Elisha, David to Jonathan, and Paul to Timothy to name a few. That approach has biblical support but I suggest it can also be quite limiting.

In *Release Your Potential,* author and mentor Elizabeth Inrig describes how limiting mentoring to a more-mature to less-mature framework constrained the potential for mentoring in her church:

> *Most women appreciate the gracious input of older women into their lives. This was brought to my attention a few years ago when our church made a choice to intentionally match older women and younger women together for mutual nourishing. Of the seventy-five women who came to fill out the profile we had created, all but one said she wanted an older woman to mentor her! We didn't have that many "older" women. We have since disbanded our contrived matches and instead have laced every one of our ministries to women with a mentoring component. It is the backbone of the way we arrange our small groups in Bible Study. …Every stage of a woman's life becomes a means by which she can encourage others regardless of their age.*[4]

My wife Elaine and I have similarly tried to match mature with less mature individuals in churches that we have led, with varying degrees of success. We ran into the same problem Elizabeth identifies—the scarcity of mature men or women available and confident enough to mentor those less mature. We longed for another way, more like what Inrig calls lacing every ministry with a mentoring component.

Mutual Mentoring Phase

Five years ago, I realized that God was teaching me a more fluid and freeing approach: mutual mentoring (two or more people who come to listen and learn from each other). The most influential person in this chapter of my life has been Don Overton. I first met Don when I was the Director of Curriculum Development for CCBT (Centers of Church Based Training). Some people I mentor treat me like a mentor-guru. From the word go, Don had a different attitude. It was as if we were lingering and learning together. We used to meet at a French-style café in Dallas (my choice), eat what Don called "health food," and process what God was doing in our lives. Sometimes we'd share insights from a book we had been reading, but mostly we were just interacting with each other about the highs and lows of life and ministry. He was a Pastor at Fellowship Bible Church North at the time (subsequently renamed Chase Oaks Church) and always peppered me with questions. We were not long into this mentoring relationship when I opened up about some of my life challenges. Don hopped straight in with intuitive questions and advice. He is an insightful strategic thinker, and often helped me gain perspective on what was really happening.

Here's how Don describes our early get-togethers:

> *The first time I met Rowland was with a small group of men. The group had been meeting for several weeks, and our leader wanted all of us to meet men that were committed to seeing other guys really grow in Christ. So he asked Rowland to come and meet with us. I don't really remember much of what he shared at the meeting (sorry, Row!) but a couple of days later Rowland invited me to meet him for coffee. At that first meeting we chatted a bit and drank some coffee, ate something not too healthy. Rowland opened his life up to me. He gave me a window into his soul. In that first meeting he shared with me what God was showing him, a sin he was struggling with, and he asked me to speak into his life. Now you have to understand, this really messed up my idea of mentoring. I thought he was the teacher and I was the student. It turned out that his intention was nothing less than a spiritual friendship that flowed in both directions. At the end of the meeting he asked if we could meet again in the next couple of weeks. That was the beginning of a friendship, a journey, a series of conversations and memories that would truly shape both of us toward Christ-likeness.*

Don and I are in a different phase of our spiritual friendship now. He is currently the Senior Pastor of North Springs Alliance Church in Colorado Springs. If you asked us now, "Who is the mentor and who is the learner?" I think we would answer, "We are." Sometimes Don mentors me and sometimes I mentor him. We linger together from time to time and both come with the attitude of a learner.

When some people hear the words "mutual mentoring" they say, "Oh you mean peer mentoring (two people at the same maturity level)?" I point out that while it includes peer mentoring, mutual mentoring is more of an attitude than a life or maturity stage. I recall visiting Henry Rogers, the Chaplain of Interstate Batteries, in his office several years ago. I told him about my transition from a curriculum writing role to become a mentor to pastors and church leaders in Dallas, Texas and in Wellington, New Zealand. Here's how Henry recalls his thought processes and our interaction:

> *I'd just finished talking to the eighth person I had hoped to mentor me. When you find a mentor, chances are they are already busy people, not looking for more to add to their plate. All had turned me down and I was discouraged by my lack of success. I just told Rowland about this because he had asked sincerely how I was doing. After I told him he said, "I'll mentor you." Shocked at first, I replied, "Really?" Then he explained that mentoring is what he does and who he is. I was floored and humbled by his invitation to linger with a guy who had never had a mentor before.*

After that we met every week for three months at "our café," and regularly whenever I visited Dallas. In those early days, Henry definitely looked to me as his mentor. Over time our mentoring partnership became mutual. The key element in this transition was the cultivation of a listening and learning attitude on the part of both of us. Because we came to learn rather than teach, to listen rather than tell, our friendship morphed into a mutual one.

Mentor-Trainer Phase

In the last five years, God has been teaching me another key ingredient in mutual mentoring: the power of training other mentors. I have over a hundred books on mentoring in my library, most of which inspire me to be engaged in mentoring. Very few show me how. That's a significant reason for the inclusion of PART TWO in *The Lost Art of Lingering*. It includes ten practices of mutual mentoring that can become habits. Those ten practices are more art than craft, more like a jazz band than a symphony orchestra. They are not sequential, rather they are ways of implementing a humble attitude toward God's Spirit and toward the people that God gives us. They are opportunities, to use David Benner's phrase, "…to point the way, not to lead the way. And the Way to which they should point is Jesus."[5]

Come join me as we learn the art of lingering, slowing down long enough to invest time and energy in each other, so that our lives are radically transformed for God's glory. And if you are a church leader, consider using this book as a tool for training mutual mentors so that your dream of a mentoring culture in your church may one day be realized.

If you long to locate a spiritual companion that may become a mutual mentor take the first step—reach out to someone that God has already placed in your pathway. Sometimes that person will be more mature than you. At other times the person will be less mature. All of us though, as Christ-followers are a little further along the road in some aspects of life than others. So reach out with the attitude of a fellow-learner. Allow this book to inspire you, but more importantly help you discover the lost art of lingering for life transformation.

Rowland Forman

Auckland, New Zealand

INTRODUCTION

"As they approached the village to which they were going, Jesus continued on as if he were going farther. But they urged him strongly, 'Stay with us, for it is nearly evening; the day is almost over.' So he went in to stay with them. When he was at the table with them, he took bread, gave thanks, broke it and began to give it to them. Then their eyes were opened and they recognized him...."
—Luke 24:28-31

"Do you want to be a resilient person, and better, one who nurtures the resiliency of your 'happy few'? Then learn a lesson from my daughter: Learn the lesson of lingering."[6]
—Gordon MacDonald

On a recent visit to Italy I spotted people who seemed to know how to linger. It looked as if they were slowing down long enough to process life. In Cortona, one filming location for the movie *Under the Tuscan Sun*, I observed three groups: a young man with an older gentleman, leaning up against a rail and chatting for an hour or more, elderly men and women who arrived in the town square around five in the afternoon and just sat and talked for ages, and a group of young people who put a rug on the ground and lingered together well into the evening enjoying each other's company. The origin of the word "linger" c.1300 is to reside or dwell, to tarry.[7] That reminded me of the request of the two disciples on the Road to Emmaus. They asked Jesus to "stay" with them, to tarry with them, or as the King James Version puts it, "...abide with them" for the evening. That's a lost art in our Western world. We know a lot about what John Ortberg calls, "hurry sickness," but we've forgotten how to linger. *In The Life You've Always Wanted* he remarks: "One of the great illusions of our day is that hurrying will buy us more time. I pulled into a service station recently where the advertising slogan read, 'We will help you move faster.' But what if my primary need is not moving faster?"[8]

The Lost Art of Lingering is an invitation for you to engage in relational slowing—to pause long enough to practice what I call mutual mentoring: two or more people taking time to linger with each other and with the Lord Jesus through his Spirit, and over his Word. Mutual mentoring is a slow process. It's slowing long enough to allow spiritual friendships to develop and life transformation to take place over time.

I'm aware that most of the stories in this book are about my experiences mentoring men. It's my sincere desire that women and men will find the material equally accessible and impactful. I do hope that you are able to take your time with this book.

PART ONE: More Than Just a Good Idea

This is my endeavor to share a straightforward theology of mutual mentoring, and some biblical guidelines for lingering together for life transformation. Each chapter includes an invitation to process the material. This invitation is firstly at a personal level, then for you to meet with another person or a small group, to reflect on what the Holy Spirit might be saying to you.

PART TWO: Practices that May Become Habits

This section contains ten mentoring skills to fold into your own life and your mentor-partnerships. As I mentioned in the Preface, these skills are more art than craft. Some of the mentoring practices may seem awkward at first. For example, if you are more of a teacher than a listener, your compulsion will be to offer advice. I believe that all ten practices can be learned, however slowly. My suggestion is to adopt the practices in the order suggested. Pray before, during and after your time together. Just focus on that the first time. Then add the second practice. Bathe the process in prayer, then attend to the second skill—meeting regularly (discovering a suitable rhythm of planned meeting times and "as needed" times), fully (giving the other person or persons your undivided attention) and purposefully (injecting intentionality through agreed goals).

Eventually, these skills will become second nature. You will be able to apply them in the way that a jazz band improvises. A top jazz band looks so effortless, but you know that they are able to do that because of endless (and what seems at times pointless) practice. Part Two could change your one-on-one mentoring times, but also your small group experiences. Maybe God will even use it to transform the way you live?

When some people hear the word "mentoring" they hear individual-to-individual. Others think of mentoring clusters or huddles. I'm fascinated by the tendency of authors to argue for one approach to mentoring over another, as if they have found the right way, or even God's way. Some present triads (mentoring clusters of three people) or even four people (quads), others again trumpet the superior benefits of mentoring "Life Groups." Certainly, one-on-one mentoring experiences have been the most life-changing for me, but I hope to show that if mutual mentoring is to become transformational for churches, we need to find ways of folding this into all of our person-to-person get-togethers as well as our small groups.

PART THREE: Mentoring Resources

These resources provide an opportunity to inject more intentionality into your mentoring meetings. When Jesus revealed himself to the two confused disciples on the Emmaus Road, their pulses quickened as he opened the Scriptures to them. At times, when we linger together in a mentoring relationship, we just need to process life. However, the conviction behind the first three Mentoring Resources is that as we pour over God's Word, we are transformed by the renewing of our minds. Resource One is an invitation to sit at Jesus' feet as he teaches his disciples in what we know as the Sermon on the Mount. In Resource Two you will saunter along the Emmaus Road with the Risen Lord and his two disciples. Resource Three, "Holy Discontent," looks at 2 Peter 1:1-11, in the quest for us to become all that God wants us to be. Other Scripture-based studies will be provided on The Lost Art of Lingering website, www.ArtofLingering.org.

Tucked away in Resource Four are questions that I've gathered over the years. Consider folding some of these into your mentoring partnerships. Resource Five provides a brief description of some books on mentoring, and other books that may maximize your mentoring get-togethers. After I read one of those books, *The Heart of Mentoring: Ten Proven Principles for Developing People to their Fullest Potential,* by David A. Stoddard in 2004, I tried to summarize the essence of mentoring. What I wrote that day captures so much of what it means to rediscover the lost art of lingering:

1. Listening: coming with open ears to listen to each other and to the Lord.

2. Learning: coming with an open heart to hear what God wants to say to me.

3. Authenticity: desiring to be open and real with another person. Taking our masks off.

4. Friendship: developing a close trust-based relationship over time.

5. Growth: through grace-filled partnerships.

Resource Six contains the biblical one-anothers because they contain the strongest argument for mutuality in spiritual mentoring. Resource Seven introduces one of the most powerful approaches to participatory, reflective learning I've come across—The WISDOM Process™.

Options

The way you read this book will depend on where you are on your spiritual journey. It is written as a flexible resource. Part One outlines some of the "why-to's" of mutual mentoring, Part Two, ten "how-to's," and Part Three, a variety of "what-to's."

Here are some options to consider:

- Read Part One and Two through without attempting to process each chapter, then come back and interact with any or all of the chapters in the section provided. The benefit of this approach is that it will ground you in the biblical framework of the book, before you work on the practices that may become habits. If the Holy Spirit has 'given' you a mentor-partner, or you are in a mentoring cluster, consider working through the chapters together at this stage.

- Read Chapter 1, then Chapter 6 and 7 ("Praying" and "Meeting"). This would work well if you are already convinced about the power of mutual mentoring for life change. It also introduces you early on to the practical "feel" of the book. Then maybe come back and read Chapter Two, followed by Chapter Eight and Nine, and so on.

- At any stage, feel free to dip into the Resources in Part 3. For example you may want to use some of the great questions in Resource 4.

As you linger together in a mutual mentoring relationship approach each other with an attitude that says: "I've come to listen to you and to the Holy Spirit through you. I've come to learn from you and I want to be real with you. I desire a spiritual friendship with you and, most importantly, I'm a work in progress so come grow with me." Join me with a dependent attitude as we pray:

Heavenly Father,
thank you for those
who have loved me enough
to pass the baton of your truth on to me.
Lead me to people you want me to learn from
and teach me to listen to your Spirit as I listen to the people you give me.
Multiply my life I pray,
for your glory alone.
Amen.

PART ONE
More than Just a Good Idea

Investing spiritually and intentionally in another person (or group) isn't just another good idea; it is at the heart of authentic discipleship. In the conviction that it's important to change our thinking before we change our behavior, Part One contains a simple theology of mutual mentoring for life transformation.

The mutuality implied in the biblical one-anothers begins to be folded into our relationships in Christ as we come together to listen and learn, rather than talk and teach.

When we linger together over the Scriptures, in the company of the Father, Son and Spirit, something more than a mere meeting takes place—like the two disciples on the Emmaus Road, our hearts burn, and our lives are transformed. That's why each chapter has an invitation to process what you have been learning.

And when we fold mutual, spiritual mentoring partnerships into every aspect of church life, we end up with something much more than a mere mentoring ministry—a mentoring/disciplemaking culture emerges for the glory of God and the beauty of Christ's Body.

CHAPTER ONE

LINGER TO MENTOR

*"I pray for them.
I am not praying for the world,
but for those you have given me, for they are yours."*
—John 17:9

*"Making disciples by going, baptizing,
and teaching people the Word of Christ
and then enabling them to do the same thing
in other people's lives—this is the plan God has for each of us
to impact nations for the glory of Christ."*[9]
—David Platt

Before we go much further, some key questions are in order: How is the word mentoring being used in this book? How does mentoring relate to Christ-focused discipleship? Are mentoring relationships bound by certain rules, or is it a more fluid, spontaneous experience? Does mentoring take place best in a one-on-one relationship with another person, or can it be optimized best in groups? Is mentoring essential for all Christ-followers, or is it best suited to reflective types? What is the relationship between spiritual mentoring and mission?

Some Definitions

The meaning of "mentoring" varies according to the context—education, business, sports, and church settings to name a few. Educator Lois Zachary describes a mentor as "…a facilitative partner in an evolving learning relationship focused on meeting mentee learning goals and objectives."[10] The Harvard Business Essentials on *Coaching and Mentoring*, defines mentoring as "The offering of advice, information or guidance by a person with useful experience, skills, or expertise to promote another individual's personal and professional development."[11] I'm using the word mentoring in a church-based setting. Earl Creps, in his insightful book, *Reverse Mentoring* captures the context I'm writing from. He remarks,

> *My goal is to prepare spiritual leaders to apply reverse mentoring as a spiritual discipline, a way of experiencing personal formation through exercising the kind of humility that invites younger people to become our tutors.*[12]

Mentoring, in the way it is being used in *The Lost Art of Lingering* is:

A mutual, transformational, spiritual relationship.

Mutual

It is one woman or man, regardless of age maturity or status, taking time to listen to and learn from another. As I've mentioned in the Introduction, mentoring in the way I'm using the word is not limited to peer mentoring. It includes more mature people learning from, and contributing to the spiritual growth of less mature folk, as well as the other way round. As we will see in Chapter Three, mutual mentoring is a reflection of "one another" biblical commands such as "encourage one another," and "pray for one another." It is a call to exercise humility whatever your current stage of spiritual maturity.

Transformational

When Jesus called his disciples to follow him, he clearly had life-change in mind. He said, "Come follow me, and *I will make you* fishers of men."[13] In this he meant, "If you come and follow me, in the process I will bring radical change about in your character and behavior. Your primary focus now is on investing in the fish business, but as you follow me, your focus will be on investing in the people business." Mutual mentoring is *intentional* and the purpose is whole-life transformation.

Spiritual

Mentoring that produces life-transformation is spiritual in the sense that it is bathed in prayer from start to finish. That's how Jesus mentored his men. He prayed earnestly before he selected them, and just before he was crucified, he was still praying for them.

Throughout his three years of public ministry Jesus was constantly surrounded by crowds, but he primarily invested in twelve ordinary men. And his primary investment was to pray for them. Listen to his prayer recorded in John 17:

> *I have revealed you to those whom you **gave me** out of the world. They were yours; you **gave them** to me and they have obeyed your word. (v. 6)*
>
> *I pray for them. I am not praying for the world, but for those you have **given me**, for they are yours. (v. 9)*
>
> *My prayer is not that you would take them out of the world but that you protect them from the evil one. (v. 15)*
>
> *Father, I want those you have **given me** to be with me where I am, and to see my glory, the glory you have **given me** because you loved me before the creation of the world. (v. 24)*

Whom has God **"given"** you at present so that you can invest in them with a view to life-transformation? At the beginning of most months I write this prayer in my journal: "Father, who are you "giving" me at the moment?" Then, on the basis of the way Jesus focused his attention on a few rather than the many, I try to write down my "3" (my Peter, James and John), my "12" (including the Three), and once a quarter I write down the names of my wider group (Jesus had 72 key followers that he sent out two by two according to Luke 10:1). If you are of a more private disposition (like my grandmother Bella-Jane) you may just have the names of your children or grandchildren, and if my life story is anything to go by, that will be eternally significant.

Keith Anderson and Randy Reese, in their outstanding book, *Spiritual Mentoring*, capture the spiritual dimension of mentoring in this way:[14]

> *Spiritual mentoring is a triadic relationship between mentor, mentoree and the Holy Spirit, where the mentoree can discover, through the already present action of God, intimacy with God, ultimate identity as a child of God and a unique voice for kingdom responsibility.*[15]

Relationship

I've been in mentoring relationships that have felt like friendships from day one. Meeting Don Overton was like that for me. We clicked straight away. Our relationship was also mutual immediately. I have also experienced mentor-partnerships that have started out as a tentative relationship and developed into a lifelong friendship. That's why my slightly extended definition of mentoring is:

> **"A mutual, transformational, spiritual relationship that may become a friendship."**

It's interesting that the Lord Jesus did not call his Twelve disciples "friends" until the end of his three ministry years. Jesus said,

> *"Greater love has no one than this, that he lay down his life for his friends. You are my friends if you do what I command. I no longer call you servants, because a servant does not know his master's business. Instead, I have called you friends, for everything that I learned from my Father I have made known to you."*[16]

I first met Dan Debenport when he was leading a "Mini-Church" (small group). His wife Barbara, and my wife Elaine became soul friends who were mutually mentoring each other almost from day one. I enjoyed Dan's company but we were little more than acquaintances until the time I felt the Spirit's prompting to have breakfast with him. On that first meeting he mentioned that he had been asked to be an elder at Fellowship Bible Church North and that he felt ill-equipped theologically for that role. So for the next 12 weeks, we used Wayne Grudem's seminal book *Bible Doctrine*, to explore theology. In between mouthfuls of yogurt (Dan) and oatmeal with brown sugar and raisins (me) we munched on theological morsels. Dan chose the topics and always came prepared with questions that probed the pastoral implications of doctrines like God's providence or original sin. Since then, Dan and I have become lifelong spiritual companions. We have sailed together, laughed and cried together, and contributed to each other's spiritual growth. Our relationship morphed into a God-given friendship.

Discipleship and Mentoring

Is mentoring a sub-set of discipleship or is it the other way round? As I understand it, discipleship is the whole deal because it refers to Christ's call to us and our lifelong pursuit of him. I became Christ's disciple, his follower, his "learner" when I came to him, admitting my sinfulness and accepting his grace-provision through his finished work on the Cross. I came to him then, and come to him every day since, admitting my weariness and helplessness, and learning how gentle and humble he is.[17] I became a disciple of Christ at age eight, and now in my late 60's I am still, by God's grace, a maturing disciple.

A church leader is also a maturing disciple. The qualifications of elders and deacons spelled out in First Timothy 3 for example, are evidences of Christian maturity. Specifically Paul tells us, they are not "recent converts."[18] In Ephesians 4, he describes some of the dynamics of bringing people to maturity in Christ:

- Those who are leaders (he describes five categories in verse 11 — apostles, prophets, evangelists, pastors and teachers), are not merely to do works of service, they are to equip fellow believers for works of service (v. 12).

- As truth (honest speech, but probably more accurately, the truth of God's Word) is spoken in love, people grow up into spiritual maturity in Christ (v. 15).

- Every person in the body of Christ plays a part in "growing and building" each other in love (v. 16).

That sounds very much like a series of mutual, transformational spiritual relationships to me. So how does mentoring relate to discipleship? My esteemed Australian friend John Mallison, mentor-extraordinaire, described the relationship between mentoring and discipleship in this way:

> *Even with its rich origins and contemporary usage, the expression mentoring...is a poor second to the word disciplemaking in the Christian context. Our spiritual guidance, coaching, counseling, teaching, sponsoring, pastoring, resourcing, modeling, encouraging, all take on a deeper, richer, Christ-oriented dimension when we operate out of this biblical framework. God, the Father, the Son, and the Holy Spirit, is our richest resource for Christian mentoring—disciplemaking.*[19]

I love the question that author Greg Ogden asks when he recruits a mentoring triad: "Will you join me, walk with me, as we grow together as disciples of Christ? I would like to invite you to meet with me and one other person weekly for the purpose of becoming all that the Lord intended us to be."[20] And I agree with whoever decided to re-name James Houston's groundbreaking book, *The Mentored Life* (published in 2002), as *The Disciple: Following the True Mentor* (re-published in 2007). In the Introduction to the 2007 edition, Dallas Willard captures the essence of spiritual mentoring as "discipleship" when he says,

> *Discipleship affirms the unity of the present-day Christian with those who walked beside Jesus during his incarnation. To be His disciple then was to be with Him, to learn to be like Him. It was to be His student or apprentice in kingdom living. His disciples heard what He said and observed what He did, then, under His direction, they simply began to say and do the same things. They did so imperfectly but progressively. As He taught: "Everyone who is fully trained will be like his teacher" (Luke 6:40).*[21]

If the goal is to make disciples, then why use the term mentoring? I believe that it has the softer connotation of mutual learning and is a call to what pastor and author Dennis McCallum refers to as "organic disciplemaking."[22]

So what about mentoring and leadership development? If it is the task of a spiritual mentor to encourage his or her mentor-friend to become a more devoted follower of Christ, then the quest of existing pastors or elders is to recognize those who are becoming mature disciples—those who have developed credibility of character with those in the church and outside—and demonstrating the qualities of a true servant-shepherd.

Both-And

"Both-And" is one of my life mantras. Unless it's a matter of core biblical orthodoxy, I'm convinced that few issues can be resolved by "either-or" thinking. "Both-and" thinking relates to questions such as:

- Does spiritual mentoring assume a one-on-one relationship?

- How can we be truth-tellers as well as grace-givers in our mentoring relationships?

- Does mentoring require us to be highly organized or can we just flow along in our relationships?

- Is spiritual mentoring mainly for the reflective types rather than those involved actively in the mission of Christ?

Both Individual and Small Group

Some books on spiritual mentoring argue that to be truly patterned after Jesus, mentoring has to take place in small groups. They maintain that if we model our mentoring on the way the Lord trained his Twelve, a watertight case can be made for mentoring in small groups. For example when Jesus pulled his disciples aside and told them that he was on his way to Jerusalem to suffer and to die, Peter objected. He said, "Never, Lord! [an interesting oxymoron!]—there's no way this will ever happen to you."[23] Addressing Peter, Jesus said "Get behind me, Satan."[24] I'm sure that the other eleven disciples were thinking, "We've wanted to say that to you for a long time!" There are many occasions with Jesus and the Twelve where mentoring took place in community. But it is a big jump to say that because most of Jesus' mentoring episodes took place with the whole group of twelve present, therefore we must avoid at all costs, one-to-one approaches.

Similarly, a case can be made for mentoring from one individual to another. As I've mentioned previously, there are many biblical examples such as Moses with Joshua, Paul with Titus, and Jesus to Peter (John's account of Jesus' threefold reinstatement of Peter that nicely corresponds to Peter's threefold denial, certainly reads like a personal encounter).[25]

Almost all of my life I have followed the one-on-one pattern. The advantages are huge. Individual-to-individual allows for an intimacy and openness on some matters that are simply inappropriate in a mixed group. More recently though, I've become convinced that if a mentoring culture is to be established in a church, it is unlikely to take place by merely training up groups of individuals to go mentor other individuals. A mentoring culture is more likely to catch fire when it flows out of existing church structures such as small groups (addressed more fully in Chapter Four).

Both Grace-Giving and Truth-Telling

In our family, my Dad was all truth and my Mom was all grace. As kids we knew who to run to when we had done wrong. Which end of the grace-and-truth spectrum are you on? I know I find it much easier to affirm than admonish, to encourage than confront. As a mentor-friend, I'm more of a grace-giver, yet know that speaking truth in a loving way is often what is most needed. As we will see in Chapter Five, the mutuality commands reflect the need to give grace and tell truth. For example, "welcome one another" confers grace and "admonish one another" requires truth-telling.

Our goal in every mentoring relationship should be to emulate the Chief Mentor. John 1:14 says that Jesus was "full of grace and truth." I find it helpful in my mentoring conversations, whether one-on-one or in a small group to ask myself, "What would the grace position be here? How can I treat this person better than they deserve?" and "What would the truth perspective be? How can I be loving but sincerely honest about this matter?" Life transforming mentoring is all about constructing a trust relationship over time, and few things build more trust than telling the truth in love.

Both Organic and Organized

Mentoring (or if you prefer the term "disciplemaking") needs to be organic as well as organized. A both-and approach doesn't mean that we somehow try to balance organic and organized, but that we fully grasp the benefits of each.

Organic (which means "relating to or derived from living organisms,")[26] mentoring emphasizes our need as Christ's disciples to depend on the Holy Spirit. Reese and Anderson put it this way:

> *Spiritual mentoring is primarily the work of the Holy Spirit.... In practical ways spiritual mentoring is the process of a mentor assisting the mentoree to pay attention to the inner working of the Spirit.*[27]

The benefit of this dependence on the Spirit is that we are open to listen to what the Holy Spirit is saying to us through our mentor-partners.

Organized mentoring delivers us from merely recycling the same topics every time we meet. I sometimes describe the practice of mentoring as "coffee, goals, and a book." By that I mean an appointment in a relaxed setting (preferably over a really good cup of coffee!), periodic reviews to establish what the goals are for our times together, and then attaching a book that informs the discussion.

For example I've used:

- *The Life You've Always Wanted*, by John Ortberg with people who wish to explore how to build spiritual practices into the rhythm of their lives.

- *Holy Fools*, by Mathew Woodley with a leadership group that wanted to learn how to lead more like Jesus.

- *The Rest of God*, by Mark Buchanan with a frantically busy friend. It enabled both of us to harmonize more with the Sabbath rhythms God has instituted.

- *Business for the Glory of God*, by Wayne Grudem with Christian businessmen that wanted to examine whether matters like competition and profit aligned or clashed with the principles of Scripture.

- *The Grace and Truth Paradox*, by Randy Alcorn with parents and pastors. His call is to confer both grace and truth.

- *The Purity Principle*, by Randy Alcorn, with men who struggle to maintain purity of mind and action in the crucible of a sex-saturated culture.

In my mentoring relationships, books like these are merely "on-the-table"—they are not used as study material. They provide common language that we may choose to flow in and out of from time to time.

Both Reflection and Mission

In his book, *Mentoring for Mission*, Günter Krallmann says of Jesus,

> *On the basis of such with-ness, he generated a dynamic process of life transference which was meant to foster wholistic maturity in his friends and to facilitate them towards effective leadership at the same time.*[28]

Krallmann observes that Jesus never made a distinction between discipling and leadership development. Jesus' approach included mentoring, spiritual formation, leadership training and coaching. And all of that was in the context of mission. Jesus was sent by the Father into the world and sent his disciples into the world to be his representatives.

I've been dreaming for some time what it might look like in evangelical churches if we adopted a mentoring model that had the "engagement" and "disengagement" flow of Jesus with his disciples. Typically Jesus engaged in an act of compassion, involved the disciples in the experience, then withdrew with them (disengaged) to process what had happened, through story or direct teaching, and above all lots of questions. Sometimes he did the reverse—taught, then involved the disciples in mission, then debriefed again.

Now there's no way we can duplicate exactly what Jesus did, but we can model the process he used in the training of the Twelve:

- He called them to be **with him** (Mark 3:14). This amounted to the development of an intentional spiritual friendship.
- He called them to **imitation** (Matthew 4:19). They did get information, but they received spiritual formation. In Matthew

11:28-30 his call was for them to see how he dealt with people and to learn from him.

- He called them to *mission*—that they would be with him and that he would send them out to bless people (Mark 3:14, Matthew 28:19-20). His goal was to make them fishers of men.

Essentially Jesus' approach was "do and learn," "learn and do." One time he asked them to row to the other side of Lake Galilee while he went up to a mountain to pray. They got into the "perfect storm!" Jesus came to them, stilled the storm, then taught them on the importance of uncomplicated faith.[29] Other times he taught them first, then sent them out two by two.[30]

What could a "do and learn," "learn and do" routine look like in your mentoring relationships and in your church?

Mentoring then, in the way it is being discussed in *The Lost Art of Lingering* is a mutual, transformational, spiritual relationship that may morph into a God-given friendship. As we invest time and energy in each other as maturing disciples of Christ, we invite others to join us, individually, or in groups, to speak grace and truth into each other's lives, in a fluid yet organized way, all in the context of Christ's mission. When we linger together in that way, Tim Elmore's great line in Regi Campbell's book, *Mentor Like Jesus* will come true:

"More time with fewer people equals greater kingdom impact."[31]

PROCESSING CHAPTER ONE

STEP 1: **DEPEND**—SOAK THE PROCESS IN PRAYER

1. Consider this prayer by Teri Lynne Underwood as you process Chapter One:

> Lord, we are often guilty of focusing on our differences.
> Teach us to celebrate what we have in common.
> Reveal to us how to encourage one another
> with the truth of Your love, grace and mercy that bless us all.
> Forgive us for the times when we belittle and judge each other,
> for those moments when malice or envy is our motivator.
> Replace those attitudes and insecurities with a love for You
> that spills over into a desire to support and encourage others.
> And, Lord, as we become encouragers to one another,
> we pray that we will be a shining light in this world.
> Amen."[32]

2. Note one or two points from this chapter and reflect on them with a spoken or written prayer:

STEP 2: **MEDITATE**—CONSIDER WHAT THE SCRIPTURES SAY

John 17:6, 9, 15, 24

> [6] *I have revealed you to those whom you gave me out of the world. They were yours; you gave them to me and they have obeyed your word.*
>
> [9] *I pray for them. I am not praying for the world but for those you have given me, for they are yours.*
>
> [15] *My prayer is not that you would take them out of the world but that you protect them from the evil one.*
>
> [24] *Father, I want those you have given me to be with me where I am, and to see my glory, the glory you have given me because you loved me before the creation of the world.*

- What are the implications of these words from Jesus' prayer for our mentoring relationships?

Ephesians 4:11-16

> [11] *It was he who gave some to be apostles, some to be prophets, some to be evangelists, and some to be pastors and teachers,* [12] *to prepare God's people for works of service, so that the body of Christ may be built up* [13] *until we all reach unity in the faith and in the knowledge of the Son of God and become mature, attaining to the whole measure of the fullness of Christ.*
>
> [14] *Then we will no longer be infants, tossed back and forth by the waves, and blown here and there by every wind of teaching and by the cunning and craftiness of men in their deceitful scheming.* [15] *Instead, speaking the truth in love, we will in all things grow up into him who is the Head, that is, Christ.* [16] *From him the whole body, joined and held together by every supporting ligament, grows and builds itself up in love, as each part does its work.*

- If leaders are maturing disciples as suggested in this chapter, what are the main elements that produce maturity according to this passage?

STEP 3: **RESPOND—**
LEARN FROM EACH OTHER AND TAKE ACTION

Reflection and Discussion:

1. Whom has God "given" you at present, so that you can invest in them with a view to life-change?

2. Reflect on and discuss Anderson and Reese's statement: "Spiritual mentoring is a triadic relationship between mentor, mentoree and the Holy Spirit, where the mentoree can discover, through the already present action of God, intimacy with God, ultimate identity as a child of God, and a unique voice for kingdom responsibility." What does this look like in practice?

3. How do you view the relationship between discipleship and mentoring? What are the implications for your church or small group?

4. Consider and discuss the "both-ands" in this chapter as they relate to mutual mentoring:

Individual and Small Group

Grace-giving and Truth Telling

Organic and Organized

Reflection and Mission

5. What are the next steps of obedience you need to take:

Personally?

As a group?

CHAPTER TWO

LINGER FOR LIFE CHANGE

"And we all, with unveiled face, beholding the glory of the Lord, are being transformed into the same image from one degree of glory to another. For this comes from the Lord who is the Spirit."
—2 Corinthians 3:18 (ESV)

"There has never been and never will be anyone else like you. But that isn't a testament to you. It's a testament to the God who created you. You are unlike anyone who has ever lived. But that uniqueness isn't a virtue. It's a responsibility."
—Mark Batterson

"Be yourself. Everyone else is taken!"
—Oscar Wilde

If the goal of spiritual mentoring is life transformation, how does God draw us into the process of life change? How does he use mutual mentors to accomplish this? How does he bring about greater Christ-likeness in such different and unique individuals, while still preserving their core identity?

As we linger together for life-change, no two of us are alike. Every time I fly from Auckland to Los Angeles I'm reminded of that. The U.S. Customs Department takes prints of both of my thumbs, then the four fingers of both hands and a picture of my iris. In doing so, they capture my unique physical identity. The Customs Department operates on the notion that there are no other Rowland Formans (some might say, "Thank God for that!") on planet earth at the moment. Maybe it's a stretch, but if I extrapolate that, there never has been and never will be another human with my thumbprint and DNA!

Mark Batterson, Lead Pastor of National Community Church opens his book *Soulprint* with a reminder that our "soul" identity is similarly unique. Our uniqueness isn't a call to narcissism, rather a charge to worship the One who created us and is sculpting us.

> *There has never been and never will be anyone else like you. But that isn't a testament to you. It's a testament to the God who created you. You are unlike anyone who has ever lived. But that uniqueness isn't a virtue. It's a responsibility. Uniqueness is God's gift to you, and uniqueness is your gift to God. You owe it to yourself to* be yourself. *But more important, you owe it to the One who designed you and destined you.*[33]

You are one-of-a-kind. That's an important understanding when you consider spiritual transformation as one of the primary purposes of mutual mentoring. Spiritual mentoring amounts to two (or more) people journeying together, fully aware of their limitations and imperfections, helping each other become more like Jesus. If we are all unique, and if the purpose of mutual mentoring is to catalyze transformation into Christlikeness, then how does God do that?

He doesn't transform us if we approach mutual mentoring as yet another task we need to accomplish in our own strength. Mathew Woodley, in *Holy Fools* calls that approach to spiritual change, "The Religion-Centered Quest," which he describes as:

> *If I obey, if I perform, if I can do it well enough...I will be accepted before God...If I keep on jumping through the right hoops, God will [transform me]....*

In contrast to that, says Woodley, the "The Gospel-Centered Quest" sounds like this:

No, because I am already loved by God in and through Jesus Christ, I will obey and surrender my life.... Pursuing a gospel-centered spiritual quest melts our sin-frozen hearts, unleashing a river of love, wonder and gratitude.[34]

How does God change us then to be more like Jesus? I believe 2 Corinthians 3:18 outlines three essential elements in that quest:

And **we all**, *who with unveiled faces* **contemplate the Lord's glory**, **are being transformed** *into his image with ever increasing glory, which comes from the Lord, who is the Spirit.*

Transformation is a Process Expected of Every Believer

And we all...are being transformed says Paul. All of us. No exceptions. Remember he's writing to the church in Corinth, which was definitely not a model church (they had been glorying in their relaxed attitudes to sexual "indiscretions," experiencing divisions, and abusing the celebration of Communion to name a few things). It is to those individuals he says, this is for all of you—every individual who is personally being hand-crafted by God himself. As I understand the Grand Story of the Bible, every human being is an image bearer of God—an image that has been defaced by the "Fall," yet not erased. An image that in Christ is being restored but is not yet perfected until we are with him forever.

Transformation Calls for Action on Our Part

We all *contemplate the Lord's glory*. We need to keep looking at Christ, not to other Christians. Our focus needs to be on him. That's one of the many things I like about James Bryan Smith's Apprenticeship Series Trilogy: *The Good and Beautiful God, The Good and Beautiful Life, and The Good and Beautiful Community.* Smith encourages his readers, as apprentices of Jesus, to engage in "Soul Training Practices." His first book is a clarion call to be enthralled with God, to focus on the character of God and how we can experience intimacy with him. That's the lifelong quest of Christ followers.

Transformation is Accomplished by the Spirit

...Which comes from the Lord, who is the Spirit. Unintentionally, promoters of particular approaches to life-transformation, who

sometimes overstate their case (whether it is life transformation through effective small groups, engaging in the spiritual disciplines, or in the case of this book—through mutual life-on-life mentoring) can send the message that if only we will follow their prescription, out will pop a Christlike individual.

My home city, Auckland in New Zealand, is sometimes referred to as "The City of Sails," because it's claimed that one in three people have a boat. I recall many occasions during the sailing of the America's Cup (in 2000 and 2003), when those sophisticated crafts, with state-of-the-art sails, and finely tuned athletes, could simply go nowhere because of lack of wind. No wind, no sailing. The spiritual realm is the same. Without the Holy Spirit, we will go nowhere. I see spiritual practices like the one outlined in this book (mutual mentoring), are mere ways of hoisting our sails to be ready so that the Holy Spirit in his time and his way can transform us.

Hand-Crafted, Not Mass-Produced

Since transformation is required, how does God change us to become more like his Son? A character study of a few of God's followers in the Old and New Testaments provides fascinating insights into this question. It is as if God has a different curriculum for each of his one-of-a-kind followers.

Abraham

As I looked at the Abraham narrative in Genesis 11 through 22, I noticed that God gave him a series of faith-stretching experiences. Abraham was called to go to a land that he would one day possess, but with no driving instructions. God said, "Just leave everything you hold dear (country, people, family) and go to the land that I will show you one day."[35] Sometimes he failed tests of character—like the times he compromised his wife Sarai to save his own skin.[36] At other times he passed the tests God gave him, such as the time he graciously allowed his nephew Lot to choose the best piece of land, or the time he passed the ultimate test of trust in God when he was asked to sacrifice the son of the promise, Isaac.[37]

So, based on the narrative about Abraham, we might be tempted to say, the way God shapes us is through a series of critical tests of integrity and patience that we sometimes get right and sometimes wrong, until such time as we trust him completely. That is true for the unique character called Abraham, but it doesn't fit other Bible characters as I found when I looked at the story of Naomi in the Book of Ruth.

Naomi

How did God transform Naomi from being a bitter (her self-description[38]) widow into a joyful grandmother[39]? It began as a series of apparently random "happenings"—things out of her control such as famine, the death of her husband Elimelech, and the passing of her two sons Mahlon and Kilion. Naomi was left with her two daughters-in-law, both from the land of Moab. One daughter-in-law, Ruth, pledged lifelong commitment to Naomi and gladly responded to Naomi's mentoring role in her life. The narrative of the Book of Ruth almost reads as if it was the mutual mentoring process (sometimes Naomi helping Ruth, or Ruth challenging Naomi) that was one of the things that helped her come out of the trough of bitterness.

Together, this mentor-pair were able to celebrate the hand of God in the provision of a kinsman-redeemer, Boaz. Naomi faced an entirely different series of circumstances than Abraham: bereavement, soul-bitterness, then eventually an outward focus through a God-given mentoring relationship (some might call her relationship with Ruth match-making!), then the sheer joy of holding in her hands, Obed, the boy through whom would come King David, and ultimately, the Messiah Jesus.

Timothy

The way God transformed Timothy was different again. He had a godly mother and grandmother who taught him the Scriptures from an early age. Then, on one of the Apostle Paul's missionary visits to Lystra, Timothy's hometown, it seems that Paul was instrumental in the young man coming to faith in Christ (at least Paul calls him his "son" in the faith). Probably one of the most formative experiences of Timothy's life (like so many Christ followers I have interviewed) was an extended mission trip. He heard Paul preach the gospel, teach new believers, plant local churches, then move on. Paul was an open book to Timothy. He said, "You, however, know all about my teaching, my way of life, my purpose, faith, patience, love, endurance, persecutions, sufferings—what kinds of things happened to me in Antioch, Iconium and Lystra, the persecutions I endured…."[40]

One huge bonus that came along with the mission trips was an ongoing mentoring relationship with Paul captured in 2 Timothy 2:2,

> *"And the things you have heard me say*
> *in the presence of many witnesses*
> *entrust to reliable people*
> *who will be qualified to teach others."*

Timothy, then, was sculpted by God through mentors (his mother, grandmother and Paul), mission trips, and the faith-stretching experience of being left behind in Ephesus so he could pass the torch of God's truth onto the next generation.

Consider others. Think of how God shaped biblical characters like Moses, Job, Hannah, Joshua, and John Mark to name a few more. All are different individuals, all skillfully grown and developed by the Master Gardener. What are some of the ways that God has been transforming you?

My life story of transformation has elements of each of the three biblical characters above: Abraham, Timothy and Naomi.

Upheaval

When I was eight years old my parents emigrated from Scotland to New Zealand. Although I can't claim that I was responding to the call of God, like Abraham, our family made a life-changing move. That was a decision of my parents. My brother Ian had pneumonia in both his lungs when he was four years old and the doctor recommended we move to a warmer climate (he recommended New Zealand or Canada—I've been in parts of Canada in the dead of winter and am glad that we moved Down Under!). The move from Scotland to New Zealand reminds me of a chapter in Robert Clinton's book, *The Making of a Leader*. Clinton calls the first phase of our lives as believers, "Sovereign Foundations." By definition, these are happenings, like my move from Scotland, over which we have no control, but God's sovereign hand is obvious.

Mentors

As I've mentioned, like Timothy, I had the privilege of a grandmother who mentored me. Some of her sayings are etched in my mind. She loved quoting from 1 Samuel 2:30, "Them that honor me I will honor" and applied that to all sorts of life situations that amounted to putting God first in my life. She modeled a love for God. When I was a boy, I recall walking past her bedroom around six o'clock in the morning and hearing her at prayer. It was the same later at night: she was again in earnest prayer to God. But her greatest legacy was her passion for God's Word. For her, characters like Abraham, Naomi and Timothy were real people. When she told me about them as a young boy, often I'd see tears streaming down her face as she recounted the dumb decisions they made at times. Into my teens and early twenties our relationship changed. Grandma plied me with questions on theology and Scripture. Our mentoring relationship became more mutual.

Low points

As I reflect on the things that have been most formative, like Naomi, it has been low points rather than exhilarating successes that have shaped me. English author and columnist in *Punch* magazine, Malcolm Muggeridge's profound words mirror my experience:

> *Contrary to what might be expected, I look back on experiences that at the time seemed especially desolating and painful with particular satisfaction. Indeed I can say with complete truthfulness that everything I have learned in my seventy-five years in this world, everything that has truly enhanced and enlightened my existence, has been through affliction and not through happiness, whether pursued or attained. In other words, if it ever were possible to eliminate affliction from our earthly existence by means of some drug or other medical mumbo jumbo, as Aldous Huxley envisaged in* Brave New World, *the result would not be to make life delectable, but to make it too banal and trivial to be endurable. This of course, is what the Cross signifies. And it is the Cross, more than anything else, that has called me inexorably to Christ.*[41]

Two life-changing events come to mind. When our third child, Craig, was three months old, he contracted pneumococcal meningitis. I vividly recall the specialist's words to Elaine and me when Craig was in the Intensive Care Ward. He said, "Your son may not pull through, but if he does, he will be like a vegetable." We prayed and called all our friends to pray. A day or so later the doctor did a brain scan and said, "He's 100%." We testified to a miracle from God. The doctor seemed unconvinced. When we got home, Elaine put Craig into his bassinette and we both knelt by our bed. I remember raising my hands as I prayed and said, "Thank You Lord for giving us Craig back. We give him back to you though. Do with him what you will." I was thinking that one day he would be a missionary in a remote part of the world and we may not see him as often as we'd like.

When Craig was five-and-a-half months old, he died of a "Sudden Infant Death Syndrome (SIDS)." I tried in vain to revive him. My mind went back to the words I'd uttered in the same bedroom. That was one of the lowest points in our lives as a married couple. My Uncle and Aunt, Dr. Will and Janette Miller, came around to our home day after day. They'd just make cups of tea and allow us to process what had happened. No pat answers, just presence, in contrast to well-meaning friends who said things like, "At least you have two other children." Cold comfort! The statement that took my breath away, though, was the person who said, "You should be glad because he might have become a Judas Iscariot." I kid you not.

That low point was formative because during that period it was as if I had 20/20 vision and saw what really mattered in life—a close walk with Christ and abandonment to his mission. It was soon after that that we moved into full-time vocational Christian ministry. I agree with author Peggy Raynoso when she says,

> *It is ironic to me that suffering can actually enhance our faith. "How is it," I asked a friend, "that the most dreadful things that happen to us are those that most increase our trust in God?" Experiences that rock our foundations, or that grind them down, cause us to choose repeatedly whether to trust God.*[42]

The second most transformative "lowlight" in my life was a car wreck—physically and metaphorically. In 1988, Elaine and I were driving to Queenstown (one of the *Lord of the Rings* filming "headquarters") where I was to speak at a Christmas convention. Three hours from Christchurch, where we lived at the time, we stopped for ice cream. To my dismay, I noticed that my trunk had popped open on the way down and my briefcase, with all my sermon notes, was missing. We backtracked, but didn't find it. That added three hours to our 7 hour car trip. I had counted on refueling at Lake Tekapo, but the gas station was closed. We were running on empty. At 11:30 pm, I drove through a concrete rail into the Roaring Meg River. Our lives should have been taken. My version is that I was distracted through lack of fuel and fell asleep at the wheel. Elaine's version is that I was driving too fast.

Driving too fast and running on empty was an accurate metaphor for the way I was living at the time—(to that I would add, and unaware of it too). I didn't know the term then but clearly I was experiencing burnout. Warning lights (such as hating things I normally loved like preaching God's Word) had been flashing on my spiritual dashboard for some time, but I ignored them. I ended up in the Cromwell Hospital for ten days with punctured lungs, pericarditis, and pneumonia. One of my visitors was a mutual mentor, Dr. Roger Raymer, who was a pastor in Christchurch at the time. He recommended that I take an extended sabbatical and said he would help make it possible for me to study at Dallas Theological Seminary (DTS). That was a lifeline for me. In fact if the car wreck was a low point, DTS was a highlight. Two or three weeks after the accident, I read Chuck Swindoll's book *Quest for Character*. Again, as with Craig's death, as I was reading, my spiritual fog lifted briefly and I saw what was really important. I wrote cryptic messages in the flyleaf of that book:

- We don't know the answers.

- Thank God for short prayers and short visits.

- Never forget Swindoll's advice—"Drink in the stillness. Linger as long as you can in the presence of your loving Shepherd. His word will restore you as 'the paths of righteousness' become clear. Even if this day is shadowed by fear or uncertainty, He is *with* you…as close as your heartbeat, as close as your next breath."[43]

If it hadn't been for the accident, I would never have met two of my lifelong friends, and co-authors of *The Leadership Baton*, Jeff Jones (Senior Pastor of Chase Oaks Church now, but a classmate then) and Bruce Miller (Senior Pastor of Christ Fellowship Church now, and one of my professors then). And I might never have met the man who taught me so much about mutual mentoring—Don Overton.

Recently I asked Don, "If you were confined to three things that have been the most formative in your spiritual life, what would they be?" Don's answer was:

- **Loss of Identify as a Worship Leader.** I was Worship Pastor at Fellowship Bible Church North (FBCN) in Plano, Texas at the time. Imperceptibly, I had shifted my dependence from listening to, and walking with the Father, to becoming a musician and leader of worship. My focus had moved from an all-out dependent worship of God as I led worship, to a self-absorbed attempt to prove something on the worship stage. As I told Jack Warren, the Executive Pastor, six months after stepping down from my role, "I'm lost." I didn't know where to turn. Up was down and down was up. Toward the end of that chapter I wanted nothing to do with church staff or vocational ministry. I was tired, burned out and spent up. That was the start of a four year desert experience. I am truly grateful for the experience of worship leading. I thank God for FBCN, but I had to get away from what had become a task master. Through that low point, God bent my ear to want him more than anything.

- **Failure of a "Shadow" Calling.** After my chapter as a worship leader, I took up a business partnership with a Christian firm that helps leaders identify their leadership style. One of my mentors, my former Pastor, Jeff Jones helped me see that my role in this business was a skill but didn't express enough of me.

- **A Mutual Mentoring Experience.** As I reflect on the most transformative experiences, it certainly has been those two desert episodes. But the consistent thing through both of those lows was the lifeline that my mutual mentoring relationship with Rowland, that God was handing to me. In one of his visits to the States, just before he returned to New Zealand, Rowland invited me to coffee. I was expecting a book, a contract, a list of accountability questions. What I got was transparent conversation. He began sharing about his life—things he longed to hear God say, mistakes he had made and he asked me to accompany him on the journey with Christ. Mentoring and discipleship had never looked like this.

A few weeks later, this mentor-with-a-difference was back. We picked a time and a place to meet. He had a book for me that we used as a springboard for conversation. Mostly though we just set the book down and explored what God was saying to us. He began speaking into my prayer and devotional life. He challenged me join him in reading through the Bible. As I think of it, he was really shaping me into the discipline of soaking in the Scripture and listening to God.

In the days, weeks, months, years that followed, that was the pattern of our relationship. We consumed a lot of soup, coffee, bread and jam. That was the excuse. But what ensued from the food was a trust and a conversation in which Rowland invited me to speak into his life and then he reciprocated by identifying something in my life where I needed to stretch and grow. He would ask about it, point to his own life and struggle with the same issue, then suggest that we walk in it together. Honestly, he convinced me that it was as much a challenge for him as me. I was either very arrogant or naive or both. It has only been in the years looking back that I could see the rhythm of our relationship: invitation, eating, talking, mutual vulnerability...work it out together. This mutual mentoring rhythm was used by God to walk me into greater intentionality in dating my wife, greater intentionality in leading worship, greater intentionality in submitting to the challenges of leading through a major leadership transition, greater intentionality with reading broadly and deeply, greater intentionality with spiritual disciplines. Here is the genius—in all of these meetings we were always listening to each other and to the whisper of the Spirit.

In summary, some of the ways God transformed the biblical and extra-biblical characters (like Don and me) above were: faith-stretching experiences and upheavals, tests of dependence and integrity, life-shattering tragedies, mentoring relationships, and engagement in Christ's mission. We must not box God in. Just when we think we have discovered a formula, he surprises us so that our focus is squarely on him.

It's God that is the "Transformer." Linger with him in the presence of spiritual companions and watch him at work.

PROCESS CHAPTER TWO

STEP 1: **DEPEND**—SOAK THE PROCESS IN PRAYER

1. Consider the following prayers "The Deeps" from *The Valley of Vision* and "Pry Me Off Dead Center" by Ted Loder, as you process Chapter Two:

The Deeps

> Lord Jesus, give me a deeper repentance,
>> a horror of sin,
>> a dread of its approach.
>
> Help me to flee it and jealously to resolve that my heart
>> will be yours alone.
>
> Give me a deeper trust,
>> that I may lose myself to find myself in you,
>> the ground of my rest,
>> the spring of my being.
>
> Give me a deeper knowledge of yourself
>> as Savior, Master, Lord and King.
>
> Give me deeper power in private prayer,
>> more sweetness in your Word,
>> more steadfast grip on its truth.
>
> Give me deeper holiness in speech, thought, action,
>> and let me not seek moral virtue apart from you.
>
> Plough deep in me, great Lord,
>> Heavenly Husbandman,
>> that my being may be a tilled field,
>> the roots of grace spreading far and wide,
>> until you alone are seen in me,
>> your beauty golden like summer harvest,
>> your fruitfulness as autumn plenty.
>
> I have no Master but you,
>> no law but your will,
>> no delight but yourself,
>> no wealth but that you give,
>> no good but that you bless me with,
>> no peace but what you bestow.

I am nothing but that you are making me to be.
I have nothing but that I receive from you.
I can be nothing but that grace adorns me.
Quarry me deep, dear Lord,
    and then fill me to overflowing
    with living water.[44]

Pry Me Off Dead Center

O persistent God,
    deliver me from assuming your mercy is gentle.
Pressure me that I may grow more human,
    not through the lessening of my struggles,
    but through the expansion of them
    that will undam me
    and unbury my gifts.
Deepen my hurt
    until I learn to share it
    and myself
    openly,
    and my needs honestly.
Sharpen my fears
    until I name them
    and release the power I have locked in them
    and they in me…

O persistent God,
    let how much it all matters
    pry me off dead center
    so if I am moved inside
        to tears
            or sighs
                or screams
                    or smiles
                        or dreams,
they will be real
and I will be in touch with who I am
and who you are
and who my sisters and brothers are.[45]

2. Note one or two points from this chapter and reflect on them with a spoken or written prayer:

STEP 2: **MEDITATE**—CONSIDER WHAT THE SCRIPTURES SAY

2 Corinthians 3:18

> NIV version: *"And we, who with unveiled faces all reflect the Lord's glory, are being transformed into his likeness, with ever-increasing glory, which comes from the Lord, who is the Spirit."*

> J.B. Phillips version: *"But all of us who are Christians have no veils on our faces, but reflect like a mirror the glory of the Lord. We are transformed in ever-increasing splendor into his image, and this is the work of the Lord who is the Spirit."*

> NLT version: *"So all of us who have had that veil removed can see and reflect the glory of the Lord. And the Lord—who is the Spirit—makes us more and more like him as we are changed into his glorious image."*

Romans 12:1-2

> NIV version: *"Therefore, I urge you, brothers, in view of God's mercy, to offer your bodies as living sacrifices, holy and pleasing to God—this is your spiritual act of worship. Do not conform*

any longer to the pattern of this world, but be transformed by the renewing of your mind.

J.B. Phillips version: *"With eyes wide open to the mercies of God, I beg you, my brothers, as an act of intelligent worship, to give him your bodies as a living sacrifice, consecrated to him and acceptable by him. Don't let the world around you squeeze you into its own mold, but let God re-make you so that your whole attitude of mind is changed.*

NLT version: *"And so, dear brothers and sisters, I plead with you to give your bodies to God. Let them be a living and holy sacrifice—the kind he will accept. When you think of what he has done for you, is this too much to ask? Don't copy the behavior and customs of this world, but let God transform you into a new person by changing the way you think."*

- What is the process of spiritual transformation according to 2 Corinthians 3:18 and Romans 12:1-2?

STEP 3: **RESPOND—**
LEARN FROM EACH OTHER AND TAKE ACTION

Reflection and Discussion:

1. What are the main elements (events, highs and lows) of spiritual transformation that God has used to shape you into the unique individual you are?

2. What does the process of spiritual transformation look like for you on a daily and weekly basis?

3. If God is hand-crafting each of us individually and not mass-producing his people, how can we avoid an individualistic approach to life transformation?

4. How does our uniqueness relate to the mutual mentoring relationships God has placed us in?

5. What steps of obedience will you take as a result of reading Chapter Two:

Personally?

As a Group?

CHAPTER THREE

LINGER WITH THE TRINITY

> *"May the grace of the Lord Jesus Christ, and
> the love of God, and the fellowship of the Holy Spirit
> be with you all."*
> —2 Corinthians 13:14

> "There is no higher privilege than serving as a soul companion to others on the spiritual journey. In this act we are allowed to enter a truly holy place—the place where people meet with their God."[46]
> —David Benner

Mutual mentoring for the purpose of life transformation is a spiritual journey—a journey of two or more people who come to listen to God through the frail instrumentality of each other, but more importantly a journey where we become attentive to the Presence of God.

Father, Son, and Spirit, God Three-in-One, are intimately involved in this mutual transformational mentoring process. Bruce Demarest, a Professor at Denver Seminary captures this truth in his chapter in *The Kingdom Life* (edited by Alan Andrews):

> *Everything that follows regarding spiritual formation flows from who God is. The God who is revealed in Scripture and who lived among us in Jesus Christ exists as a loving*

community of grace in three persons. From eternity past to eternity future, Father, Son and Holy Spirit relate to each other with grace, love, mutual submission, and unity of heart and by honoring their roles practicing functional submission—the Holy Spirit to the Son and the Father and the Son to the Father. Marvelously, this triune God has invited us, in relationship with Himself, to participate in this culture of grace.[47]

How then can mentoring as a genuine interchange between us and the Trinity take place in practice?

Talk to Your Father

As we have seen in Chapter One, when the Son was reviewing the primary thrust of his three years of public ministry, he said to his Father, "I have revealed you to those whom **you gave me** out of the world. They were yours; **you gave them to me**...."[48] In other words our Heavenly Father is the one who gives people to us to be in a mentoring relationship with. He is intimately involved in the process. This is no mere accident. We need to pray frequently, "Father, whom are You giving me to invest my life in at the moment?" Involve your Heavenly Father in the process. These are his people that he is entrusting to you.

One of our goals should be to live and lead like Jesus. We can do that as we cultivate a daily dependent relationship with our heavenly Father. The Holy Son of God did that. John records these words from Jesus about his interaction with his Father:

> *"...I tell you the truth, the Son can do nothing by himself;*
> *he can do only what he sees his Father doing,*
> *because whatever the Father does, the Son also does.*
> *For the Father loves the Son and shows him all he does."*[49]

Note the word "nothing"—not one thing. The Holy Son of God, though eternally equal with the Father, chose to humbly wait for the Father's directions for his every move while on Planet Earth. Is that true of you? Too often I'm like the shepherds of Israel who Jeremiah talked about: "The shepherds are senseless and do not inquire of the LORD; so they do not prosper and all their flock is scattered."[50]

That's why the first skill we need to acquire is to pray before, during and after every mutual mentoring meeting (see Chapter Six). To be like Jesus is to intimately relate to our heavenly Father—to interact with him constantly.

When did you last speak intimately with the Father about those he has entrusted to you?

Walk with the Son

Mutual mentoring relationships involve constant interaction with the Father but also an awareness of the Presence of Christ with us. In the Great Commission (Matthew 28:19-20) Jesus said that as we go and make disciples (evidenced by them going public in baptism), and teaching them to obey everything he commanded, he will be *with us*.

The cameo of a true mentoring relationship in Luke 24:13-35 captures the fact that the Lord Jesus is right alongside us as we meet in his name—he is *with us* more than we ever realize! Two confused disciples were on a street that wound its way to a village called Emmaus. They were discussing the strange happenings of the last few days—and maybe the meaning of the empty tomb? While they processed those events, the Lord walked alongside them. It sounds strange, but they didn't recognize him. Strange until you realize how infrequently you are aware of the presence of Jesus as you meet with someone with a view to mutual transformation. The Model Mentor did what all good mentors do: he conferred grace by asking a question: "What are you discussing as you walk along?"

One of the two disciples, Cleopas, ironically (and from our perspective almost humorously) asks "Are you the only one who doesn't know what has happened in these days?" Or course he did! Jesus followed that question up with another, "What things?" They recounted items about his life, death and peculiar happenings relating to his resurrection. Then Jesus lovingly chided them for being slow to believe all that the prophets had spoken of, and directed them to one of the great themes of Scripture—that Messiah would suffer then enter into his glory.

They stopped near the Emmaus Village, and Jesus said he would move on. The two men persuaded him to linger with them. Jesus had table fellowship with them, then shared a meal. Suddenly their eyes were opened. It was Jesus! Author and scholar Darrell Bock says,

> ...It is no accident that Jesus is revealed as he sits having table fellowship with the two disciples. The table was a place for fellowship in the ancient world. Here family and friends gathered to share time with each other. Luke had underscored the importance of meal scenes through his gospel. The table was a place where Jesus was heard and his presence came across most intimately. This fact suggests that Jesus reveals himself in the midst of the basic moments of life. He is at home in the midst of our everyday activity.[51]

Bock's description of table fellowship at Emmaus reminds me of a tradition Earl Lindgren (a senior mentor-friend) and I have every time I visit Dallas. We go to a café in Plano. Earl is usually there before me and he sets the table. He has the bread and the cup all ready. We catch-up on our lives first. Usually it's about family, sometimes we ask the profound question J.R.R. Tolkien and C.S. Lewis reputedly asked each other when they met at The Inklings: "What has become clear to you since last we met?" Earl and I are both avid journalers and will often share things that are clear, or still cloudy in our lives and ministry.

Once we have caught up, we thank the Lord Jesus for his presence with us at the table and thank him for his death and resurrection and coming again. I love that! Two people, sometimes clear, sometimes like the two friends on the Emmaus Road, a bit confused, but most importantly, processing life in the company of Christ. We are practicing of the Presence of the Lord Jesus—acknowledging him as we interact with each other.

He is with you as you meet one-on-one, or in a mentoring cluster. Walk with him, talk to him and discuss life with him and with each other.

Recently I dipped into Lance Witt's book *Replenish*. One of his very convicting and refreshing word pictures was of the difference between an Eastern and Western wedding. In Western culture the Bride is everything. Witt says:

> *"The lowly groom…is an afterthought. He's filler, the warm-up act for the main attraction." In contrast, in Eastern weddings the groom gets all the attention. For example in the wedding ceremony in heaven, John writes, "Let us rejoice and be glad and give him glory! For the wedding of the Lamb has come, and his bride has made herself ready." What are the implications for the church in our generation?*
>
> *In the last thirty years within the church world, there has been a subtle shifting of the spotlight. Inadvertently, in many places, it has become all about the bride (the church) rather than the groom (Jesus). But as John reminds us, the bride belongs to the bridegroom. Or to say it another way, the bride exists for the groom."*[52]

When you linger together as mentor-partners, make it your goal to make much of the Bridegroom. Talk about him often. Refer to him as you meet. He is present with you.

Keep in Step with the Spirit

Paul's question in Galatians 3:3 continually haunts me: "After beginning with the Spirit, are you now trying to attain your goal by human effort?" It haunts me because too often I have engaged in mentoring relationships by human endeavor alone. Spiritual transformation is the work of the Spirit. There is no other way. Scripture after Scripture calls us to be transformed as we depend on the Holy Spirit:

- "…through Christ Jesus the law of the Spirit of life set me free from the law of sin and death." —Romans 8:2

- "…if by the Spirit you put to death the misdeeds of the body you will live." —Romans 8:13

- "And we, who with unveiled faces all reflect the Lord's glory, **are being transformed** into his likeness with ever increasing glory, **which comes from the Lord who is the Spirit**." —2 Corinthians 3:18

- "So I say, live by the Spirit and you will not gratify the desires of the sinful nature." —Galatians 5:16

- "But the fruit of the Spirit is love, joy, peace, patience, kindness, goodness, faithfulness, gentleness and self-control…Since we live by the Spirit let us keep in step with the Spirit."
  —Galatians 5:22, 23, 25

Mentoring relationships in the flesh are powerless and ineffective. As Bruce Demarest puts it:

> *The Spirit is like refreshing water splashed on a thirsty people (see Isaiah 44:3-41). The Spirit is the wind of God (see John 3:8; Acts 2:1-4), who enlivens (see John 6:63), encourages (see Acts 9:31), and empowers (see Acts 1:8). Apart from the Spirit's ministry in our hearts, we are like branches without sap, coals without fire, and ships without sails.*[53]

Prayer is the channel by which the ministry of the Spirit is released in our lives. In most of the mentoring times I have with those the Father has given me (I wish I could say all), I ask for the filling of the Spirit. I ask the Holy Spirit to fill us, control us, and orchestrate our conversation. Make it one of your goals to have a mentoring partnership that simply cannot be explained apart from the power of the Spirit!

What does it look like then to linger together with the Trinity? C. S. Lewis once compared it to a dance. He wrote:

> *The whole dance, or drama, or pattern of this three-Personal life is to be played out in each one of us: or (putting it the other way round) each one of us has got to enter that pattern, take his place in that dance. There is no other way to the happiness for which we were made.*[54]

The Father, Son, and Holy Spirit have been in an eternal dance—forever delighting in each other. We are invited into that dance. In his must-read book on spiritual transformation, *Christ Formed in You*, Brian Hedges says,

> *For God is not a solitary personality, but a community of three persons who eternally coexist in mutual, indwelling, self-giving relationships of love with one another.… You and I must be drawn into the choreography of this eternal dance.… The*

> *problem, of course, is that we sometimes refuse to dance.... We all have a...tendency to shrink from personal relationships, especially when they stretch us beyond our comfort zones. But in doing so, we miss the opportunity to grow closer to the people God has put in our lives.*[55]

In our mentoring relationships that may become spiritual friendships, let's delight in the Father, Son and Spirit and emulate them by delighting in the people God has placed in our lives.

PROCESSING CHAPTER THREE

STEP 1: **DEPEND** —SOAK THE PROCESS IN PRAYER

1. Consider the following prayers by A.W. Tozer, (O God, I have tasted…), Thomas Ken ("To God the Father…") and Catherine of Siena ("You, O eternal Trinity…") as you process Chapter Three:

> O God, I have tasted Thy goodness,
> and it has both satisfied me
> and made me thirsty for more.
> I am painfully conscious of my need of further grace.
> I am ashamed of my lack of desire.
> O God, the Triune God,
> I want to want Thee;
> I long to be filled with longing;
> I thirst to be made more thirsty still.
> Show me Thy glory, I pray Thee,
> that I may know Thee indeed.
> Begin in mercy a new work of love within me.
> Say to my soul, "Rise up, my love, my fair one,
> and come away."
> Then give me grace to rise
> and follow Thee up from this misty lowland
> where I have wandered so long.
> In Jesus' Name,
> Amen.[56]

To God the Father,
> Who first loved us,
> > And made us accepted in the beloved Son:

To God the Son,
> Who loved us
> > And washed us from our sins in his own blood;

To God the Holy Spirit,
> Who sheds abroad the love of God in our hearts;

> To the one true God
>> Be all love and all glory
>>> For time and eternity.[57]

Eternal Trinity,

> You are a deep sea,
> into which the more I enter the more I find,
> and the more I find the more I seek.
> The soul ever hungers in your abyss,
> Eternal Trinity,
> Longing to see you with the light of your light,
> and as the deer yearns for the springs of water,
> so my soul yearns to see you in truth.[58]

2. Note one or two points from this chapter and reflect on them with a spoken or written prayer:

STEP 2: **MEDITATE**—CONSIDER WHAT THE SCRIPTURES SAY

John 5:19-23

> [19] Jesus gave them this answer: "I tell you the truth, the Son can do nothing by himself; he can do only what he sees his Father doing, because whatever the Father does the Son also does. [20] For the Father loves the Son and shows him all he does. Yes, to your amazement he will show him even greater things than these. [21] For just as the Father raises the dead and gives them life, even so the Son gives life to whom he is pleased to give it. [22] Moreover, the Father judges no one, but has entrusted all judgment to the Son, [23] that all may honor the Son just as they honor the Father. He who does not honor the Son does not honor the Father, who sent him.

- From this paragraph, how does the Lord Jesus model the relationship we should have with our heavenly Father in our mentoring relationships?

John 15:4-5

> [4] Remain in me, and I will remain in you. No branch can bear fruit by itself; it must remain in the vine. Neither can you bear fruit unless you remain in me. [5] I am the vine; you are the branches. If a man remains in me and I in him, he will bear much fruit; apart from me you can do nothing.

Colossians 2:6-7

> [6] So then, just as you received Christ Jesus as Lord, continue to live in him, [7] rooted and built up in him, strengthened in the faith as you were taught, and overflowing with thankfulness.

- How do these Scriptures capture the need we have to be walking with Jesus on a daily basis? What does that look like in everyday terms?

2 Corinthians 3:18

> *¹⁸ And we, who with unveiled faces all reflect the Lord's glory, are being transformed into his likeness with ever-increasing glory, which comes from the Lord, who is the Spirit.*

Galatians 5:22-26

> *²² But the fruit of the Spirit is love, joy, peace, patience, kindness, goodness, faithfulness, ²³ gentleness and self-control. Against such things there is no law. ²⁴ Those who belong to Christ Jesus have crucified the sinful nature with its passions and desires. ²⁵ Since we live by the Spirit, let us keep in step with the Spirit. ²⁶ Let us not become conceited, provoking and envying each other.*

- From these passages and others you know, how would you describe the role of the Holy Spirit in a transformational mentoring relationship?

STEP 3: **RESPOND—**
LEARN FROM EACH OTHER AND TAKE ACTION

Reflection and Discussion:

1. As you reflect on the mentoring relationships that God has given you, to what extent are you:

Talking with your heavenly Father?

Walking with the Lord Jesus?

Depending on the Spirit?

2. Discuss the quote from Lance Witt (page 41) on the extent to which we have taken more notice of the "Bride" (our churches) than the "Bridegroom," our Lord Jesus Christ.

3. What does it mean to you personally, to be invited into the eternal "dance of delight" of the Trinity?

4. What are the implications of delighting in the Father, Son and Holy Spirit, and in each other, for our mentoring partnerships?

5. What steps of obedience will you take as a result of reflecting on this chapter?

Personally?

As a group?

CHAPTER FOUR

LINGER IN COMMUNITY

*"His intent was that now, through the church,
the manifold wisdom of God should be made known
to the rulers and authorities in the heavenly realms,
according to his eternal purpose which he accomplished
in Christ Jesus our Lord."*
—Ephesians 3:10-11

*"In recent years the church has been tragically marginalized
as a provider of soul care. If the church is to be restored to its
rightful place of relevance to and preeminence in supporting the
care and cure of souls, we must equip and encourage people to
offer themselves to others in relationships of soul friendship and
spiritual companionship."*[59]
—David Benner

Imagine a church that is a mirror of the Trinity in community described in Chapter Three:

- An affirming community where the people genuinely delight in each other, regardless of race, gender, or social status.

- An authentic community where, to use James Emery White's description, "we can love and be loved, know and be known, serve and be served, and celebrate and be celebrated."[60]

- A discipling community where people linger together to mentor each other with the aim of radical life transformation.

- A committed community that reflects the spirit of Luke's description of the church in the First Century:

> *They devoted themselves to the apostles' teaching and to the fellowship, to the breaking of bread and to prayer. Everyone was filled with awe, and many wonders and miraculous signs were done by the apostles. All the believers were together and had everything in common. Selling their possessions and goods, they gave to anyone as he had need. Every day they continued to meet together in the temple courts. They broke bread in their homes and ate together with glad and sincere hearts, praising God and enjoying the favor of all the people. And the Lord added to their number daily those who were being saved.*[61]

Do you have to stretch your imagination to think of your church as an encouraging, authentic, devoted community like that? The letters of Paul, Peter and James, plus Jesus' letters to seven representative churches in Asia Minor, remind us that over time, enthusiasm wanes, commitment to genuine fellowship slips, and a sense of the powerful presence of God can become a distant memory. Individually, and in our local churches, we are in various stages of broken-wholeness.

Brokenness—evidenced by pretending that our church is "fine" even when we are spiritually beige, dominated by recurring sins, or indifferent to each other's needs. Wholeness—shown by unselfish loving deeds, occasional times of worship when it feels as if heaven has come down, and small groups that experience community for the sake of the community.

In *Prayers from the Pew*, author Terri Lynne Underwood probes into some of those broken elements:

> *What makes the 21st century church a place where people go for connection and leave feeling even more alone? Why are we losing a whole generation who find attending, and especially joining a church to be a waste of time? What is the difference between the modern church and the 1st Century church?*[62]

I love her answers. Some people say the difference is due to the modern church being more like a business than a "body." Others talk about changing the forms of church, such as returning to home churches and the likes.

Underwood, who describes herself as "...a messed up, falling down, failing constantly, clinging to grace believer" says,

> *I found...that God has very specific desires for those gathered in His name. We have clear instruction about His plan for the Church. While many things in Scripture can be elusive, the truth that God intends us to worship, serve, and fellowship together is not one of them. That "together" must begin with prayer: prayer for the Church, for our churches, for pastors and leaders, and for ourselves....*[63]

The clarion call of *Prayers from the Pew* is to repent of our cynicism about the local church and start praying that in our day, our churches will rediscover that first flush of love for God and each other described in Acts 2:42-47, and be known as "houses of prayer."

If your desire is for your church or the small group you are leading to experience a fresh sense of biblical community, where people are mutually mentoring one another, and lives are being radically changed, the place to start is on our knees. But then we need to put some practical steps in place. How do we move from shallow-relationship churches to ones where deep spiritual friendships become the norm? How can we implement the lost art of lingering for life transformation through mutual mentoring in our churches?

In our ministry lives, my wife Elaine and I have tried two approaches.

Model It

The first is to "model what it means to be a mentor, and gradually it will catch on." I believe we need to model what it means to be a mentor first (repeatedly Paul says, "imitate me as I am imitating Christ)[64], but some Western churches put so much effort into programs—organizing weekend services, organizing youth and children's programs and so on—that mentoring can become a poor cousin, something that is nice to have but a non-essential.

Mentoring Ministry

The second approach is to launch mentoring as a separate ministry. In the early 90's my wife Elaine implemented Vicki Kraft's mentoring program, "Heart to Heart." In our small church in Christchurch, New Zealand, Elaine tried to match more mature women with less mature. She experienced the same problem Elizabeth Inrig encountered (see page vii in the Preface)—there were simply not enough more experienced women available. A few years back, I had the privilege of visiting Janet Thompson, who heads up the "Woman-to-Woman" mentoring ministry in Saddleback Community Church. Scores of women have been trained in mentoring through her well thought out mentoring program. Women apply for the semester based process. The ministry links mentors up with "mentees," with a huge emphasis on prayer. Janet's team take a whole day to pray over possible mentor-mentee matches. Her book, *Woman to Woman Mentoring*, provides guidance on how to start, grow, and maintain a mentoring ministry.[65]

Existing Groups

The call of this book though is to go a step beyond merely introducing mentoring as a separate ministry. It is to engage the whole church in mutually mentoring one another. It's a call to start with whatever structures you have in your church.

Does your church have a pastoral staff? Then part of their job description needs to be mentoring other leaders to pass the baton of God's truth onto other leaders. If you are a pastor, my question to you is: Who is your Timothy or Ruth? Does your church have elders (maybe you give them another name)? Then my question to each elder (no exceptions!) is, "Who are you in a mentoring partnership with at the moment?

Does your church have Ministry Team Leaders (worship, youth, children, etc.)? Who are they investing in at present? Do you have Small Group Leaders? "Who are they mentoring at the moment?" Do you have Small Groups? Then encourage each group member to be listening to each other with a view to flowing into connections that the Holy Spirit wants to make.

Currently, I have the joy of leading a small group in the church we attend (BotanyLife Community Church in Auckland, New Zealand). It's a men's group of 15. We call ourselves "Ironmen" (a wish more than a reality!). Here's how mutual mentoring works in our group:

- The leadership structure of our group is a leader and three "champions" (each one in charge of an aspect of our group's life: one for Bible Study and prayer, one for connection and communication, and one for an outward focus). My mutual mentoring role is primarily with these three men. We meet as a group regularly for encouragement and accountability.

- One of the primary job descriptions of the four leaders is to listen attentively to what the men say on a given study evening. We are also listening to the Spirit's prompting—asking ourselves, "Who, Lord, might you be 'giving' us at the moment?"

- A member of the group might express a challenge he's facing at home or business. One of us meets informally with that man with a view to listening to him and praying with him.

- At times, all that is needed is a single mentoring session. At others, we flow into a longer mentoring relationship.

- There is an organized side of what we do but it is also very organic. We mutually build into each other's lives but we also flow along with the prompting of the Holy Spirit on a given night.

My friend Eric Paul, Senior Pastor of Beth El Bible Church in El Paso, Texas, has found a similar way to fold a mentoring philosophy into the fabric of church life. He promotes mentoring partnerships in the context of their Life Group ministry. Mentoring partners are encouraged to either come earlier to the group meeting and spend an hour together, or stay later.

Forming New Mentoring Groups

I read three books that capture the spirit of this church-based approach to mentoring:

- *Transforming Discipleship* by Greg Ogden.

    Greg Ogden's disciple-making model is "…one person inviting two others into a covenantal relationship structured around a Bible-based curriculum."[66] For approximately a year they meet weekly for about an hour and a half per session. Built into Ogden's process is multiplication. The three people are investing in each other's lives for about a year, then each person invites two others into a fresh triad. It's the same content but different relationships.

- *Organic Disciplemaking* by Dennis McCallum.

    Although Dennis McCallum's book is called *Organic Disciplemaking*, my impression is that there is a great deal of organization involved in the implementation of this approach at Xenos Christian Fellowship. A compelling aspect of the process at Xenos is the comprehensive understanding of discipleship. It includes nurturing new believers throughout coaching well-established believers.[67] McCallum describes the basic steps of establishing discipleship with a friend as: "…friendship-building, a regular meeting time, enhanced inter-personal sharing, appropriate biblical and theological content to study together, times of prayer, counseling and helping your friend in areas of weakness, helping your friend develop a ministry, and releasing your friend to pursue a life of service to God."[68]

- *Building a Discipling Culture* by Mike Breen and Steve Cockram.

    Breen and Cockram's approach aims to emulate what Jesus did with his twelve disciples:

    > *Put simply, we invite only a few people into a discipling relationship with us. If Jesus invited twelve people, we're going to assume right off the bat we can't do as many as he did. And we invite these people into a Huddle.*

    > *A Huddle is the group of four to ten people you feel God has called you to specifically invest in, and you will meet with them regularly (at least every other week)*

> to intentionally disciple them in a group setting. The best discipling relationships always have an intentional, "organized" component to them, as well as a less formal "organic" component. Having a regular Huddle meeting is the "organized" component.
>
> Ultimately, we are talking about creating a discipling movement in the place you live. Huddles do not grow by adding new members; Huddles grow when members of your Huddle start their own. Why do it this way? Because we take seriously the principle that Jesus established: Every disciple disciples. You can't be a disciple if you aren't willing to invest in and disciple others. That's simply the call of the Great Commission....
>
> While a Huddle is an important part of discipling people, it isn't enough. An **organic** part of discipling people happens outside a Huddle. That means you need to give these four to ten people much higher ACCESS to your life than other people get or than you are probably accustomed to giving the people you currently lead.[69]

What I admire about these three approaches is the commitment to making disciples. They are genuine attempts to be true to the Great Commission: going to make disciples of all nations, baptizing them (seeing new believers publicly confess their faith in Christ) in the name of the Father and of the Son and of the Holy Spirit, and teaching them to obey everything Christ commanded, in the sure knowledge of his abiding presence.[70]

My only reserve is the tendency of some authors to give the impression that they have found the right way to implement discipleship or transformational mentoring in our churches. I don't believe there is one right way. There are multiple pathways to reach the goal of life change through mutual mentoring. There is no right way, and no formula to mass produce disciples. Allow David Platt's words on the Great Commission to reignite your passion for mutual mentoring in your local church:

> Making disciples by going, baptizing and teaching people the Word of Christ and then enabling them to do the same thing in

other people's lives—this is the plan God has for each of us to impact nations for the glory of Christ.

This plan is so counterintuitive to our way of thinking. In a culture where bigger is always better and flash is always more effective, Jesus beckons us to plainly, humbly, and quietly focus our lives on people. The reality is, you can't share life like this with masses and multitudes. Jesus didn't. He spent three years with twelve guys. If the Son of God thought it necessary to focus his life on a small group of men, we are fooling ourselves to think we can mass-produce disciples today. God's design for taking the gospel into the world is a slow, intentional, simple process that involves every one of his people sacrificing every facet of their lives to multiply the life of Christ in others.[71]

Implementing *The Lost Art of Lingering*

- **One-on-One**

    At the simplest level, I hope that as you read this book you will implement it with any one-on-one spiritual friendships you have at the moment. Try to fold the practices we will see in Part Two into your meetings and access the Scripture-Based studies from Part Three.

- **Existing Groups**

    Whatever group/s God has you in at the moment consider reading Part One together with a view to changing your thinking before you change your behavior. Then progressively fold Part Two and Three into your meetings together.

- **Mentoring Huddles**

    Form new mentoring clusters, maybe triads, or huddles of four to ten people by invitation and work through the material in each of the three parts of this book. My caution is to avoid overload on the part of your most highly committed people. If you choose the "Huddle" option, consider the possibility of the people opting out of their existing small group for a season.

In an age when so many people (young and old) are opting out of church, and espousing what some call "a churchless faith," we need to recapture what Bruce Miller calls "the glory of the church." He says,

> ...people have largely lost the significance and glory of the Church.... The Church is not simply a non-profit organization; the Church is a divine organism instituted by God Himself. The local church is on the very short list of God ordained institutions: marriage, family and Church. We dare not miss this!
>
> The glorious Church of Jesus Christ is so much more than simply a nice place to go on Sunday morning. The Church is the family of God, the body of Jesus Christ, the temple of the Holy Spirit. If you want your life to count, get involved in what God is doing.[72]

I love those images—family, body, temple. Imagine a local church that comes close to that! And most importantly recognize that you are incapable of producing that. Invite the Father, Son and Spirit to do what only they can do—produce a passionate group of disciples that love Christ passionately and with all their imperfections, begin to practice the biblical one-anothers in a fresh and vital way, so that the world will know we are his disciples.

PROCESSING CHAPTER FOUR

STEP 1: **PRAY**—SOAK THE PROCESS IN PRAYER

1. Consider this prayer by Timothy Jones as you process this chapter:

> "Lord, I'm tempted sometimes to go inside myself.
> I think I can make my spiritual life a do-it-yourself project.
> But you have said in your Word that two are better than one,
> that Jesus is present where two or three
> are gathered in his name.
> May my life with you find a dwelling
> amid a community of friends.
> Help me find partners and mentors
> who can encourage my faith and to whom I can go as well.
> Lead me to those with whom I can join arms
> and find new strength to move forward.
> Amen."[73]

2. Note one or two points from this chapter and reflect on them with a spoken or written prayer:

STEP 2: **MEDITATE**—CONSIDER WHAT THE SCRIPTURES SAY

Acts 2:42-47

> [42] *They devoted themselves to the apostles' teaching and to the fellowship, to the breaking of bread and to prayer.* [43] *Everyone was filled with awe, and many wonders and miraculous signs were done by the apostles.* [44] *All the believers were together and had everything in common.* [45] *Selling their possessions and goods, they gave to anyone as he had need.* [46] *Every day they continued to meet together in the temple courts. They broke bread in their homes and ate together with glad and sincere hearts,* [47] *praising God and enjoying the favor of all the people. And the Lord added to their number daily those who were being saved.*

- How would you describe the main elements of biblical community from this description of the early days of the First Century church in Jerusalem?

Ephesians 3:10-12

> [10] *His intent was that now, through the church, the manifold wisdom of God should be made known to the rulers and authorities in the heavenly realms,* [11] *according to his eternal purpose which he accomplished in Christ Jesus our Lord.* [12] *In him and through faith in him we may approach God with freedom and confidence.*

- What is the place of the church in God's eternal plan according to this passage? How does this relate to how we implement mutual mentoring in our churches?

STEP 3: **RESPOND**—
LEARN FROM EACH OTHER AND TAKE ACTION

Reflection and Discussion:

1. Chapter Four suggests that our churches are in various stages of "broken-wholeness." When you think of your church (or small group), in terms of biblical community, describe its:

"Wholeness" (encouraging signs of community):

"Brokenness" (matters that need attention to be able to experience anything like the biblical community described in Acts 2:42-47:

2. Who are you investing in personally with Jesus Christ as center?

3. Who should you be approaching to invest in personally?

4. Which of the three approaches to folding discipleship/mentoring into your church (Ogden, McCallum, Breen) appeals to you most? Why?

CHAPTER FIVE

LINGER WITH ONE ANOTHER

"Don't just pretend to love others. Really love them. Hate what is wrong. Hold tightly to what is good. Love each other with genuine affection, and take delight in honoring one another."
—Romans 12:10-11 (NLT)

"God has so ordained things that we grow in the Spirit only through the frail instrumentality of one another."
—Alan Jones

What is the biblical basis for mutual mentoring for life transformation—that is, cultivating a spiritual friendship where we come to listen to the Spirit through each other and in the process experience life change? Is this just an idea that fits our postmodern culture, where authority has been challenged and in many cases diminished and even abandoned? Doesn't the Bible promote the notion of older or more mature people passing the baton to younger, less mature individuals?

The answer to that last question is definitely "Yes!" Moses was more experienced and wiser than his understudy Joshua. Paul had vastly more maturity than "Timid Timothy." And, having been mentored by the more mature Apostle Paul, Titus was instructed to:

> *...teach the older women to be reverent in the way they live, not to be slanderers or addicted to much wine, but to teach*

what is good. Then they can train the younger women to love their husbands and children, to be self-controlled and pure, to be busy at home, to be kind, and to be subject to their husbands, so that no one will malign the word of God.[74]

There is power and biblical warrant for a spiritual father or mother investing time and energy in a spiritual son or daughter. As mentioned in the Preface, I am living testimony to the effectiveness of "more-mature" to "less-mature" mentoring. Yet spiritual transformation is more accessible when all Christ-followers come to listen deeply to each other and to the Spirit, regardless of their stage of maturity. How does that happen? Do the Scriptures give us any clues?

Iron-on-Iron

At the simplest level, the Scriptural basis for lingering together with a view to transformational mentoring is embodied in Proverbs 27:17 (NLT):

As iron sharpens iron,
so a friend sharpens a friend.

Mutuality is implied in that principle of life. Each piece of iron has an effect on the other. Similarly, one person (young or old, more mature or less) can whet another.

Old Testament scholar Tremper Longman III translates Proverbs 27:17:

As iron sharpens iron,
so people sharpen the edge of their friend.

What does "sharpening" a person imply? Longman places this timeless principle into the context of the book of Proverbs:

It is usually understood, and there is no argument against this interpretation, to mean that friends help each other prepare for the ups and downs of life. In the context of the book of Proverbs, this in the first place likely means mutual instruction in matters of wisdom, which would help a person navigate life successfully. It would certainly include receiving and giving correction to foolish behavior and speech. In this way, the friends could avoid making the same mistake in the future. The wisdom enterprise is a community effort.[75]

In practice, it is rare for mentoring partners to sharpen each other's edges every time they meet. One person will likely need more honing than the other. The important factor though is the attitude of both partners—willingness to come to the whetstone to be sharpened. And sharpening can at times be painful. Here's how Don Overton describes one of our iron-on-iron episodes:

Rowland and I were three or four years into our friendship. Deep mutual trust had taken place courtesy of copious cups of coffee, much laughter, and trading wits and words. To create iron-sharpening opportunities takes time and intentionality. So here goes: Tamara and I had attended leadership training conferences that seemed to help us improve communication. We were rather outspoken about the conference and managed to persuade many of our friends inside and outside our church to participate with us. One of my blind spots is that I leap before I look, hoping to find a parachute on the way down! I had not researched the underpinning philosophy of the organization. The leadership training was teaching us to depend more and more on our own strengths and less and less on Christ.

Rowland took me to lunch one day to ask questions about the program. He saw the core issue and confronted it. Then he did the redemptive thing. He sat with me for hours and just listened. Over the weeks he called me to confront where my true identity lay—in Christ.

Iron sharpening iron in my experience is seldom a single conversation. Earning the right to confront involves much investment of time. That's what friends do. They love well.

Two Better than One

Iron-on-iron mentoring can be painful, but when it is done well it is life-transforming. And when two or more people choose to trade independence for interdependence, there are multiple benefits according to Ecclesiastes 4:7-12:

⁷ Again I saw something meaningless under the sun:
⁸ There was a man all alone;
he had neither son nor brother.
There was no end to his toil,
yet his eyes were not content with his wealth.
"For whom am I toiling," he asked,
"and why am I depriving myself of enjoyment?"
This too is meaningless—
a miserable business!

⁹ Two are better than one,
because they have a good return for their work:
¹⁰ If one falls down,
his friend can help him up.
But pity the man who falls
and has no one to help him up!
¹¹ Also, if two lie down together, they will keep warm.
But how can one keep warm alone?
¹² Though one may be overpowered,
two can defend themselves.
A cord of three strands is not quickly broken.

The "Preacher," most likely King Solomon, describes:

The Problem of Isolation—"There was a man all alone." (verse 8).

Isolation is one of the harsh realities of life spelled out in the early part of Ecclesiastes 4. Some people in Solomon's day were oppressed and without comfort (v. 1-3). Others were competitive, pursuing success out of envy (v. 4-6). Still others were isolated like the discontented, workaholic materialist (v.7-8). The writer saw that all were alone, engaged in a meaningless exercise—like chasing after soap bubbles, or dining on cotton candy. In a different era, St. John of the Cross, put it this way: "A soul which remains alone…is like a burning coal which is left by itself: it will grow colder rather than hotter."[76]

The Power of Partnership—"Two are better than one..." (verse 9-12).

Two are more beneficial than one because of:

- The **support** they supply to each other. If one falls down, the other picks him up (v. 10). The reality is we all stumble and sometimes fall. The metaphor is of two people lurching along. One stumbles, the other supports.

I recall a mentoring partnership when I was Senior Pastor of a church in Hamilton, New Zealand. Once a month, Steve Thurman (then Senior Pastor of Auckland Bible Church) and I would meet at a café midway between our two cities. Sometimes Steve would be down, and I'd encourage him. Other times my chin would be on the floor and Steve would pick me up. Once in a while, we'd both be down and somehow our mentoring relationship sustained us. On those occasions we were like two people, both with a limp, lurching along and making progress, however slow.

- The **encouragement** of companionship. Verse 11 talks about two people keeping warm. On a mountain pass, if you are snowed in, your chances of survival are much greater with two or three people huddling together than if you are isolated.

Recently I felt the chill of discouragement as if all my emotional energy had been drained. But encouragement was found through meeting with a much younger lead pastor, Jonathan Dove, who was also experiencing some of the hits of pastoral life. We helped each other up and warmed our chilled souls.

- The **protection** it provides. One person is vulnerable but two can defend themselves. (v. 12)

I thank God for mentors who have spoken up for me when I've been unjustly maligned. Clive Hanna comes to mind. When I was the principal of a Bible College in Te Awamutu, New Zealand, a story circulated that Elaine and I had failed to pay our share of a fence a builder had erected between our property and that of our neighbor. As soon as Clive (a fellow elder at the time) heard the rumor, he went to the builder and the neighbor and established that everyone was happy with the payment. He then called all the people that had spread the story and set things right. Clive did what it would have been more difficult for me to do. I experienced the blessing of Ecclesiastes 4:12.

Those three word pictures from Ecclesiastes 4 are one another situations. There is mutuality about the support, warmth and protection these mentor-friends give each other. This leads to the strongest biblical warrant for lingering together with a view to life transformation: the mutuality commands of Scripture.

One Anothering

The "one anothers" of Scripture describe a rich texture of human relationships. They add something to the concepts of iron sharpening iron (Proverbs 27:17), and one person supporting another (Ecclesiastes 4:7-12). They call for mutuality in our mentoring/discipling relationships. Consider this sample:

- **Greet** one another (Romans 16:16)
- **Welcome** (accept) one another (Romans 15:7)
- **Meet with** one another (Hebrews 10:25)
- **Submit to** one another (Ephesians 5:21)
- **Honor** one another above yourselves (Romans 12:10)
- **Show hospitality** to one another (1 Peter 4:9)
- **Encourage** one another (Hebrews 3:13; 10:25)
- **Build up** one another (Romans 15:2; 1 Thessalonians 5:11)
- **Confess your sins** to one another (James 5:16)
- **Admonish** one another (Colossians 3: 16)
- **Bear with** one another (Ephesians 4:2)
- **Be kind, tenderhearted, and forgiving** towards one another (Ephesians 4:32; Romans 12:10)
- **Bear** one another's burdens (Galatians 6:2)
- **Serve** one another in love (Galatians 5:13)
- **Be devoted** to one another (Romans 12:10)
- **Pray** for one another (James 5:16)

Picture what it would look like if the biblical one anothers functioned in one direction only. One person greets the other warmly. The other hardly even responds. One person forgives the other repeatedly for major hurts, the other person harbors a grudge for months. One person is very devoted to the other. The second person is transparent, the other has a mask on.

Mutual Relationships

Imagine on the other hand what a grace-filled, reciprocal approach to these one-anothers might look like! Both mentor partners are so enthralled with God's welcoming grace, undeserved yet lavishly bestowed, that they gladly welcome and fully accept each other, flaws and all.

- They **love one another** because they have experienced the love of Christ that will not let them go. Jesus said, "A new command I give you: Love one another...."[77] A command. It's not optional or trivial. This command was based on the practical example Jesus had just given by washing the dirty feet of his disciples.

- They **welcome and accept each other** because they have experienced God's undeserved welcome into his family. They "accept one another...just as Christ accepted [them]..." (Romans 15:7). Notice the benchmark. Their acceptance of one another is modeled on the way that Christ has welcomed them.

- They **meet together** often. Like the First Century Church, they meet to pray and be taught from God's Word, but they meet in each other's homes in between those corporate gatherings.

- They humbly **submit to one another** out of respect for Christ (Ephesians 5:21). The biblical word for submit means to "come under." That is, we are willing to lay down our rights and preferences for the sake of another. In his excellent book, *Love One Another*, Gerald Sittser says,

  > *Mutual subjection is God's way of nurturing harmony in a discordant world, unity in broken relationships, healing in a sick society, and love in a divided church. It is applicable to imperfect people—like you and me— who belong to imperfect families, work imperfect jobs,*

> *participate in imperfect organizations, belong to imperfect churches and live in an imperfect world.... Mutual subjection takes the world as it is, not as we want or expect it to be. It requires us to surrender ourselves to God, discerning how we can do his will in circumstances that are less than ideal.*[78]

When two or more people in a mentoring relationship submit to each other and surrender to Christ, they are like two harmonious dancers. Ted Koppel interviewed Ginger Rogers, after Fred Astaire's death. She said he was so good, that he never seemed to be the leader and she the follower. "There was a fluidity between the two of them, a seamlessness, an elegance, as if two people were dancing as one."[79]

- They **honor** each other as fellow citizens of a new kingdom (Ephesians 2:19; Romans 12:10). In his commentary on Romans, Chuck Swindoll puts it this way:

  > *Honoring someone begins with a willingness to let another have his or her preference in non-essential matters. We are to listen when someone speaks and give his or her words careful consideration. We must allow others to disagree, respecting their opinions even though we disagree.*[80]

- They constantly **encourage and build each other up** because they are captivated by Christ's love (2 Corinthians 5:14) and like the Lord Jesus they are looking out for each other's interests more than their own (Philippians 2:1-11).

- They **admonish one another** in a loving way because, at their very best, they are just greatly forgiven sinners, who need to be reminded of God's truth.

- They **forgive each other** again and again and are so taken with the magnitude of God's forgiveness that they live in the knowledge that greatly forgiven sinners forgive greatly (Matthew 18:21-35).

- They openly and appropriately **confess their sins** to each other and **pray for each other** (James 5:13-17) because they are aware of their own brokenness and feel secure in God's unending love for them in Christ (Romans 7:21-8:4).

In mutual mentoring relationships, one person may be more mature than the other, but it's the one another attitudes that make all the difference. Essentially they are unselfish, humble attitudes, and humility attracts grace. When a more experienced older mentor comes to a relationship to learn rather than teach, to receive rather than to give, to accept rather than to judge, genuine spiritual transformation takes place.

As I touched on in *The Leadership Baton*,[81] a turning point in my mentoring journey was when I met weekly with Rick Murphy while we were both students at Dallas Seminary. I was ten years Rick's senior. Prior to meeting with Rick, I had assumed that if I was to be an effective mentor, I had to be the "guru" in the relationship, and a closed book when it came to anything that would reveal my personal brokenness. Times with Rick changed all that. Early on in our lunch meetings, he opened up to me about struggles he was having. That seemed to flick a switch in me. It was a call to take off my mask. Most of my life I'd been a leader: a Bible Class leader when I was 15, a church elder at age 29, principal of a small Bible College at 32. And, wrongly, my reasoning was, "I can't tell my fellow elders about the things I'm really struggling with or I might lose my position. I can't tell fellow staff members at the Bible College about the inner conflict between my flesh and the Spirit, because they all seem to look up to me."

The lunch times with Rick simply unmasked me. We were sharpened as iron clashed with iron, we experienced the support, encouragement and protection described in Ecclesiastes 4. There was a one another flow as we accepted, forgave and held each other lovingly accountable.

Mutual mentoring, as an opportunity to practice intentional lingering, allows us to flow naturally into the biblical one anothers, to sharpen and support other believers, and to put ourselves in a place where life transformation is more likely to occur.

PROCESSING CHAPTER FIVE

STEP 1: **DEPEND**—SOAK THE PROCESS IN PRAYER

1. Consider the following prayer by B. F. Westcott as you process Chapter Five:

> "Almighty and most merciful God,
> who hast given us a new commandment
> that we should love one another,
> give us also grace that we may fulfill it.
> Make us gentle, courteous, and forebearing.
> Direct our lives so that we each look to the good of others
> in word and deed.
> And hallow all our friendships
> by the blessing of thy Spirit;
> for his sake who loved us and gave himself for us,
> Jesus Christ our Lord."[82]

2. Note one or two points from this chapter and reflect on them with a spoken or written prayer:

STEP 2: **MEDITATE**—CONSIDER WHAT THE SCRIPTURES SAY

Ecclesiastes 4:9-12

> [9] *Two are better than one, because they have a good return for their work:* [10] *If one falls down, his friend can help him up. But pity the man who falls and has no one to help him up!* [11] *Also, if two lie down together, they will keep warm. But how can one keep warm alone?* [12] *Though one may be overpowered, two can defend themselves. A cord of three strands is not quickly broken.*

- What are the benefits of partnership with one or two people according to this passage?

John 15:9-14, 17

> [9] *"As the Father has loved me, so have I loved you. Now remain in my love.* [10] *If you obey my commands, you will remain in my love, just as I have obeyed my Father's commands and remain in his love.* [11] *I have told you this so that my joy may be in you and that your joy may be complete.* [12] *My command is this: Love each other as I have loved you.* [13] *Greater love has no one than this, that he lay down his life for his friends.* [14] *You are my friends if you do what I command....* [17] *This is my command: Love each other.*

- What should our primary motive be if we are to keep on loving one another?

Greet one another with a holy kiss. —Romans 16:16

Accept one another, then, just as Christ accepted you, in order to bring praise to God. —Romans 15:7

But encourage one another daily, as long as it is called Today, so that none of you may be hardened by sin's deceitfulness.
—Hebrews 3:13

Carry each other's burdens, and in this way you will fulfill the law of Christ. —Galatians 6:2

Therefore confess your sins to each other and pray for each other so that you may be healed. —James 5:16

- How does this sample of the biblical one-anothers relate to the reciprocal mentoring described in Chapter Two?

- When you reflect on this selection of the biblical one-anothers, what are some implications for our mentoring relationships?

STEP 3: **RESPOND**—
LEARN FROM EACH OTHER AND TAKE ACTION

Reflection and Discussion:

1. How have you experienced "iron-sharpening-iron" relationships in the way described in Proverbs 27:17?

2. Meditate on Ecclesiastes 4:8-12. To what extent have you experienced the truth that "two is better than one"?

3. Consider the biblical one-anothers listed in this chapter.

    - How can our mentoring relationships move from being one-way to become two-way (mutual)?

    - Which of the one-anothers of Scripture mentioned in this chapter are weak points that need to be folded into your mentoring relationships?

4. What steps of obedience will you take:

Personally?

As a group?

PART TWO
Practices that May Become Habits

The following ten mutual mentoring practices may be adopted one-by-one, or in pairs: Praying and Meeting, Listening and Asking, and so on.

As the interlocking circles suggest, there is an interplay between the various practices. Initially, it may pay to fold each practice into your mentoring gatherings, as you go, but eventually they will become habits.

Having said that, many of the practices, such as praying before, during and after our sessions, can easily slip. That's why we suggest that you read this book, and adopt these practices along with another person or a group, so that you hold each other lovingly accountable.

Note that each chapter gives you an opportunity to process what you are learning, with the addition of "Mentoring Practices"—suggestions on how you can fold the skills into your mentoring sessions.

CHAPTER SIX

PRAYING

*"Therefore, confess your sins to each other and
pray for each other so that you may be healed."*
—James 5:16

*"Prayer is a mighty instrument, not for getting man's
will done in heaven, but for getting God's will done in earth."*
—Robert Laws

One mentoring practice transcends, and is foundational to all others—prayer. Pray before you meet, during your meeting, and after the scheduled meeting time. Jesus did that. He was forever praying for his disciples. He chose them after a night of prayer (Luke 6:12), he taught them to pray (Luke 11:1-4), he prayed for them in a time of crisis (Luke 22:31-32, 40) and he focused on them in his High Priestly prayer, just before he was crucified (John 17).

Pray Before

Do you pray before you meet with your mentor-friends? Too often I just proceed in my own strength (one of my bad habits!). When you remember to pray before a mentoring meeting, does the time always flow perfectly? Sometimes it does for me, sometimes no. What does happen though is that our attitude changes. Invariably we have a sense of expectancy, looking to see what God will do. And if the time together has a touch of the divine, we pause and thank God.

Prayer is not, as some people describe it, a *given* (something routine and less important). It is central and crucial. Jesus' words in John 15:5 (ESV)—"I am the vine; you are the branches. Whoever abides in me and I in him, he it is that bears much fruit, for *apart from me you can do nothing.*"—need to be etched into our brain. Prayer in our day is more like a missing ingredient. In *Gospel-Centered Discipleship*, Jonathan Dodson asks, "How often do we start our day by requesting a fresh filling of the Spirit's power for the day that lies ahead? Instead, we assume his presence and barrel forward. Instead, of starting and continuing our days in our own strength, what would it look like to fight for faith with utter dependence upon the power and direction of the Holy Spirit?"[83]

The First Century Church was different. They practiced the power of believing prayer. Greg Ogden says,

> ...when I open the book of Acts...and observe the picture of the church there...I see a small band of timid disciples huddled together in an upper room. They know they need God's power. They are Galileans, disrespected by the higher classes in Jerusalem as lower-class, rural, uneducated commoners.... So what are they doing? They are not plotting strategies. They are "joined together constantly in prayer." They are not busy putting faith in themselves or relying on themselves. They are pleading for the power of God, and they are confident that they are not going to accomplish anything without his provision. Then God sends his Spirit in power, and everything changes."[84]

To emulate the disciples in the book of Acts, before you meet with your mentor-friend, maybe pray a prayer like this:

> *Heavenly Father, I know you have given my friend to me, and me to my friend. Grace us with your Presence as we meet. Lord Jesus, too often I'm like those friends who trudged on toward Emmaus, all confused. Open our eyes so that we are aware of you as we meet to mentor each other. Holy Spirit, activate our conversation, lead us into the truth I pray. Amen.*

Pray During

Interactive Praying

One of my mutual mentors, Stu Henderson, Co-Pastor of "The King's Arms Church" has a favorite activity for our mentoring times: to go for a walk. We've done that often along beaches in Auckland, and along the stunningly picturesque walkway in Wellington harbor. We share concerns quite naturally as we stride along, and talk to the Lord about the matter as if he is right there. He is. And we don't close our eyes! It feels natural to go in and out of talking with each other and with the Lord Jesus, as if we are the two disciples on the Emmaus Road after they recognized Jesus.

Most of my mentoring meetings take place in cafés. I'm conditioned to pray with my eyes closed (a helpful idea to aid concentration, but definitely not a biblical requirement) and have them closed in a café regardless of what people think. Other times I keep my eyes open while praying to the Lord like when Stu and I go on mentoring-prayer walks. What you do with your eyes is not the issue. A prayerful attitude is.

Nehemiah is a great example of this. When he was cupbearer to King Artaxerxes, he was unable to disguise his sadness at the mess Jerusalem was in. The King asked him why he was so sad. Nehemiah was terrified as you were not supposed to convey sadness in the presence of royalty in those days. The King asked Nehemiah what he wanted. Right then and there he "prayed to the God of heaven" and answered the King.[85] I imagine Nehemiah kept his eyes open as he prayed and simply sent up an inaudible prayergram to heaven. That's a great option for us in any mutual mentoring meetings.

Another way to activate prayer during a mentoring session is to ask for prayer or to offer to pray. If trust has been built, share your concerns openly and ask, "Would you please pray for me now about that?" When your mentor-companion, or someone in your mentoring huddle opens up about one of their concerns, say, "Let me pray about that right now." After a while the ebb and flow of conversation and mutual prayer feels like the most natural thing in the world. For most of us it feels awkward initially.

The call of this first "Essential Practice" is to cultivate an interaction, not just with your mentor-friend, but with the God of heaven. To do that, requires the aspiration Eugene Peterson expresses:

> *I want to cultivate my relationship with God. I want all of life to be intimate—sometimes consciously, sometimes unconsciously—with the God who made, directs and loves me. And I want to be a person in this community to whom others can come without hesitation, without wondering if it is appropriate, to get direction in prayer and praying.*[86]

Vulnerable Praying

James calls us to "pray for one another," always in the context of human brokenness. In this verse he urges us to, "…confess your sins to each other and pray for each other…."[87] First confess, then pray. In other words, as you humble yourselves before each other you will need to pray for each other as never before.

In James 5:13-15 this half-brother of Jesus tells us it is always the right time to pray. He says, if you are in trouble, pray. If you are happy, then lift up praise. If you are sick, call your elders to pray with you. He describes one of the primary tasks of church elders: to pray with and for their people. The initiative in this case is with the person who is sick, but the elders communicate in various ways that they are always available for prayer. They anoint the person with oil and offer prayers of faith, and God raises the person.

When James says, "Therefore confess your sins to each other…," I believe he is widening the circle. He's built his case for the necessity of vulnerability in our relationships as he demonstrated in the case of the sick person and the church elders. Now he says all of the believers are to confess their sins with each other and pray for each other.

Confession and prayer form one mutuality command. As Gerald Sittser says in *Love One Another: Becoming the Church Jesus Longs For*:

> *Confession exposes; prayer heals. Confession takes responsibility for wrongdoing; prayer asks God to help us do what is right. Confession acknowledges the human condition; prayer draws on the transcendent power of God. Confession admits to sin; prayer leads us to salvation. Confession challenges us to risk being weak and vulnerable before our brothers and sisters in Christ. We can, of course, choose not to confess, because in many cases no one will ever know our sins. But in the long run we will suffer loss, for we will not be known and still loved for the sinners we are, nor will be receive the grace of God through the ministry of others. Prayer, in turn, requires us to intercede on behalf of those who have been weak and vulnerable before us. This mutuality command appeals directly to God, who alone has the power to forgive, restore and heal broken sinners—such as we all are.*[88]

I was 46 when attending Dallas Seminary as a student. I had been the Principal of a small Discipleship and Missions Bible College for 14 years and was badly burned out. God put me together again in those two and a half years in seminary. A huge element in my restoration was a friendship with Rick Murphy. As mentioned in Chapter Five, it was when he confessed his sins that it freed me to admit my sins to him. Before that I longed to be open and vulnerable but always talked myself out of it.

As I reflect on my reticence to confess my sins to another human being, there are some pertinent lessons for mutual mentoring, such as:

- Fellow believers are more broken, needy and imperfect than they let on.

- Confession to God through the mediation of Christ alone (and embodied in the prayer at the conclusion of this chapter) is our primary port of call.

- When deep respect and trust has been built between two Christ-followers, we need to be appropriately vulnerable with each other.

- When we confess our sins to each other and pray for each other, spiritual healing (and sometimes physical) can take place as well.

What God taught me through that mutual mentoring relationship with Rick, is best captured in Greg Ogden's words:

> When we (1) open our hearts in transparent trust to each other (2) around the truth of God's Word (3) in the spirit of mutual accountability, we are in the Holy Spirit's hothouse of transformation.[89]

Pray After

"I'll pray for you!" I've said that hundreds of times. As I say those words it feels so spiritual and reassuring, but it is meaningless when I neglect to pray. Here are some practical ways I'm attempting to overcome my tendency to promise to pray then promptly forget:

- I keep a journal or notebook with me and during the mentoring session I jot down any items from our conversation that could be triggers to pray for my mentor-friend.

- When I get home, or sometimes the next day, I send an email that says in effect, "Here's what I am praying for you" (the Apostle Paul seemed to do that almost every time he wrote to individuals or a church). Sometimes this will include specific and personal items that arise during our time together. Other times I believe it is important to pray bigger prayers. Prayers like the one Paul prayed for the Colossian believers:

  > *...we have not stopped praying for you and asking God to fill you with the knowledge of his will through all spiritual wisdom and understanding. And we pray this in order that you may live a life worthy of the Lord and may please him in every way: bearing fruit in every good work, growing in the knowledge of God....*[90]

  As I read that incredible prayer, I realize that my prayers are often too small.

- If I know that the person I am mentoring has an important appointment coming up, I put a note in my calendar to pray for them and at times supplement that with a text to say I have been praying.

This first essential mentoring practice that may become a habit—praying before, during and after—is hinted at in Psalm 127:1. Admittedly the Psalmist is talking about building a godly family, but the principle is transferrable and timeless: "Unless the LORD builds the house, its builders labor in vain. Unless the LORD watches over the city, the watchmen stand guard in vain."

As you together build this mentoring friendship, never forget that dependence on God through prayer is at the center of spiritual mentoring. Unless you do, it could be a fleshly exercise and potentially be in vain. If you bathe your relationship in prayer, then when your relationship morphs into a spiritual friendship, all credit goes to God.

Maybe like me, your default life habit is to do things in your own strength. At least we are not on our own! Paul chided the Galatian churches for that bad habit. He said, "Are you so foolish? After beginning with the Spirit, are you now trying to attain your goal by human effort?"[91] Self-reliance is foolish and deep-seated. And deeply ingrained habits are hard to break.

That's why we need each other. Ideally, as you read this book you will be in a mentor-partnership with another person, or in a mentoring huddle. If you are convinced that you need to bathe your mentoring relationships in prayer, commit to engaging in this first habit and keeping each other gently accountable. I say "gently" because there are few things more exhausting than an intensely legalistic check-up session. Maybe on the day of your next meeting text each other with the pray-before-during-after reminder? When you meet, try introducing the Lord into your conversation, however awkward it feels at first. He is with you. And after you have met, send a text or an email with a "here's what I am praying for you…" message.

PROCESSING CHAPTER SIX

STEP 1: **DEPEND**—SOAK THE PROCESS IN PRAYER

1. As you process Chapter Six, consider my prayer "Before, During, After" and "The Simplest Form of Speech" by James Montgomery:

Before, During, After

Living Lord,
Before each mentoring meeting I pray—
- for you to go ahead of us and prepare our hearts,
- for the Holy Spirit's guidance,
- for a sense of your Presence.

During our meetings I pray—
- for sensitivity to listen deeply to each other and to your Spirit,
- for the energy to be fully present,
- for your prompting on which questions to ask,
- for wisdom to know when to affirm and when to lovingly admonish.

After we have met I pray—
- for boldness as we take action on what you have said to us,
- for your prompting on how and when to send messages of encouragement,
- for our eyes to be on you Lord and not on each other.

The Simplest Form of Speech

Prayer is the simplest form of speech
    that infant lips can try;
    prayer the sublimest strains that reach
    the Majesty on high.

Prayer is the contrite sinner's voice,
    returning from their way,
    while angels in their songs rejoice
    and cry, "Behold, they pray!"

> Prayer is the Christian's vital breath,
>> the Christian's native air;
>> their watchword at the gates of death;
>> they enter heaven with prayer.
>
> O Thou, by whom we come to God,
>> the Life, the Truth, the Way:
>> the path of prayer thyself hast trod;
> Lord, teach us how to pray![92]

2. Note one or two points from this chapter and reflect on them with a spoken or written prayer:

STEP 2: **MEDITATE**—CONSIDER WHAT THE SCRIPTURES SAY

Psalm 5:2-3

> ² Listen to my cry for help, my King and my God, for to you I pray. ³ In the morning, O LORD, you hear my voice; in the morning I lay my requests before you and wait in expectation.

Psalm 55:16-17

> ¹⁶ But I call to God, and the LORD saves me. ¹⁷ Evening, morning and noon I cry out in distress, and he hears my voice.

Daniel 6:10

> ¹⁰ Now when Daniel learned that the decree had been published, he went home to his upstairs room where the windows opened toward Jerusalem. Three times a day he got down on his knees and prayed, giving thanks to his God, just as he had done before.

1 Timothy 2:1-3

> ¹ I urge, then, first of all, that requests, prayers, intercession and thanksgiving be made for everyone—² for kings and all those in authority, that we may live peaceful and quiet lives in all godliness and holiness. ³ This is good, and pleases God our Savior....

James 5:16

> ¹⁶ Therefore confess your sins to each other and pray for each other so that you may be healed. The prayer of a righteous man is powerful and effective.

- How do these passages relate to the topic of praying before, during and after each mentoring encounter?

STEP 3: **RESPOND**—
LEARN FROM EACH OTHER AND TAKE ACTION

Reflection and Discussion:

1. What are the main things you have learned from your study of the Scripture passages listed above?

2. What causes us to neglect to pray before, during and after the times we meet together for mutual mentoring?

3. What are the roadblocks to prayer as a way-of-life?

4. What are the boundaries we need to keep in mind as we seek to be more vulnerable in our mentoring relationships, such as confessing our sins to one another?

Mentoring Practices:

1. This week, as you meet with your mentoring partner or mentoring cluster, aim to put this chapter into practice. Before you set off for the meeting, pause to pray. When you meet, explore ways to fold prayer into your time together. As you leave each other, pause to pray for your mentoring partner/s.

2. To make this a spiritual practice that becomes a habit, seek to fold the pray-before-during-after routine into as many aspects of your life as possible.

CHAPTER SEVEN

MEETING

"Let us not give up meeting together, as some are in the habit of doing, but let us encourage one another—and all the more as you see the Day approaching."
—Hebrews 10:25

"Our presence matters....
We are good news when we have nothing to offer but our availability. We are quiet support—like the foundation of a house, present but not often noticed."[93]
—Rochelle Melander

The first two mentoring practices (Praying and Meeting) amount to **prayer** and **presence**. If you soak your relationship in prayer, in the realization that life transformation is the work of God, yet fail to meet together (with what Rochelle Melander calls "a generous presence"[94]), one of God's primary means of life-change is removed. While God doesn't need us to accomplish his purposes, he chooses to use us to help build up one another. He demonstrates his amazing humility by accomplishing his purposes primarily though frail human vessels. Showing up in another person's life is a way of releasing ourselves from focusing on ourselves and our interests. It is one way to apply Paul's words to the church at Philippi: "Each of you should look not only to your own interests, but also to the interests of others."[95]

How do *you* decide whom to meet with as you pursue a mentoring partnership? While I am more of a planner—who organizes mentoring appointments in my calendar (typically on a Sunday afternoon), my wife Elaine, has a free-flow approach to mentoring connections. Typically she prays a prayer in the morning something like this: "Lord who do you want me to visit today?" She waits and if someone comes into her mind she calls them. Sometimes it's a young mother who needs advice on child-rearing. Sometimes it's a woman from her Small Group. Invariably it is just what the person needed on that day. Whether you plan your visits or respond to promptings of the Holy Spirit, the key thing is to show that your sail is set towards your mentor-partner or partners.

Showing up in another person's life is implied in several of the one-anothers of Scripture:

Meeting Together

- *"Let us not give up meeting together, as some are in the habit of doing, but let us encourage one another—and all the more as you see the Day approaching."* —Hebrews 10:25

It's so easy to find excuses not to bother meeting with another person for mutual encouragement—in the words of Scripture to just "give up." Tiredness, busyness, and at times, the sheer inconvenience of making time to arrange a meeting, can result in us disobeying God's call in this one-another. Implied in this verse is one of the most powerful motivations for mutual mentoring—knowing how encouraging it is to another human being that you took the time to contact them.

Greeting Each Other

- *"Greet one another with a holy kiss. All the churches of Christ send greetings."* —Romans 16:16

- *"All the brothers and sisters here send you greetings. Greet one another with a holy kiss."* —1 Corinthians 16:20

- *"Greet one another with a kiss of love. Peace to all of you who are in Christ."* —1 Peter 5:14

To greet one another with a holy kiss means that when we meet together we do so with purity and affection. We show warm acceptance and genuine interest.

Showing Hospitality

- *"Offer hospitality to one another without grumbling."* —1 Peter 4:9

The biblical word for hospitality implies love of strangers. Hebrews 13:2 spells that out—"Do not forget to show hospitality to strangers, for by so doing some people have shown hospitality to angels without knowing it." In a mentoring context this includes reaching out to people who may not realize you are thinking of them. This one-another also implies how we show up. According to the American Heritage Talking Dictionary, hospitality is "The quality of being pleasant and friendly: friendliness, affability, amiableness, amiability, amicability, cordiality, geniality, agreeability, agreeableness, kindliness, pleasantness, warmth, warmness, good-naturedness, graciousness...."[96] How then should we show up in the lives of the people we mutually mentor?

Meet Regularly

The writer to the Hebrews captures the need for regularity and frequency in our mentoring relationships by saying:

- *"But encourage one another daily, as long as it is called Today, so that none of you may be hardened by sin's deceitfulness."* —Hebrews 3:13

The frequency of mutual mentoring meetings is determined by the nature of the relationship. There have been seasons in my mutual mentoring relationship with Don Overton where we met every week. That was true when we worked together in Fellowship Bible Church North. It was also true when Don was at a crossroads ministry-wise, and I was in need of advice about writing this book. As I write, our frequency is about once a month or on an as-needed basis. Thank God for internet video connections! Sometimes we make an appointment to meet at a particular time. At other times we just let each other know we are online. The bottom line is that I know that I am on Don's radar screen and we are thinking of each other.

I've been mentoring Warren Henderson, Deputy Principal of Onslow College, in Wellington, New Zealand off and on for the last seven years. He's in Nice, France at the moment with a group of his students. Here's a text that has just come in: "I'm in a confectionary shop in Nice, waiting for the kids and thanking God for friends like you." I replied, "And I'm in an Auckland café, sipping a latte, writing about mentoring, and thanking God I ever met you. Stay close to Christ!" Warren and I show up in each other's lives spontaneously, but our commitment to each other is just as real as if we met every week. And he mentors me every now and then by texting Scripture verses.

Meet Wholly

It's one thing to merely meet, and another to show up generously—to be wholly present. It is the practice of giving the other person the gift of full attention. Rochelle Melander captures the reality of half-hearted presence:

> *Many of our encounters…lack this quality of presence. We are distracted or distant. Most of us are pretty good at faking presence. We say "uh-huh" into the phone as a friend recounts her day, all the while checking email. At a conference, a colleague moves his head up and down while scanning the room for someone more important to talk to....*[97]

And she suggests the following actions to support the practice of being "fiercely present":

> **"Put other work aside.** *Close folders, books, the Internet connection, and anything else that might pull your attention.*

Minimize potential distractions. In the office, shut the door, turn off the phone's ringer, and shut down the computer. At a public venue, take the non-power seat—so that all concentration can be on the person you are talking with. Avoid looking at your watch.

Pray. On many days it seems that it is only by God's grace that I can focus on anything.... For that reason, I always ask God to center me, to calm my worried mind, and to create a space where I can pay attention to the needs of the one before me at the moment.

Focus your body. Both my piano and clarinet instructors believed that the proper posture laid the foundation for playing good music. Good posture doesn't hurt in our interpersonal relationships either. Turn your body toward the person you are speaking to. Lean forward. Keep your hands and arms in an open position.

Open your mind. In a conversation, we open our mind to the other person. Our personal thoughts and distractions are quieted so that we can be open to receive the gift of the other— his or her thoughts, emotions, and needs. Our agenda is put aside. This time is not about us but about them.

Stay present. Inside the conversation, the only time that matters is now.... Intrusive thoughts are shooed away, like flies. Important inklings—persistent insights we want to share with the other—are jotted down for a later time.[98]

And at times, when Christ graces us with the gift of being fully present, the net result is what one of my more artistic mentor-friends John Maikowski, calls disruption. He wrote a poem about our times together:

There's something disruptive about you.
Normally I'm able to maneuver through life running,
directing, jumping, acting, reacting,
all the while keeping the call of the wild a whisper.

There's something disruptive about you.
Usually I'm able to abort the processing of call,
cause, creation, connection, communion,
effectively silencing the whisper of the Holy.

There's something disruptive about you...
that speaks of a different way
and of being okay at the end of the day
having had less to pay.

There's something disruptive about you...
that screams softly of wholeness and boldness
to eschew the faithless space that leads to emptiness.

There's something disruptive about you.
I pray that one day soon
I'll know what to do
with the disruption.[99]

What moved me most when I received this poem in the form of an email was the nature of my mentoring journey with John. John is at his core an artist. He's a deep thinker. When we first met, I was in my "mentor-to-pastors" role at Fellowship Bible Church North. We'd meet for lunch at a restaurant near our church office. I recall the first meetings as fairly formal. It felt as if we were both at arms-length. What changed all that was a visit to China with John, his wife Linda and our friends Greg and Tina Joseph. John and I began to open up to each other in a new way. Now our relationship felt more like a father and son. God knit our hearts together.

More recently we have connected via internet video and walked together as John has been responding to God's "disruptive" call to leave the comfort of his influential role as Worship Arts Pastor at Chase Oaks Church for the uncertainty of a move to Denver, Colorado to live among artists to communicate Christ's love. As we have shown up fully in these encounters, we have become disruptive soul-brothers.

Meet Purposefully

After the Patriarch Job experienced unrelenting tragedy and excruciating pain, Job's three "friends", Eliphaz, Bildad and Zophar, showed up and gave him the gift of a generous presence. Job 2:12-13 says, "When they saw him from a distance, they could hardly recognize him; they began to weep aloud, and they tore their robes and sprinkled dust on their heads. Then they sat on the ground with him for seven days and seven nights. No one said a word to him...." They were emotionally, physically and appropriately present with him.

They had a purpose for this meeting though: Job 2:11 says, "...they set out from their homes and met together by agreement to go and sympathize with him and comfort him." They showed up at Job's place intentionally—to provide support and comfort. As we know from the rest of the story of Job, the three comforters did a great job initially, but ended up more like discouragers than encouragers.

I've found that listening to each other's life stories is a powerful way to encourage each other, to forge community, and ultimately deep trust. A simple way to do that is to share one uplifting experience and one challenging experience in each decade of your life. Be ready to pray for each other at appropriate junctures in the conversation. Much of the impact of this exercise depends on how much time you have available. Don't rush it. Better to just unpack a couple of decades then come back to that on another occasion than race through it.

Uplifting	10	20	30	40	50	60+
Challenging						

Early on in mentoring meetings it's important to determine what our goals are for the times together. And if mutual mentoring is to occur, the goals should be mutual. Many of my mentoring relationships include "coffee, goals and a book." My first mentoring meeting with Greg Joseph involved those three things. We met for lunch at a café, and explored what we wanted out of this relationship. Greg's goal was to learn how to make his faith more meaningful in the workplace. I just "happened" to be reading *Business for the Glory of God* by Wayne Grudem. Greg bought Grudem's book that day and had several chapters read by the time we met the next week. Over lunch each week we chewed on business issues like ownership, productivity, profit and how these matters can glorify God.

My goal when Greg and I met, was character development. I needed someone to speak grace and truth into my life. I hardly needed to spell that out though. I could tell two things about Greg from the very first time we met: First, he cared about me. I could tell this was a mentor-friendship made in heaven. Second, I didn't intimidate him. From day one he spoke boldly and lovingly about strengths and weaknesses he had seen in me.

At other times it is clear that the goal of a fellow mentor is to seek advice. That's what it was like when Pastor Allan McPherson and I met at an Auckland café. He was at a crossroads in ministry and expressed his need for sound advice from someone further along the road that he had known for many years.

In Edward Smither's book *Augustine as Mentor*, he describes how Augustine of Hippo (354-430 A.D.) mentored leaders in the 4th and 5th Century. Augustine's main method was through copious letters that amounted to mutual advice-giving. Smither says "…on account of his letters and writings, became a mentor of the clergy and bishops through correspondence."[100] There are 252 surviving letters that include 23 to five different leaders that are most definitely examples of mutual mentoring. His seven letters to Paulinus of Nova reveal "…a growing, intimate friendship between two spiritual leaders desperate to learn from each other. In *Letter* 27, written in 396, Augustine responded to Paulinus's initial letter, expressing how he had been encouraged by it and that he desired to get to know his new friend in Christ.[101]

Just meeting, as one of the primary practices of a mutual mentor, doesn't sound all that significant. However when it is coupled with prayer (before, during and after) and when you linger regularly (enthusiastically and purposefully), the effect is profound. What you are saying as you meet in this way is: "I'm here for you, to invest time in you, to listen to you, to learn and grow with you, to be authentic with you, to walk alongside you as a companion, and to leave a little of me (and hopefully a lot of Christ) in you."

The first two mentoring practices amount to being present to God and present to people. Both require a humble attitude. The practices in Chapters Eight and Nine, "Listening" and "Asking," are no different. They are a call for an unselfish approach to human relationships.

PROCESSING CHAPTER SEVEN

STEP 1: **DEPEND**—SOAK THE PROCESS IN PRAYER

1. As you plan to "meet" in the way described in this chapter, meditate on, and praying this great prayer of Francis of Assisi:

> Lord, make me an instrument of your peace.
> Where there is hatred, let me bring love;
> Where there is injury, pardon;
> Where there is doubt, faith;
> Where there is darkness, light;
> Where there is sadness, joy.
>
> O Divine Master, grant that I may not
> So much seek to be consoled as to console,
> To be understood as to understand,
> To be loved as to love.
> For it is in giving that we receive,
> It is pardoning that we are pardoned,
> And it is in dying that we are born to eternal life.[102]

2. Note one or two points from this chapter and reflect on them with a spoken or written prayer:

STEP 2: **MEDITATE**—CONSIDER WHAT THE SCRIPTURES SAY

Greet one another with a holy kiss. All the churches of Christ send greetings. —Romans 16:16

Accept one another, then, just as Christ accepted you, in order to bring praise to God. —Romans 15:7

Offer hospitality to one another without grumbling. —1 Peter 4:9

- How do these "meet and greet" biblical one-anothers capture how to "show-up" in our mentoring relationships?

Hebrews 3:12-15

[12] See to it, brothers, that none of you has a sinful, unbelieving heart that turns away from the living God. [13] But encourage one another daily, as long as it is called Today, so that none of you may be hardened by sin's deceitfulness. [14] We have come to share in Christ if we hold firmly till the end the confidence we had at first. [15] As has just been said: "Today, if you hear his voice, do not harden your hearts as you did in the rebellion."

- What does this passage tell us about the frequency of and motivation for our mentoring times?

STEP 3: **RESPOND**—
LEARN FROM EACH OTHER AND TAKE ACTION

Reflection and Discussion:

1. What are some of the things that hold us back from bothering to "show up" in the lives of our Christian companions?

2. What are some guidelines as we decide how often to meet together in a mutual mentoring relationship?

3. How can you tell if the other person in a mentoring relationship is wholly or half-heartedly present?

4. What should be some of the primary purposes of meeting for mutual mentoring?

5. What steps of obedience do you need to take after reading Chapter Seven:

Personally?

As a group?

Mentoring Practices:

1. Remember to pray before during and after your meeting.

2. The three skills in this mentoring practice are: meeting regularly, meeting wholly, and meeting purposefully.

- **Meeting regularly**. Review the frequency of your mentoring meetings. Does this accomplish the purpose of your times together? Review the people you mentor on an "as needed" basis. Should you meet more regularly with them?

- **Meeting wholly**. Discuss this skill as you meet together after reading this chapter. Talk about the things that distract you most easily. Possibly read out the statement on page 96 to each other that begins: "I'm here for you, to invest time in you…." and then renew your commitment to being "fiercely" present when you meet.

- **Meeting purposefully**. Take this as an opportunity to visit or revisit your mutual goals for the times you spend together.

3. The important thing in this time is to practice both of the first two skills: praying and meeting.

CHAPTER EIGHT

LISTENING

"Listen to advice and accept instruction,
and in the end you will be wise."
—Proverbs 19:20

"He who has an ear, let him hear what the
Spirit says to the churches."
—Revelation 2:7; 17, 29; 3:6, 13, 22

"Mentoring is not about telling. It is about listening—
to the Holy Spirit and to the life of the other....
It is true that there are times of instructing, guiding and sharing
of wisdom, but mentoring is primarily about discernment
and learning to recognize where God is already
present and active in the heart of the other."[103]
—Anderson and Reese

Learning to listen well is essential for effective transformational mentoring. And self-awareness is a great starting place. I know that I am naturally more of a teacher, more of an advice-giver than a listener. What about you? Are you more talker than listener; or listener than talker? When you are in a small group setting are you quick to offer your opinion? Or do you tend to hang back and listen, then say something profound (well, maybe helpful)?

I've had to learn and hone the skill of listening. Nothing gives me more pleasure as a mentor than to hear someone say, "Thank you. You really listened to me."

Listen Attentively

Healthy mentoring relationships require active reciprocal listening. Listening is much more than a passive, "I speak, you listen; you speak, I listen" routine. It calls for us to be actively present with each other. In *A Generous Presence*, Rochelle Melander says that ideally, a fully engaged listener communicates some of the following attitudes:

- **"I am fully present with you."** Melander describes this as being "fiercely attentive." The listener dismisses as many distractions as possible.

- **"I care about you."** The person sets aside his or her time and enters into our world.

- **"I accept you."** The attentive listener exudes warmth and welcomes the other person just as they are.

- **"Is this what you are saying?"** An attentive listener asks for clarification with a view to deeper understanding.

- **"I understand."** The listener is more interested in understanding us than in being understood.[104]

The reality though is that our world is full of internal and external distractions:

Internal:

- Your mind wanders to your work or whatever you were doing before meeting,
- What the person says reminds you of something you need to attend to,
- Multitasking,
- Listening with an agenda,
- You hear what the person says and are already marshaling your answers or formulating the next question.

External:

- Your mobile phone is on and although you have it on mute, it vibrates and your curiosity gets the better of you,
- There are intriguing things going on in the café where you meet,
- You watch the clock,
- You are sitting at your work desk and your mind goes in a hundred directions.

I'm convinced that listening is a discipline that can be learned. And that discipline starts with self-awareness. What are some internal and external factors that really distract you? In the Mary and Martha story (Luke 10:38-42), if you asked that of Martha after her interaction with Jesus, she may have said, "Much serving. I get so involved in doing that I neglect to listen."

In my role as a mentor-coach I ask mentor-trainees to give me an approximate percentage of how much listening, and how much talking they did during a mentoring session. Invariably they talk more than they listen. My challenge is to change that next time. What about you? Are you more of a talker than a listener? To engage in the discipline of listening, this next week, try to just listen to people. Resist the desire to give your opinion. I know it will be a bit contrived and awkward, but you will be training yourself to listen.

In his book, *Leader Mentoring*, what Michael Shenkman says about leaders is true of all mentor-friends:

> *To be a great leader mentor, you must listen not only for what is said, but also for what isn't said.... You must be less interested in telling your own stories, and more interested in the story of your mentees. People who talk too much don't make good mentors. People who can be silently active, with strong eye contact...are stronger candidates than those who feel the need to put all their thoughts into words.*[105]

Those comments from Shenkman capture the essence of good listening—focusing on the other person, physically, and most importantly, internally. Rein in your tendency to give advice. Turn off the conversation inside your head and just listen. The benefits will be unbelievable. It's almost magical as Tony Stoltzfus puts it:

> *...When I sit down with a friend who is really listening, something magical happens. As he listens patiently, asks me questions and helps me look at my situation from other angles, the truth comes into focus. My objective and subjective insights begin to mesh. I push through the fog of emotions or preconceptions until suddenly I break out of the box I'm in and see the solution clearly. When we verbalize our thoughts to someone else who is listening, we think more clearly and confidently than we do alone.*[106]

Listen Humbly

Listening with a view to understanding requires humility. It is firstly a heart attitude that says, in effect, "I'm here to listen to you and what God might be saying to me through you." Advice-giving has its place in the mentoring relationship, as we will see in some of the other mentoring practices, but listening attentively is another way of implementing Paul's instructions in Philippians 2:3-4: "...in humility consider others better than yourselves. Each of you should look not only to your own interests, but also to the interests of others." A person with a listening ear is essentially other-oriented. It amounts to putting a brake on whenever you are tempted to dish out advice.

The words of the Teacher in Ecclesiastes about the best heart attitude when we go into the house of God are true for transformational mentoring relationships as well:

> *Guard your steps when you go to the house of God. Go near to listen rather than to offer the sacrifice of fools, who do not know that they do wrong. Do not be quick with your mouth, do not be hasty in your heart to utter anything before God. God is in heaven and you are on earth, so let your words be few.*[107]

In this passage the Teacher is concerned with how worshippers listen but also with how they speak. They are to approach God with a listening ear, eager to hear his Word. They are also to be slow to make rash promises in God's presence. The principle is the same when we come to a mentoring friendship: be eager to listen and slow to speak.

There was a period in my marriage when I was on serious overload in life and ministry. I was the Principal of the GLO Bible College at the time, as well as National Director of Gospel Literature Outreach (GLO). I had been asked to give a plenary address at the GLO International Conference in London. The day before I left for a three week speaking tour, I met Elaine after work and could tell that something was amiss. I asked, "What's wrong?" She replied, "Nothing" (which being interpreted means, trouble brewing). When I pressed that point she said, "It's not worth telling you—you never listen." Something happened in me that day. Usually I would have been my own attorney. I would have dissected the phrase, "you never listen" focusing on the word "never." That day though, all I said was "I really want to listen." And that's all I did. No justification of my inattentiveness. No springing to my own defense. And when Elaine explained her feelings I merely said, "Tell me more." That day I uncovered the power of humble listening. Our marriage has been better ever since. Humble listening will be a challenge if you are an answer-giver (like me). There is a time for that, but in most mentor meetings, listening begins with turning off the flow of answers.

God is our example when it comes to listening. The Book of Job demonstrates that. The godly Patriarch Job experiences unrelenting tragedy: the death of his sons and daughters, excruciating sores all over his body, and "friends" who increase his agony by suggesting that he must have sinned to be suffering as much as that. Initially Job dealt with tragedy and suffering well—he praised Yahweh, but his friends ground him down. As the emotional and physical pain got the better of him, he told God exactly what he thought of him. According to the Book of Job, God just listened (Chapter 3 through 37). No answers. There's no doubt God could have told Job about the Cosmic Council with Satan (Chapter 1 and 2) and lots more. Yet, even when Yahweh spoke, essentially all he did was to ask questions such as, "Where were you when I laid the earth's foundation" (38:4)? Wisely, after God's interrogation, Job says, "I am unworthy—how can I reply to you? I put my hand over my mouth" (40:4). So if we are to emulate God in our mentoring relationships, we need to humbly listen as our first instinct.

Listen Spiritually

Skillful mutual mentors listen deeply and humbly to each other. But if spiritual transformation is to take place, they also listen to what the Holy Spirit is saying through each other. It amounts to being more taken up with the concerns of others and with God's agenda rather than our own. Anderson and Reese put it this way:

> *Mentoring is not about telling. It is about listening—to the Holy Spirit and to the life of the other.... It is true that there are times of instructing, guiding and sharing wisdom, but mentoring is primarily about discernment and learning to recognize where God is already present and active in the heart of the other.*[108]

Spiritual listening amounts to asking the question: "What might the Holy Spirit be saying to me and to us?" According to Jesus' letters to the Seven Churches of Asia, church leaders need to ask, "What is the Spirit saying to our church?" In every one of Jesus' letters in Revelation Chapter 2 and 3 he says, "He who has ears let him hear what the Spirit is saying to the churches."[109] Similarly, in our mentoring pairs or huddles we need to become detectives of what the Spirit may be whispering to us. How do we hear from the Holy Spirit in our mutual mentor partnerships?

Ask

First we need to ask for his help. Chapter Six was a call to pray before, during and after we meet. James says "You do not have, because you do not ask God"[110] and I'm sure that is true of listening to the Spirit. Before you meet, ask God to speak to you both by His Spirit (or to your mentoring huddle), and maybe during your meeting, pause and express your desire to hear from him. After your mentoring session, ask the Lord, "What were you saying?" Those prayers before, during and after convey an open heart—a willingness to listen and respond, akin to Samuel's words, "Speak LORD for your servant is listening."[111] The Samuel story is instructive because the young apprentice to Eli, initially didn't realize God was speaking. That's so like me. I'm often quick to speak and slow to listen to the Spirit. How about you?

Reflect

Second we need to reflect. The words of Ecclesiastes 4:9 are true here—"Two are better than one." I've been through several phases in this quest to listen to what the Spirit may be saying in my mentoring relationships. For years, I had a general desire to listen to the Spirit, but wasn't comfortable to claim that the Spirit had spoken. Then one day while mentoring Allan McPherson, I asked him to send me an email with anything that he sensed the Spirit might be saying to him from our mentoring meeting. His response blew me away by capturing so much of our time together. This is addressed more fully in Chapter Thirteen, but Allan's email showed me the power of an open heart and reflective spirit. Now, in most of my mentoring partnerships or huddles, we send each other emails that try to capture what the Spirit may have said to us individually, to the other person, and occasionally what the Spirit has said to us as a unit.

Obey

Third we need to obey what the Spirit has said. As we obey his promptings (always and only in harmony with the Scriptures), he will reveal more and transform us in the process. Richard Foster captures the goal of spiritual listening with these words:

> *In our day heaven and earth are on tiptoe waiting for the emerging of a Spirit-led, Spirit-intoxicated, Spirit-empowered people. All of creation watches expectantly for the springing up of a disciplined, freely gathered, martyr people who know in this life, the life and power of the kingdom of God. It has*

happened before. It can happen again.... Such a people will not emerge until there is among us a deeper, more profound experience of an Emmanuel of the Spirit—God with us, a knowledge that in the power of the Spirit Jesus has come to guide His people Himself, an experience of His leading that is as definite and as immediate as the cloud by day and fire by night.[112]

We come then to our mentoring relationships with a dependent attitude. We bathe the process in prayer. Then we meet (and linger) unselfishly and generously in the life of a person God has "given" us. When we meet, our primary approach as we linger, is to listen intently to them, and to what the Holy Spirit is saying through them.

PROCESSING CHAPTER EIGHT

STEP 1: **DEPEND**—SOAK THE PROCESS IN PRAYER

1. As you listen, humbly and receptively, consider this prayer "Lord, I Believe," by Ted Loder and the hymn by E. May Grimes: "Speak Lord in the Stillness."

Lord, I Believe

>Lord,
>I believe
>>my life is touched by you,
>>that you want something for me,
>>and of me.
>
>Give me ears
>>to hear you,
>
>eyes
>>to see the tracing of your finger,
>
>and a heart
>>quickened by the motions
>>of your Spirit.[113]

Speak Lord in the Stillness

>Speak Lord, in the stillness,
>While I wait on Thee;
>Hushed my heart to listen
>In expectancy.
>
>Speak, O blessed Master,
>In this quiet hour,
>Let me see Thy face, Lord,
>Feel Thy touch of power.[114]

2. Note one or two points from this chapter and reflect on them with a spoken or written prayer:

STEP 2: **MEDITATE**—CONSIDER WHAT THE SCRIPTURES SAY

Proverbs 13:3

> [3] He who guards his lips guards his life, but he who speaks rashly will come to ruin.

Proverbs 19:20

> [20] Listen to advice and accept instruction, and in the end you will be wise.

Proverbs 25:12

> [12] Like an earring of gold or an ornament of fine gold is a wise man's rebuke to a listening ear.

- What do these proverbs say about the issue of really listening to each other?

Ecclesiastes 5:1-2

> [1] Guard your steps when you go to the house of God. Go near to listen rather than to offer the sacrifice of fools, who do not know that they do wrong. [2] Do not be quick with your mouth, do not be hasty in your heart to utter anything before God. God is in heaven and you are on earth, so let your words be few.

- In what should our attitudes when we mentor each other, reflect what the "Preacher" says here about listening to God when we come before him as worshippers?

Revelation 2:7; 17, 29; 3:6, 13, 22

⁷ He who has an ear, let him hear what the Spirit says to the churches.

- What might the Lord Jesus say to you personally, to your mentoring group, or even to your church, if he was to write you a letter?

STEP 3: **RESPOND**—
LEARN FROM EACH OTHER AND TAKE ACTION

Reflection and Discussion:

1. In your mentoring interaction (one-on-one or mentoring huddle) are you more of a talker than listener or the other way round? Why?

2. Why is humility so important as we aim to become better listeners in our mutual mentoring relationships?

3. What are the things that distract you most when you are seeking to really listen to your mentor-partner?

4. How can we cultivate an ear to listen to what the Lord Jesus is saying to us through his Spirit as we meet for mutual mentoring?

Mentoring Practices:

1. The whole idea of this section is to keep adding a new skill and continuing to practice the ones before.

- Praying before you meet, as you meet, and after you meet.

- Meeting regularly, wholly and purposefully.

2. The skill of listening (for most of us, doesn't come easily). Try to implement the three aspects of listening mentioned in Chapter Eight:

- **Listening attentively.** Both of you, or your whole mentoring cluster needs to get rid of any distractions and focus on the other person physically, and internally (note what Shenkman says about this on page 104).

- **Listening humbly.** Deliberately take the humble place in the next conversation (could be interesting and a very quiet time if you both practice this together!).

- **Listening spiritually.** As you meet, pause to pray for a special filling of the Spirit, and ask him to speak to you individually and as a pair or group.

CHAPTER NINE

ASKING

"When they had finished eating, Jesus said to Simon Peter, 'Simon son of John, do you truly love me more than these?'"
—John 21:15

"Nothing pries us open like a question. A key attitude of prayer is listening, and what we listen for most are God's questions: 'Where are you?' 'Where is your brother?' 'Where are the other nine?' 'Why do you call me Lord, Lord and not do the things I say?' 'Who do you say I am?'"[115]
—Mark Buchanan

One thing that reveals an unselfish listening attitude in a mentoring relationship is when our default setting is to ask questions rather than give answers. The Master Mentor, Jesus, exemplified that. Sometimes he would follow someone's question with yet another of his own. When the Pharisees quizzed Jesus on paying taxes to Caesar for example, Jesus followed their question, "Tell us then, what is your opinion? Is it right to pay taxes to Caesar or not?" with several of his own: "You hypocrites, why are you trying to trap me...? Whose portrait is this? And whose inscription?"[116]

On other occasions Jesus employed questions to probe a little deeper into the lives of his followers. Consider this sample:

- *You of little faith, why are you so afraid?*[117]
- *Why do you worry?*[118]
- *Can you drink the cup I am going to drink?*[119]
- *Who do you say that I am?*[120]
- *Who was the neighbor?*[121]
- *Were not all ten cleansed? Where are the other nine?*[122]
- *What do you want me to do for you?*[123]
- *Do you want to get well?*[124]
- *Simon, son of John, do you truly love me more than these?*[125]

Even if you are a born answer-giver, you can learn to be a good listener. And if you are relatively unskilled in the art of posing perceptive questions, you can develop that skill. Evaluate your proficiency in asking questions from this list of mistakes:

> **Closed Questions:** These usually contain an obvious answer such as "Yes," or "No," and invariably shut the conversation down. They have their place in the early days of your mentoring partnership (such as asking how many children they have, providing you know they have some!). Even then a more open question such as "Tell me about your family?" is a better way to go.

> **Leading Questions:** Sometimes these can be manipulative, for example, "How would you describe that? Confused?" Questions that require a right answer or a right number of answers need to be weeded out as well. I recall driving along the highway in Dallas on route to the airport. One of my seminary friends was sitting in the rear seat of our old beaten up Cadillac with our son. He asked him, "What were the seven highlights of your two years

here in the United States?" My son gave one or two answers then left it wisely at that. "What were some highlights of your time in the US?" would have been more appropriate.

Multiple Questions: However good your questions are, they need to stand alone. I attended a church leadership conference and still cringe when I think about the questions of an interviewer to a distinguished panel of leaders. He asked, "How do you care for your own soul while caring for others?" A great question! It became clouded when he continued without a pause: "How have you failed to look after yourself in your leadership role?" and "Why do you think leaders neglect to engage in personal soul care?" The audience laughed when the first panelist said, "Which question do you want me to answer?" Undeterred the interviewer proceeded to re-frame all three questions!

"Closed," "leading," and "multiple" questions reveal a lack of skill in the art of questioning. What then constitutes a great question? In *Leading with Questions*, author and business leader Michael Marquardt suggests that there is no single correct answer, and instead offers the following benefits of great questions. They:

- Cause the person to focus and to stretch.
- Create deep reflection.
- Challenge taken-for-granted assumptions that prevent people from acting in new…ways.
- Generate courage and strength.
- Lead to breakthrough thinking.
- Contain the keys that open the door to great solutions.
- Enable people to better view the situation.
- Open doors in the mind and get people to think more deeply.
- Test assumptions and cause individuals to explore why they act in the way that the do as well as why they choose to take action.
- Generate positive and powerful action.[126]

So how do you hone your asking skills as you aim to go from poor, to good, to great, as a mutual mentor? Journalism's "Five 'W's and an 'H'" are not bad places to start: Why? Who? Where? What? When? and How? But there's something a bit mechanical about merely applying those in a mentoring relationship. Here are three things I have learned as I seek to become a more skillful questioner: asking generally, asking specifically, and asking perceptively.

Ask Generally

A few years ago I had the privilege of interviewing John Mallison in Sydney, Australia. He had just retired after many years as a mentor and author. Humbly, he put all of his material onto a website: www.johnmallison.com. I had a video crew ready to record our interview, but before the video-shoot, John and I had coffee together. I asked him what he had learned about the art of asking questions. He said, "Oh, my approach is really simple. I just ask 'How are you doing?'" John follows that very general question up (if necessary) with, "How are you doing emotionally?" "How are you doing spiritually" or "How are you doing physically?" Then based on how the person answers, he asks other questions. I've employed that simple approach again and again. Occasionally I throw in a twist to that general question, "How are you being?" (which usually elicits a smile). In other words, I want to probe, not what the person has done, but how they really are.

The Risen Lord Jesus asked a couple of general questions when he strolled alongside two of his confused disciples on the Emmaus Road. He asked, "What are you discussing together?" and when they quizzically replied, "Are you only a visitor to Jerusalem and do not know the things that have happened here in these days?" rather than answering them, he asked a second general question: "What things?"[127]

Ask Specifically

As you get to know each other, come ready to ask questions that relate to where the person is up to at that stage of their spiritual pilgrimage. Jesus did that. In John 21, when Jesus prepared breakfast on the beach for his disciples, three times over, he asked variations of the question, "Do you love me more than these?"[128] While that sounds like a closed question that merely needed a yes or no answer, it was a very pointed question when you think of the events prior to Jesus' crucifixion. When Jesus explained he was on the way to be crucified, Peter proffered his undying love to Jesus. All the other eleven disciples might desert Jesus, but not him. Jesus predicted that before a rooster crowed twice, Peter would deny him three times.[129] Tragically that came true. Now on the beach, Jesus' three questions mirrored Peter's three denials and probed the extent of Peter's love. Questions like that require insight and deep trust.

As you develop the ability to ask intuitive and appropriate questions, it's also helpful to access, or memorize a series of questions that fit your situation. Keith Farmer suggests these questions:

Spirituality: *How are you and God doing?*

Relationships: *How are you doing with those closest to you?*

Emotions: *How are you doing emotionally?*

Rhythms: *What rhythms have you established that will help you live well?*

Vulnerabilities: *If Satan was to take you out, how would he be likely to do it?*[130]

When I prepare for my next mentoring meeting, I pray then gather questions such as the ones above. I keep the questions in mind but hold them very loosely. I've tried the list of 20 accountability questions that ends up with the question that always gets a laugh: "Have you been lying to me?" The approach of laboriously going through a long list of questions seems a bit too much like an interrogation. A more important task is to develop the art and skill of probing questions. Tony Stoltzfus in *The Coaching Process* includes these great questions:

- "Tell me a little more about that."
- "Give me some background that led up to this situation."
- "What did you mean when you said _____?"
- "What would be the most important for us to focus on?"
- "How did that happen?"[131]

Author Parker Palmer describes the time he was given the opportunity to become the president of a small educational institution. He called on a "clearness committee" (half a dozen trusted friends) that refrained from giving advice, but merely asked questions. Here's his description of the encounter:

> *For a while, the questions were easy, at least for a dreamer like me: What is your vision for this institution? What is its mission in the larger society? How would you change the curriculum? How would you handle decision making? What about dealing with conflict?*
>
> *Halfway into the process, someone asked a question that sounded easy but turned out to be very hard: "What would you like most about being a president?"*
>
> *The simplicity of that question loosed me from my head and lowered me into my heart. I remember pondering for at least a full minute before I could respond....*
>
> *"Well," said I, in the smallest voice I possess, "I guess what I'd like most is getting my picture in the paper with the word* president *under it."*
>
> *...Finally, my questioner broke the silence with a question that cracked all of us up—and cracked me open: "Parker," he said, "can you think of an easier way to get your picture in the paper?"*[132]

In our mentoring relationships we need to model ourselves on that "clearness committee"—where we discipline ourselves to listen well and ask questions rather than jump to giving answers.

In Resource Four: "The Art and Craft of Great Questions," I have included various categories of questions such as: Character, Attitudes, Marriage, Family and Friendships. This list provides a comprehensive source of questions to use once you know each other reasonably well. One way of using these questions is to mutually prepare for your time together by reviewing the questions in Resource Four, and email or text each other either the question you would like to be asked or one that you would like to explore with your mentor-partner.

Ask Perceptively

Knowing each other, regardless of your group size, is of the essence, and preparing questions beforehand, or having a stock of pre-prepared questions is a great way to develop the skill of questioning in your mentoring relationship. However, both of those approaches can become a bit mechanical. A third way to approach the questioning process is to simply depend on the Holy Spirit to lead you. Certainly this harmonizes with the concept of praying before, during and after your mentoring session.

According to the Lord Jesus, one of the roles of the Holy Spirit is to lead us into all truth. How important it is then to seek the Spirit's guidance before we meet on which questions to ask, or to ask him to prompt us when we meet to ask perceptive questions.

Developing the skill of asking good questions calls firstly for the right attitude: we need to be genuinely interested in the other person or persons, probing to find out more about them, and asking questions to help them clarify their own thinking. Secondly, we can hone our ability to ask questions by utilizing general and specific questions—to use intuitively or purposefully. Thirdly, we will develop this skill as we humbly ask the Holy Spirit to guide us. As we do that, I believe that Linda Miller and Chad Hall's prediction will be realized: "Questions that are based on focused listening, that are worded carefully, and that are well-timed can catapult a person forward in discovery and action."[133]

PROCESSING CHAPTER NINE

STEP 1: **DEPEND**—SOAK THE PROCESS IN PRAYER

1. Consider this anonymous prayer written by a confederate soldier in the US Civil War as you process the importance of asking good questions and asking God to transform you:

A Soldier's Prayer

> I asked God for strength, that I might achieve,
> > I was made weak, that I might learn humbly to obey.
> I asked for health, that I might do greater things,
> > I was given infirmity, that I might do better things.
> I asked for riches, that I might be happy,
> > I was given poverty that I might be wise.
> I asked for power, that I might have the praise of men,
> > I was given weakness, that I might feel the need of God.
> I asked for all things, that I might enjoy life,
> > I was given life, that I might enjoy all things.
>
> I got nothing that I asked for
> but everything that I had hoped for,
> almost despite myself, my unspoken prayers were answered.
> I am among all men most richly blessed.[134]

2. Note one or two points from this chapter and reflect on them with a spoken or written prayer:

STEP 2: **MEDITATE**—CONSIDER WHAT THE SCRIPTURES SAY

Job 42:1-6

> *[1] Then Job replied to the Lord:*
>
> *[2] "I know that you can do all things; no plan of yours can be thwarted. [3] You asked, 'Who is this that obscures my counsel without knowledge?' Surely I spoke of things I did not understand, things too wonderful for me to know. [4] You said, 'Listen now, and I will speak; I will question you, and you shall answer me.' [5] My ears had heard of you but now my eyes have seen you. [6] Therefore I despise myself and repent in dust and ashes."*

- What does this passage (and the context of God's repeated questions in Job Chapter 38-41) teach us about the need to ask questions rather than dispense answers?

John 21:15-17

> *[15] When they had finished eating, Jesus said to Simon Peter, "Simon son of John, do you truly love me more than these?"*
>
> *"Yes, Lord," he said, "you know that I love you."*
>
> *Jesus said, "Feed my lambs."*
>
> *[16] Again Jesus said, "Simon son of John, do you truly love me?"*
>
> *He answered, "Yes, Lord, you know that I love you."*
>
> *Jesus said, "Take care of my sheep."*
>
> *[17] The third time he said to him, "Simon son of John, do you love me?"*

Peter was hurt because Jesus asked him the third time, "Do you love me?" He said, "Lord, you know all things; you know that I love you."

Jesus said, "Feed my sheep."

- What is the significance of this sequence of questions from Jesus to Peter? What can we learn about the art of questioning from this passage?

STEP 3: **RESPOND—**
LEARN FROM EACH OTHER AND TAKE ACTION

Reflection and Discussion:

1. What are the main differences between a good question and a poor one?

2. How do you know when to ask general questions or when to get more specific and personal?

3. Discuss the quote from Mark Buchanan at the start of this chapter: "Nothing pries us open like a question. A key attitude of prayer is listening, and what we listen for most are God's questions: 'Where are you?' 'Where is your brother?' 'Where are the other nine?' 'Why do you call me Lord, Lord and not do the things I say?' 'Who do you say I am?'"

4. What are some next steps you need to take as a result of reading Chapter Nine:

Personally?

As a group?

Mentoring Practices:

1. Next time you meet, try to practice the "clearness committee" approach mentioned in this chapter. One person should pose an issue that they are concerned about or struggling with at present. The other person (or persons) is only allowed to ask questions. Then swap. Discuss how this felt. It is a great way to learn to listen and to practice the art of good questions.

2. Review the three kinds of questions mentioned in Chapter Nine:

- General questions.

- Specific questions

- Perceptive questions

3. Discuss how you plan to implement these questions in your mentoring get-togethers.

CHAPTER TEN

AFFIRMING

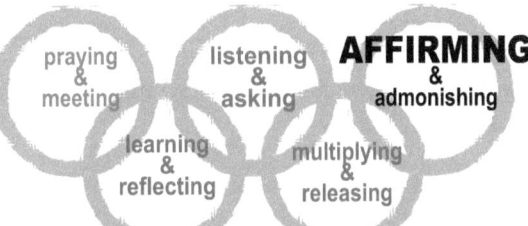

"But encourage one another daily, as long as it is called Today, so that none of you may be hardened by sin's deceitfulness."
—Hebrews 3:13

*"Kind words are the music of the world.
They have a power that seems to be beyond natural causes, as if they were some angel's song that had lost its way and come on earth. It seems as if they could do what in reality only God can do—soften the hard and angry hearts of men."*
—Frederick Faber

Some people are born encouragers (or have that spiritual gift according to Romans 12:8). Most of us mere mortals have to work at it. All Christ-followers, according to passages like Hebrews 3:13 listed above, are required to encourage each other—and in your quest to become a more effective mutual mentor, this is a primary skill. What about you? Do you see yourself as an encourager? How do others perceive you?

Affirm Repeatedly

I love the title of one of the chapters in Johnson and Ridley's book, *The Elements of Mentoring*: "Affirm, Affirm, Affirm and Then Affirm Some More."[135] That resonated with me because I'm certain all of us need encouragement. I know I do. Hebrews 3:13 says, "But encourage one another daily, as long as it is called Today, so that none of you may be hardened by sin's deceitfulness." That means day by day by day we need to encourage each other and never give up. This verse also gives us one solid reason for unremitting affirmation: our hearts can easily become calloused by sin. It's as if a well-chosen word of affirmation can keep our hearts soft toward God. To put it another way, "One kind word can warm up three winters" according to a Japanese proverb.

I know that's true. In my case one kind word has warmed up twenty winters. When I was leaving Dallas Seminary in 1991, one of my professors, Dr. Howard Hendricks gave me a book he had written (*Living by the Book*) and wrote words of affirmation on the first page:

> *What a delight that the Lord caused our paths to cross. There is nothing with which I resonate more than your vision for New Zealand. Praying that God will give you grace and wisdom in implanting your burden for developing quality leadership. Thanks for being you! Isaiah 54:17*

From time to time, when I feel discouraged, I pull the book off my shelves, soak in his kind words, and am ready to go on.

Howie (as we affectionately called him) indelibly marked me because I so often descend into sinful thought patterns. I'm not talking about blatant disobedience, rather, negative (often stupid) thought patterns such as, "If only people knew me as I am, they would never bother with me," or "I feel like quitting, my life doesn't amount to much." Negative thoughts like that plague me. My hunch is I'm not alone in that. That negative tendency reminds me why I need to affirm, affirm and then affirm some more.

We need encouragement but we can't require it. It feels hollow when we solicit affirmation. I believe it's better to take responsibility for being a better encourager and leave the need for encouragement to God. Imagine mutual mentoring relationships where constant, meaningful affirmation was the norm. That means when we meet together, one of our instinctive questions would be, "How can I affirm fellow mentor-friends today?" Try to fold that question into your mentoring mind-set in the next month.

Affirm Significantly

Recently, a book found me, called *Practicing Affirmation: God-Centered Praise of Those Who Are Not God,* by Sam Crabtree. It has given me a new perspective on the art of affirmation. Here are some lessons (among many) I have learned from his book:

- **Affirm God-Like Qualities**

In the past, most of my affirming words have amounted to variations of "Good job!" That's not insignificant—it is worthwhile to catch someone doing something well, and then tell them how much it has blessed you. Crabtree's call though, is to affirm God-like qualities. One of the big ideas of Scripture is that God originally made us in his image, and tragically, because of the "Fall" that image has been defaced but not erased. However, through Christ, the image of God is being restored but is not completed until we get to heaven.

God-centered affirmation amounts to spotting the image of God in people, however imperfect it may be. I did that recently with my hairdresser/barber (not that I have much hair to dress!). When I was about to pay, I said, "When I leave your salon I always feel happy. You are a very joyful person." She looked at me with a tear in her eye and said, "No one has ever said that to me. Thank you." Next time you spot one of your friends speaking truth, showing great courage, or being incredibly kind to someone, instead of just saying, "Good job," affirm the God-like quality in them. Crabtree puts it this way:

> God-centered affirmations point toward the echoes, shadows, and reality of a righteousness not intrinsic to the person being affirmed. These qualities are gifts, coming from outside people and being worked in them. Even without yet being fully complete, these qualities are nevertheless commendable,

and are to be seen and highlighted. We can truthfully say to an unregenerate four-year-old, "God is helping you become more..." and fill in the blank with qualities such as: careful with your things (as a steward), cheerful around the house as a singer, cautious around dangerous things like hot stoves, and so on. While the child's growth in character is commended, God is identified as the source.[136]

That's what the man in Jesus' parable about the talents did (Matthew 25:14-30). He said to the servants who invested their talents (money), "Well done, good and faithful servant!" They had done a good job, but it was the God-like qualities of goodness and faithfulness that he affirmed.

There are attributes of God that we can delight in but never emulate. He is all-powerful, all-knowing, all-present, and sovereign. We will never be. However, God's moral attributes, such as: truth, kindness, love, grace, and holiness, can all become categories for affirmation of one another. As Chapter Three indicated, we can always affirm and delight in God for all that he is. Delighting in God is the most transformative experience we can ever engage in.

- **Put Deposits in Your Relational Bank**

Think of the last time you met with your mentor-friend or mentoring-huddle. What proportion of your interaction was encouragement and how much was correction in one form or another? Crabtree says that words of encouragement are like deposits in your relational checking account. Corrections are withdrawals. "If you write too many checks in relation to the deposits, your checks bounce—they're no good. It will take additional deposits to restore your credit."[137] Crabtree's book, *Practicing Affirmation*, is not calling for sugary praise with no correction, but multiple affirmations for each correction (which is explored more fully in Chapter Eleven).

- **Discover Each Other's Encouragement Language**

Gary Chapman's insightful book, *The Five Love Languages* has helped Elaine and me in our marriage relationship. I don't recall my Scottish dad doing chores of any note around the house. That was left to my mother (or us kids). So, soon after Elaine and I were married, I thought I'd pull all the stops out and vacuum the entire house. Elaine arrived home, and I was waiting for accolades. I waited until I could stand it no longer and said, "Did you notice anything?" Elaine said, "No." I mentioned my herculean task. To my disappointment all she said was, "Oh good." When we discussed this episode later I found that her Irish dad often joined in on household chores. He wasn't so good at affirmation however, or doing more romantic things like giving flowers. I learned early on that Elaine's love languages are words of affirmation, well-chosen gifts, and spending significant uninterrupted time with her. My hunch is that we all have "encouragement languages" as well. What is your encouragement language? What might the encouragement language of your mentor-friend be?

Here are some of mine:

- At the top of my list are any comments relating to positive things about my character (maybe that's why Sam Crabtree's book had such impact on me?). My co-mentor, Don Overton calls me "Caleb," (I refer to him as Josh) and I love that. The thought that I am in any way like the biblical character Caleb—who was forever climbing fresh mountains, inspires me to reach higher.

- Small meaningful gifts. In the case of my grandmother, it was often just a few biblical meditations she had gleaned from a tear-off calendar. What it told me was that she was thinking of me.

- Unsolicited praise. I know there's a dark side to needing praise, but when I conduct a seminar, preach a sermon, or lead a spiritual retreat, and someone interacts with the seminar or sermon, and says positive words, I am hugely encouraged.

- It sounds insane, but almost any word of encouragement (even if it only amounts to "Well done!") from someone whom I respect deeply, keeps me going.

Affirm Promptly

Romans 12:8 says: ***If it* [your gift] *is to encourage, then give encouragement....***[138] Those with that gift are to practice it unrelentingly. Those of us without that gift are not off the hook. Meditate on this selection of Scriptures:

1 Thessalonians 4:18	*Therefore encourage one another with these words.*
1 Thessalonians 5:11	*Therefore encourage one another and build each other up, just as in fact you are doing.*
1 Thessalonians 5:14	*And we urge you, brothers and sisters, warn those who are idle and disruptive, encourage the disheartened, help the weak, be patient with everyone.*
Hebrews 10:25	*Let us not give up meeting together, as some are in the habit of doing, but let us encourage one another—and all the more as you see the Day approaching.*

Most of us nod in agreement when we read those Scriptures, yet my hunch is that many of us have difficulty practicing continual encouragement. Why is that? Sam Crabtree maintains:

> *The absence or sparseness of our commendations is generally not because we jump out of our chair one sunny afternoon and announce, "No more affirmations from me! No siree!" Instead, we become preoccupied, distracted. Life happens.... And before we know it, a lot of drifting water has passed under the bridge, the weeds of indifference have grown, and we can't remember when we last passed out the blessings. ...Yesterday's refreshment doesn't refresh permanently. You can't stockpile freshness.*[139]

One way to make sure that we practice affirmation is simply to do it straight away. That means when you meet as mutual mentors, actively think of ways to encourage each other, and when the Spirit prompts you, say it straight away. Don't wait for a more appropriate moment.

It may never arrive. Similarly, when you are prompted to give encouragement and the person isn't present, take action right away.

A few weeks ago, I was blessed by a prayer that someone prayed in a worship service. I didn't see them after church and intended to send an email to them when I got home. I forgot. Just last week, at the church where I am a member (BotanyLife Community Church, Auckland, New Zealand), it was one of those days when heaven came down. I was drawn to worship God through the unobtrusive and Christ-exalting worship team. Then there was a sermon from Brad Carr, our Lead Pastor, that felt as if the Lord was speaking directly to me. That time, as soon as I arrived home, I sent an email to the individuals telling them that I had been drawn to adoring worship and had heard the voice of God. Affirming people blesses them, it opens them like a flower, and in the process we are blessed. Is there someone you need to affirm, do it now!

John Maxwell tells about a time he visited his father Melvin in 2004. John needed a quiet spot for a conference call, so his dad let him use his office. As he sat at the desk, he noticed a card right next to the phone, with these words in his father's handwriting:

#1 Build people up by encouragement.

#2 Give people credit by acknowledgement.

#3 Give people recognition by gratitude.[140]

Those words were a reminder to encourage people right then and there. Don't let the moment pass if you know you should say appropriate words of affirmation. Here are some practical suggestions on ways to encourage your mentor-friends:

- When you see a God-like character quality in someone, tell them then and there. Don't wait for the perfect moment.

- Review what the person means to you. Compose an email that affirms a Christ-like quality in them.

- Choose or make a card and write it out in your own hand. Strange, but I've found that nowadays a handwritten card can be more impactful than an email.

- When you get to your car after a mentor-meeting, take a couple of minutes to compose an encouraging text.

- Next time you meet, have a gift such as a book you have bought for your friend and do the Howie Hendricks thing: write words of encouragement in the flyleaf.

- Think of something practical you can do for your mentor-friend, such as recommending them to a prospective employer. Don't just do it, tell them that this is just another way of showing what they mean to you.

- Email or text them with a prayer you are praying for them. My mentor-friend Earl Lindgren signs off his emails with: "Look for the best, not the worst. Look for all you can praise God for and be glad about."

- Stop and pray now, asking God to change you to be more affirming.

- Ask your mentor-friend what their "Encouragement Languages" are.

- Ask God to make you as (wise, kind, faithful, enthusiastic, etc.) as someone you know who excels at that quality. Then tell that person you are praying that way.[141]

When I think of the power of affirmation my mind goes back to the days when our children were in Elementary School. Each year the School held a Cross Country Race. One year, our eldest, Rochelle, was in the race. They had to complete two laps of an undulating course, over an emerald green farmland. I situated myself about 200 yards from the finish line. Toward the completion of the first lap, Rochelle came round in third place. I called out words of encouragement. She was in the same position after the second lap. Again I shouted out encouraging words and she did come in third. On the way home in the car, Rochelle said words I will never forget. She said, "Dad, thanks for your words of encouragement. If you hadn't, I wouldn't have made it."

There are people out there, maybe your mentor-partners, who won't make it, unless you affirm, affirm, affirm, then affirm some more.

PROCESSING CHAPTER TEN

STEP 1: **DEPEND**—BATHE THE PROCESS IN PRAYER

1. As you consider the importance of being an encourager, pray this prayer by John Henry Newman (used daily by the Missionaries of Charity):

The Poor and Hungry

> Dear Jesus, help me to spread your fragrance everywhere I go.
> Flood my soul with your spirit and life.
> Penetrate and possess my whole being so utterly that all my life
>   may be only a radiance of yours.
> Shine through me and be so in me that every soul we come into
>   contact with may feel your Presence in my soul.
>
> Let them look up and see no longer me, but only Jesus.[142]

2. Note one or two points from this chapter and reflect on them with a spoken or written prayer:

STEP 2: **MEDITATE**—CONSIDER WHAT THE SCRIPTURES SAY

1 Thessalonians 5:8-11

> *⁸ But since we belong to the day, let us be self-controlled, putting on faith and love as a breastplate, and the hope of salvation as a helmet. ⁹ For God did not appoint us to suffer wrath but to receive salvation through our Lord Jesus Christ. ¹⁰ He died for us so that, whether we are awake or asleep, we may live together with him. ¹¹ Therefore encourage one another and build each other up, just as in fact you are doing.*

- What is the basis of the encouragement according to this passage (see the full context in 1 Thessalonians 4:13-5:11)?

Hebrews 3:12-13

> *¹² See to it, brothers, that none of you has a sinful, unbelieving heart that turns away from the living God. ¹³ But encourage one another daily, as long as it is called Today, so that none of you may be hardened by sin's deceitfulness.*

- Why should we encourage one another according to this passage?

STEP 3: **RESPOND**—
LEARN FROM EACH OTHER AND TAKE ACTION

Reflection and Discussion:

1. Discuss this quote from Frederick Faber: "Kind words are the music of the world. They have power that seems to be beyond natural causes, as if they were some angel's song that had lost its way and come on earth. It seems as if they could do what in reality only God can do—soften the hard and angry hearts of men."

2. Why is it important to constantly encourage one another?

3. What is your response to the concept of affirming God-like qualities you see in others? How might you do this in practice?

4. What is your encouragement language?

5. What steps of obedience do you need to make as a result of reading Chapter Ten:

Personally?

As a group?

Mentoring Practices:

1. Review the spiritual mentoring practices you have been developing so far. You will know that these practices are becoming a godly habit when you do them instinctively: Praying (before, during and after), Meeting (regularly, wholly and purposefully), Listening (humbly, attentively and spiritually), Asking (generally, specifically and perceptively) and Affirming (repeatedly, significantly and promptly).

2. Discuss the practical suggestions on ways to encourage your mentor-friends on pages 131-132. Which ones might you fold into your encouragement kit?

CHAPTER ELEVEN

ADMONISHING

"Let the word of Christ dwell in your richly
as you teach and admonish one another with all wisdom...."
—Colossians 3:16

"A man who loves you most
is the man who tells you the most truth about yourself."
—Robert Murray M'Cheyne

"One of the best definitions of tough love I know is action for the well-being of the beloved. We need more people who love others with such devotion that they will risk their current comfort level in the relationship, and say whatever needs to be said in order to protect the other person's well being."[143]
—Bill Hybels

Of all the biblical mutuality commands, (see Resource Six for a more extensive list) "admonish one another" is probably the least popular and least employed by Christ-followers. "We would rather keep the peace than deal with a strained relationship, hurt feelings, misunderstanding or anger."[144] Maybe that's because of our permissive Western culture, or because of previous clumsy attempts at admonition on our part, or because we are aware of our own failings and don't wish to appear judgmental. An even scarier possible reason why we sidestep the biblical call to admonition is that imperceptibly we have "become conformed to this world." What would once have shocked us and prompted us to admonish a fellow-believer, now hardly registers on our corrective radar screen.

Maybe we have become too much like Lot in the story about his Uncle Abraham (Genesis 13-20)? Lot made a series of unwise choices, such as choosing to pitch his tent near Sodom, even though he knew how immoral the people of that city were. It was all downhill from there—one sad compromise after another until he finished his days in a drunken incestuous relationship with his two daughters. One of Lot's choices that few commentators mention is the decision to move out of Uncle Abraham's orbit. No longer could his spiritual father admonish him.

When it comes to admonition, I find it so much more convenient to err on the grace side of the spectrum. I find it easy to talk myself out of the need to offer correction to a fellow mentor. My default is to leave matters of admonition to one side in the hope things will right themselves. Take a few moments of self-assessment to consider these questions:

- How often have I held back in mentoring sessions because I am concerned I might lose their friendship?

- How many times have I heard my mentor-partner say something that should be challenged, and chosen the easy option to say nothing?

- How often have I wanted to say something and hoped that a better opportunity might arise?

I cringe when I think of my clumsy attempt at admonition of a fellow mentor around 20 years ago. Sam[145] and I had been meeting weekly for most of the year and I sensed that this chapter of our mentoring relationship was coming to an end. I felt a responsibility to admonish him about his somewhat prideful attitudes and demeanor. I did. It was a disaster! He asked why, and without thinking I said, "Other people have remarked to me about your arrogance." You guessed it! He wanted to know which people. There was no way to dig myself out of that attempt at admonition. Thankfully I learned from that massive mistake. Now, when I meet with a new mutual mentor I ask, "How do you feel about pushing into things that need correction in our lives from time to time?" Since then I haven't met a person that doesn't want loving correction—especially when I invite them to speak into my own life. It's as if we are both committing ourselves to the mutuality command: "admonish one another"—you admonish me, I admonish you.

I quoted from the British hymn writer and theologian, Frederick Faber in Chapter Ten:

> "*Kind words are the music of the world.*
> *They have a power that seems to be beyond natural causes,*
> *as if they were some angel's song that had lost its way and come on earth.*
> *It seems as if they could do what in reality only God can do—*
> *soften the hard and angry hearts of men.*"

The full quote concludes:

> *No one was ever corrected by a sarcasm—*
> *crushed perhaps, if the sarcasm was clever enough,*
> *but drawn nearer to God, never.*"

Sarcasm is a world away from biblical admonition, but Faber does raise a valid point. Kind words heal, inappropriate correction hurts. What then does appropriate admonition look like?

Admonish Sparingly

I subscribe to Ken Blanchard's suggestion of "one-minute-praisings" (catching anyone doing something right and commending them for that), and to the folk wisdom in these lines from Dorothy Nolte's poem:

> *If children live with criticism, they learn to condemn....*
> *If children live with encouragement, they learn confidence....*
> *If children live with praise, they learn appreciation.*[146]

Because of our fallenness, frequent encouragement needs to be the norm in any healthy mentoring relationship. A constant diet of correction will shrivel the soul of your mentor-partner. Well-timed, infrequent and loving admonition is as Proverbs 25:11 says, "...like an apple of gold in settings of silver."

Admonish Courageously

In *Love One Another,* Gerald Sittser describes the biblical admonition to "admonish one another" in this way:

> *The Greek word for* admonish *means to "set right, correct, warn, lay on the heart of someone." It denotes confrontation, challenge, correction. Behind it lies the assumption that something is very wrong with that person's life. If comforting requires that we stop at the side of the road to be with grieving people, if bearing burdens requires that we get people back on their feet again, so, if stirring up requires that we get inert Christians moving, then admonition demands that we turn disobedient Christians around. We see what will happen if they do not. Appealing to their conscience, we challenge them to make a choice.*[147]

To do that requires backbone, and more importantly a strong relational bridge (through listening, affirming and burden bearing over time) that can stand the weight of loving correction. When I think of that my mind goes to the Prophet Nathan when he admonished King David after David's sordid adultery, deceit, and murder episode. Less well known is the strong friendship he had established with the King well before his epic confrontation. Nathan was the man who first encouraged David in his desire to build a Temple for the Lord.[148] That night, after his words of encouragement,

God asked Nathan to tell David that he was not the one to build a house for the Lord. That called for courage, built on a deep friendship. Even greater courage must have been required for Nathan to confront David after the King's adulterous affair with Bathsheba. Where did that courage come from?

2 Samuel 12:1 starts this way: "Then the LORD sent Nathan to David…." The timing was right and Nathan was the right person to admonish this powerful man. Nathan's courage came from obedience. He knew he was sent from the Lord. He could have lost David's friendship, he might even have lost his life, but he responded to the Spirit's prompting. Chuck Swindoll describes the courage we need to be able to admonish wisely:

> *You will have nothing to lose if you walk in the strength of the Lord. Don't fear the loss of a friendship. God honors the truth. After all, it is the truth—and only the truth—that sets people free. If the Lord is really in it, you'll be one of the best friends this person ever had by telling him the truth. Remember the phrase, "Faithful are the wounds caused by the bruising of one who loves you"? Be certain you are confronting out of love.*[149]

Recently my mentor-friend, Don Overton, admonished me. No, it wasn't over a sin in my life (though I'm no saint). I told him about an up-coming trip from New Zealand to Dallas, Texas. He asked me why I was going. I'll never forget two of his questions: "Is your ego involved?" (I told him my motivation was primarily to serve but that my ego was involved) and "Is this in keeping with your primary calling to be a mentor and train others to develop spiritual friendships?" (I answered, "No!"). God used that admonition to recalibrate me. I heard the Spirit's call through Don to live within my limits and stay focused on my primary calling.

Admonish Biblically

Biblical admonition doesn't mean just throwing Bible verses at a person. Yes, God's Word is powerful and capable of getting right to the core of an issue, but the Bible is not a hand grenade that we hurl in the direction of fellow believers in need of correction. In Colossians 3:16, Paul calls the Colossian churches to "Let the word of Christ dwell in you richly as you teach and admonish one another with all wisdom...." That's the key. We need to so soak in the Scriptures, allowing them to shape us, that when we do admonish a fellow-sinner, we do so wisely.

Like our Savior, we need to be full of grace and truth. We need to find a way to treat people much better than they deserve, yet speak honestly into their lives. The Prophet Nathan, referred to above, did that when he addressed King David. Instead of just gunning him down with a few choice Scriptures (which he would have been able to do), he graciously told a story about a ewe lamb that drew David in. Then when the King fumed, Nathan delivered the truth: "You, David are the man!"[150] Jesus did the same in his interaction with the "woman taken in the act of adultery." He dealt with her accusers (the Pharisees) first, then spoke words of healing to the woman: "Neither do I condemn you." And followed up with words that called her to a life of holiness: "Go and sin no more."[151]

Notice that neither Nathan, nor Jesus, sugar-coated sin. They were not building the person up first, then confronting their sin. Rather they spoke words of admonition in a gracious way. When we admonish one another in this way, the benefits are immense. George Mueller, founder and director of the Ashley Downs Orphanage in 1849, described the benefits this way:

> *As to the importance of the children of God opening their hearts to each other, especially when they are getting in a cold state, or are under the power of a certain sin, or are in especial difficulty; I know from my own experience how often the snare of the devil has been broken when under the power of sin; how often the heart has been comforted when nigh to be overwhelmed; how often advice, and great perplexity has been obtained, by opening my heart to a brother in whom I had confidence. We are children of the same family, and ought therefore to be helpers of one another.*

We help one another when we warn one another in a gracious way, fully aware of our own tendency to sin. Biblical admonition though is more than gracious admonition, it is admonition in keeping with the whole of Scripture. "All Scripture is inspired by God and is profitable for…reproof…."[152] And it is in the Scripture that we discover the offenses and behaviors in need of admonition. How do we know what to admonish? In *Love One Another*, Gerald Sittser identifies two categories worthy of correction that relate to mutual mentoring:

- Theological problems, the most vital of which is our view of Jesus Christ.

- Moral problems, involving defiance against God.

Sittser says,

> *Admonition addresses attitude as well as action, corrects character flaws before they become moral tragedies, toes the mat over small compromises before they erupt into big crises.*[153]

If you have built a strong bridge of trust, you are in the best place to warn a mentor-partner, whether the issue is theological, moral or just an unwise decision. Even then, Paul's words to believers in Galatia must be ever in our minds: "Brothers, if someone is caught in a sin, you who are spiritual should restore him gently. But watch yourself, or you also may be tempted."[154] Paul's charge here is to step forward and admonish one another, but to do so gently and humbly (realizing our propensity to sin), and spiritually (walking in step with the Holy Spirit).

PROCESSING CHAPTER ELEVEN

STEP 1: **DEPEND**—SOAK THE PROCESS IN PRAYER

1. As you add the practice of admonition to your mutual mentoring toolkit, cultivate a soft heart, and a non-judgmental spirit. Consider this prayer of confession by Peter Nott:

Confessing Sin and Seeking God's Forgiveness

> O Lord, open our minds to see ourselves as you see us,
> And from all unwillingness to know our weakness and our sin,
> > *Good Lord, deliver us.*
>
> From failure to be truthful;
> from pretence and acting a part; from hypocrisy;
> from all dishonesty with ourselves and with others,
> > *Good Lord, deliver us.*
>
> From impurity in word, in thought, and in action;
> from failure to respect the bodies and minds
> of ourselves and others;
> from any kind of addiction,
> > *Good Lord, deliver us.*
>
> From failure to see our sin as an affront to God;
> from failure to accept the forgiveness of others,
> > *Good Lord, deliver us....*[155]

2. Note one or two points from this chapter and reflect on them with a spoken or written prayer:

STEP 2: **MEDITATE**—CONSIDER WHAT THE SCRIPTURES SAY

Acts 20:31

> [31] *So be on your guard! Remember that for three years I never stopped warning each of you night and day with tears.*

Romans 15:14

> [14] *I myself am convinced, my brothers, that you yourselves are full of goodness, complete in knowledge and competent to instruct one another.*

Galatians 6:1

> [1] *Brothers, if someone is caught in a sin, you who are spiritual should restore him gently. But watch yourself, or you also may be tempted.*

Colossians 3:16

> [16] *Let the word of Christ dwell in you richly as you teach and admonish one another with all wisdom, and as you sing psalms, hymns and spiritual songs with gratitude in your hearts to God.*

- What are the main principles from these Scriptures that could guide you as you warn your mentor-friend?

STEP 3: **RESPOND**—
LEARN FROM EACH OTHER AND TAKE ACTION

Reflection and Discussion:

1. Share the principles you gleaned from the biblical passages above.

2. Why are many of us so reticent to admonish one another?

3. What do we learn from the way that the prophet Nathan admonished King David?

4. How can we inject Scripture passages into our words of loving correction in a way that is not perceived as hitting them over the head with the Bible?

5. Discuss this quote from Gerald Sittser: "Admonition addresses attitude as well as action, corrects character flaws before they become moral tragedies, toes the mat over small compromises before they erupt into big crises."[156]

6. What steps of obedience do you need to take after reading Chapter Eleven:

Personally?

As a group?

Mentoring Practices:

1. At the start of a new mentoring relationship, mention your need to be admonished (from time to time), and gain permission to do the same in their life.

2. Put such an emphasis on affirmation in your mentor-partnership that words of loving correction are more likely to be received well.

3. When you become aware that a word of admonition needs to be given, ask God for courage and the right timing, and then step forward in faith.

4. Consider whether an indirect approach (such as Nathan telling a story to King David) or a more direct approach is more appropriate.

5. As you admonish each other, keep Galatians 6:1-2 in mind. Do it gently and humbly.

CHAPTER TWELVE

LEARNING

*"Come to me, all you who are weary and burdened, and I will
give you rest. Take my yoke upon you and learn from me, for I am
gentle and humble in heart, and you will find rest for your souls.
For my yoke is easy and my burden is light."*
—Matthew 11:28-30

*"When I mentor someone, I come prepared—and expecting—to
learn, not just to teach and advise. As I step into another person's
world and he steps into mine, we begin to see the world afresh,
from different perspectives. Neither of us will ever be the same."*[157]
—David A. Stoddard

My much loved Professor at Dallas Theological Seminary, Dr. Howard Hendricks inspired me with a love of lifelong learning. In *Teaching to Change Lives* he wrote,

> *"Learning is always a process. It's going on all the time.*
> *Every moment you live, you learn; and as you learn, you live.*
> *Stop learning today, and you stop living tomorrow."*[158]

When we approach a mentoring relationship, to learn and listen, life-changing mutual mentoring takes place. I saw that first hand when my friend Bruce Miller, at that time Pastor of Leadership Development at Fellowship Bible Church North (FBCN), led a group of elders and spouses through the BILD (Biblical Institute of Leadership Development) course on the book of Acts. Elaine and I were invited to join the group, and Dr. Gene Getz, then Senior Pastor of FBCN, and his wife Elaine, were also participants. The thing that I remember most about those evenings was Gene's enthusiasm for learning. His body language conveyed that he was there to listen and learn. Someone would make an observation. Gene would lean forward and say, "Please repeat that." And he'd write down what the person said. What was most engaging was that he had written several of the articles in the course!

Learn Humbly

How then can our mentoring relationships become opportunities for maximum learning? Firstly by learning humbly from each other, as Gene Getz did. Learning of this kind involves:

Lingering—allowing ample time to process what our Heavenly Father is teaching us.

Loving—offering lavish grace as we think out loud on what the Holy Spirit may be saying.

Listening—at the feet of Jesus, and at the coffee table with each other.

Note the emphasis on who we learn from. We must learn at the feet of Jesus before we learn at the coffee table from each other. Humble learning of this kind is Jesus' on-going call to us in every mentoring relationship. To his twelve disciples, and to his 21st Century followers, every single day he says:

> *"**Come to me**,*
> *all you who are weary and burdened,*
> *and I will give you rest.*
> ***Take my yoke** upon you*
> ***and learn from me**,*
> *for I am gentle and humble in heart,*
> *and you will find rest for your souls.*
> *For my yoke is easy and my burden light."*[159]

The daily process is: "Come," "Take," "Learn." The requirements are an admission of need (overworked, burdened down, and in various states of exhaustion), acceptance of Jesus' yoke (not a self-made yoke, or a yoke imposed by church members, but one that fits well) and a willingness to keep on learning from Jesus.

The curriculum content in this learning process according to Matthew 11:28-30 is the gentleness and humility of Jesus. Where do we find that? In a wide-angled sense, we learn about the Lord Jesus in all of Scripture. When Jesus unraveled the confusion of his two followers on the Emmaus Road, he taught them from all of the Scriptures, the things "concerning himself."[160] But in a more focused sense we learn about him in the Gospels: Matthew, Mark, Luke and John.

The main moves in each of the four gospels highlight Jesus' humility and gentleness. Rather than a grandiose entrance, his birth and early years were the epitome of lowliness. Rather than work experience fit for a King, his first thirty years were spent working alongside his carpenter dad. Rather than investing in the best of the best, he chose and discipled twelve men of no great repute. Rather than mingling with the influential people of his day, he hung out with the disadvantaged and despised people of his day: "tax collectors and sinners…."[161] Rather than death in a palace bed, his death was on an ignominious cross fit for murders. How does Jesus' call to come and learn from him relate to our mentoring partnerships?

Christ Centered Attitude

When we come to learn from Jesus daily, our attitudes are transformed. In Paul's hymn in Philippians 2:5-11 (NASB), he began with "Have this attitude in yourselves which was also in Christ

Jesus." We need to approach our mentoring relationships with gentleness—shedding harsh and unbending attitudes. When I think of gentleness embodied in a person, my mind goes to William (Bill) MacDonald. During my years as Principal of the GLO Bible College, Bill was a visiting lecturer. His lectures received the highest ratings, but my lasting memory is how gentle he was with our children and with people who interpreted Scripture differently. When someone disagreed with him theologically he would listen politely, then with a smile, quote his friend Harry Ironside:

> *"Well dear brother, when we get to heaven*
> *one of us is going to be wrong,*
> *perhaps it will be me."*

As you come to learn together in your mentoring relationships, keep that gentle attitude in mind. When we learn from Jesus, we will have an unselfish attitude as well. We will be much more interested in the needs of our mentor-partner than our own. We show gentleness and unselfishness when we choose to listen and ask genuine questions rather than take center stage in the conversation.

Christ Centered Content

We become like the people we emulate. If we accept Jesus' invitation to **learn from me**, how do we do that? One obvious way is to study the way he treated people gently and humbly. Take a look at Luke Chapter 5 and 7 for example:

- When he called the Twelve to follow him, note the way he related to Simon Peter when the Big Fisherman was overwhelmed with a sense of his sinfulness. Jesus didn't scold him, instead he said, "Don't be afraid; from now on you will catch men…" (5:1-11).

- In the same chapter, study the way Jesus related to the leprous man and the paralytic. He touched the untouchable leper, and he called the paralyzed man "friend" and forgave his sins (5:12-26).

- Look at the way Jesus called Levi. Tax collectors were considered to be the scum of society. Jesus accepted him fully, to the consternation of the Pharisees (5:27-31).

- Take time to soak in the story of Jesus being anointed by the "sinful" woman and ask God's Spirit to grace you with the gracious attitudes that our Lord displayed (7:36-50).

Search the gospels for Jesus' relationships—focusing on Jesus' humility and gentleness, with the prayer that God will make you more like his Son.

Christlike Choices

When we come to learn from Jesus, this will influence whom we choose to build mentoring relationships with. We have so much to learn from people who are different from us. Reflect on the people our Savior interacted with. Isaiah prophesied that the coming Messiah would not break a "bruised reed" and wouldn't snuff out a "smoldering wick."[162] Jesus applied those words to himself when he spoke to the crowds.[163]

When you are choosing whom to invest in, or form a mentoring relationship with, the question is not: "Who are the sharpest, most talented, most mature people I can learn from?" but "Who is the Holy Spirit leading me to invest in or learn from?" Everything changes when we pray and make those choices with a humble attitude.

What happens when we come to Jesus, take his yoke and learn how gentle and humble he is? We experience deep soul rest. Invariably I leave a mentoring session (with an individual or a cluster) with the thought that this is how Jesus created me to be used. I know that some would say, "That's because it is your spiritual gift." Maybe? But remember that Jesus' invitation is to all of us disciples. If any of us choose to apply the principles of Matthew 11:28-30 to our daily lives and our mentoring partnerships, a deep settled soul rest will be the outcome.

Learn Intentionally

Approaching your mentoring relationship to learn rather than to lecture, creates a culture where a true human and divine interchange can take place. It still leaves us with the question, "How can we turn our mentoring meetings into intentional learning opportunities?" Here are three examples of adding intentionality into your mutual mentoring experience:

Multiply

In his book, *Multiply: Disciples Making Disciples*, Francis Chan provides a comprehensive course on disciplemaking. He addresses what it means to live as a disciple maker, how to fold this into church life, how to study the Bible, and provides an outstanding overview of how to understand the Old and New Testament. Mutual, transformational mentoring, as described earlier in Chapter One, is really a way of making disciples. Chan's book, which is a well-constructed course, could provide you with the intentional discipleship material you are looking for.

Memorize

Bible memorization is one of the forgotten spiritual disciplines of the Christian life. The ultimate goal of spiritual mentoring as suggested in this book is life transformation for God's glory. To achieve that we need to start with the transformation of our minds, and Scripture memorization is one of the best ways to fill our minds with God's thoughts.

Regi Campbell in *Mentor Like Jesus* describes how he has used Bible memorization with mentoring groups at Northpoint Community Church. The participants memorize twenty-three Scriptures that Regi feels are very impactful. In what he calls "next generation mentoring groups," he assigns these Scriptures for memorization.[164] For example:

Priorities	But seek first his kingdom and his righteousness, and all these things will be given to you as well. Matthew 6:33
Fruit	But the fruit of the Spirit is love, joy, peace, patience, kindness, goodness, faithfulness, gentleness and self-control. Against such things there is no law. Galatians 5:22-23
Humility and Gentleness	Take my yoke upon you and learn from me, for I am gentle and humble in heart, and you will find rest for your souls. Matthew 11:29
Time	Be very careful, then, how you live—not as unwise but as wise, making the most of every opportunity, because the days are evil. Ephesians 5:15-16

Discover

In a mentoring group setting, some of my best memories have been with the excellent resources that the Centers of Church Based Training (CCBT) has produced. This third recommendation is an intentional discipleship pathway contained in the four part *Discovery Series* (*Discovering the Christian Life, Discovering Intimacy with God, Discovering Your Role in God's Family,* and *Discovering How to Share Your Faith*).[165]

Part of the power of the *Discovery* material is the educational design. It is based on The WISDOM Process™ and allows your mentoring cluster to interact with each other with the aim of cultivating godly wisdom (see more in Resource Seven).

- **W**ork the Issue (What is really at stake here?)

- **I**nvestigate Scripture (What does God say?)

- **S**eek Counsel (What do wise people say?)

- **D**evelop Your Response (What do I think?)

- **O**penly Discuss (What do we think together?)

- **M**ove to Action (What will I/we do?)

This framework has a nice mix of personal reflection and facilitated learning that can help you apply the mentoring principles from *The Lost Art of Lingering* in a small group setting.

Learn Interactively

When I think of the need for interactive learning exemplified in The WISDOM Process™, one of the laws of learning in Hendricks' book, *Teaching to Change Lives* comes to mind: "The Law of Activity: Maximum learning is always the result of maximum involvement."[166] That reminds me of the "do then learn; learn then do" method of Jesus. Sometimes the disciples had to fail before they could really learn:

> *Picture the situation: The disciples have been sent out two by two, and they're having a ball. They come back to Jesus and say, "Lord, even the demons are subject to us!"*
>
> *But one day they run into a difficult case. They're unable to cast out a demon from a boy. The boy's father in exasperation goes to Jesus and says, "I went to your disciples, but they were not able." So Jesus casts the demon out.*
>
> *Sure enough, the disciples get Jesus off to the side and say, "Lord, what happened?" "I'll tell you," he says. "This kind comes out by prayer and fasting only." As so often happened the disciples' taste of failure provided one of their greatest learning experiences.*[167]

In your mentoring pair or huddle, consider emulating Jesus' method. Follow a time of learning (maybe you are working through one of the *Discovery* courses mentioned above, or a Scripture passage) with a ministry opportunity. Or engage in an act of purposeful kindness, debrief, then explore what the Scriptures or other authors have said on this topic.

What could that "do and learn," "learn and do" practice look like in your church? When I was a Mentor to Pastors at Fellowship Bible Church North, in Plano, Texas, I had the privilege of facilitating what I called a "Leadership Formation Group." We met for a semester. I constructed the syllabus with the life-on-life, interactive approach of Jesus in mind. Here is a brief overview of the three modules:

> **Module One** was entitled "Spiritual Friendship." We explored what it meant to become sacred companions who invested in each other's lives. A key component was a lesson from the *Life Development Planner*[168] called "Life Development Timelines." We concluded the module with a weekend retreat where we shared our timelines. Given that I'm a teacher by training, I was tempted to give each person a fixed time to tell their life story, then ring a bell! Wisdom prevailed and I suggested that each person share their highs and lows, their key mentors,

and their learning experiences without any time restriction. I recall tears and laughter. We moved from mere acquaintances to become a spiritual community in one weekend.

Module Two focused on "Spiritual Disciplines." We read and discussed Chapter 9, "Some Main Disciplines for the Spiritual Life," from *The Spirit of the Disciplines* by Dallas Willard and Chapter 6, "Interrupting Heaven: The Practice of Prayer," from *The Life You've Always Wanted* by John Ortberg. That was the learning part. The doing element was a one day "Silent Retreat." That was the greatest faith stretching experience for our group of 6 couples. Some said that they didn't know how to be silent for an hour, far less a whole day. Several still refer to that day as one of the most life-transforming markers on their spiritual journey. A highlight for me was the extended time of reflection together as a group. My question was, "In what ways did you hear from God's Spirit today?" (making it clear that it was totally acceptable to say, "I didn't hear anything, but had a good sleep").

Module Three was on building bridges to the community. We read chapters from Robert Lewis's book, *The Church of Irresistible Influence*, and culminated the module with a visit to a homeless shelter in downtown Dallas. Again it was the time of review and reflection after the time among the hundreds of homeless people that heightened the learning experience. The lasting impression of the time with the Leadership Formation Group was the way this emulated how Jesus mentored his men. He taught them (mainly in parables) and followed that with faith-stretching experiences. Then, together they processed what they had learned and experienced.

Learning is an attitude that mutual mentors need to cultivate. The essence is a humble, teachable stance which says, "I am here, not to be your teacher, but to learn along with you." It is also an interactive and intentional practice where we linger together over God's Word and spur one another on to love and good deeds. Most importantly, it's an invitation to come and learn from Jesus. Listen to him as he addressed the disciples of his day, and addresses you today:

> *Are you tired? Worn out? Burned out on religion? Come to me. Get away with me and you'll recover your life. I'll show you how to take a real rest. Walk with me and work with me— watch how I do it. Learn the unforced rhythms of grace. I won't lay anything heavy or ill-fitting on you. Keep company with me and you'll learn to live freely and lightly.*[169]

PROCESSING CHAPTER TWELVE

STEP 1: **DEPEND**—SOAK THE PROCESS IN PRAYER

1. As a student at the feet of the Lord Jesus, consider this prayer by Thomas à Kempis:

> Grant, O Lord ... to know what is worth knowing,
>   to love what is worth loving,
>   to praise what delights You most,
>   to value what is precious in Your sight and
>   to reject what is evil in Your eyes.
>
> Grant [us] true discernment to distinguish between
>   different things.
>
> Above all may [we] search out and do
>   what is most pleasing to You;
>   Through Jesus Christ our Lord.[170]

2. Note one or two points from this chapter and reflect on them with a spoken or written prayer:

STEP 2: **MEDITATE**—CONSIDER WHAT THE SCRIPTURES SAY

Proverbs 24:30-34

> [30] *I went past the field of the sluggard, past the vineyard of the man who lacks judgment;* [31] *thorns had come up everywhere, the ground was covered with weeds, and the stone wall was in ruins.* [32] *I applied my heart to what I observed and learned a lesson from what I saw:* [33] *A little sleep, a little slumber, a little folding of the hands to rest—* [34] *and poverty will come on you like a bandit and scarcity like an armed man.*

Matthew 11:28-30

> [28] *"Come to me, all you who are weary and burdened, and I will give you rest.* [29] *Take my yoke upon you and learn from me, for I am gentle and humble in heart, and you will find rest for your souls.* [30] *For my yoke is easy and my burden is light."*

Philippians 4:10-13

> [10] *I rejoice greatly in the Lord that at last you have renewed your concern for me. Indeed, you have been concerned, but you had no opportunity to show it.* [11] *I am not saying this because I am in need, for I have learned to be content whatever the circumstances.* [12] *I know what it is to be in need, and I know what it is to have plenty. I have learned the secret of being content in any and every situation, whether well fed or hungry, whether living in plenty or in want.* [13] *I can do everything through him who gives me strength.*

- Consider the three passages about how we learn and grow in God. What are some of the principles that arise out of each passage?

- In what way do these passages on learning relate to the task of learning through a mutual mentoring relationship?

STEP 3: **RESPOND**—
LEARN FROM EACH OTHER AND TAKE ACTION

Reflection and Discussion:

1. How do we cultivate a humble attitude as we approach a reciprocal mentoring relationship?

2. What are some ways you could inject more intentionality into your mentoring get-togethers?

3. Discuss Howard Hendricks' Law of Activity: "Maximum learning is always the result of maximum involvement."

4. Share your findings from the Scripture passages above.

5. What steps of obedience do you need to take as a result of reading Chapter Twelve:

Personally?

As a group?

Mentoring Practices:

1. Become a student of the Gospels and learn how humble and gentle Jesus was.

2. Evaluate your own attitudes as you learn about Jesus' gentle and humble dealings with people.

3. When you choose a new person or mentoring cluster for the next round of mentoring relationships, resist the temptation to invite only the brightest and best people. Humbly choose people the Spirit directs you to.

4. Inject intentionality into your mentoring meetings by studying Scripture or chapters from godly authors into your times together.

5. Ensure that your mentoring encounters are truly interactive by choosing resources that call for participative learning.

CHAPTER THIRTEEN

REFLECTING

praying & meeting · listening & asking · affirming & admonishing · **learning & REFLECTING** · multiplying & releasing

> "Do not let this Book of the Law
> depart from your mouth; meditate on it day and night,
> so that you may be careful to do everything written in it.
> Then you will be prosperous and successful."
> —Joshua 1:8

> "The fruit *of a reflective life should be a changed life. The changes
> should affect not only who we are but how we live, branching
> from our soul to our schedule.*"[171]
> —Ken Gire

The book of Psalms opens with a description of the truly blessed person:

> Blessed is the one who does not walk in step with the wicked
> or stand in the way that sinners take
> or sit in the company of mockers,

> *but whose delight is in the law of the LORD,*
> *and who meditates on his law day and night.*[172]

According to Psalm One, the people whom God congratulates (the "blessed" ones) choose their friends wisely, and soak in the Scriptures as a way of life. They meditate on God's Word continually. The original word for *meditate* means to ruminate, to mull over, to reflect on. Warren Wiersbe says,

> *Meditation is to the spirit what digestion is to the body. When we meditate on the Word, we allow the Spirit of God within us to "digest" the Word of God for us.*[173]

Our daily meditative attitude to God's Word needs to spill over into every aspect of our mentoring relationships. We need to reflect on what God is saying to us through his Word but also in his world. We need ears to hear, and eyes to see what God is saying or what he is showing us. The poet Elizabeth Barrett Browning put it this way:

> *Earth's crammed with heaven,*
> *And every common bush afire with God;*
> *But only he who sees takes off his shoes;*
> *The rest sit round it and pluck blackberries.*[174]

I've learned to "take off my shoes" in mentoring relationships in at least three ways: promptly, electronically and obediently.

Reflect Promptly

If I merely *intend* to reflect on what God is up to through various mentoring partnerships, I usually do nothing. Maybe that is my inertia, slothfulness or just an expression of my fallenness. So as much as possible my aim is to reflect on what God may be saying as soon as possible.

Consider the mutual mentoring practices you have been learning so far:

- **Praying and Meeting.** Reflect on what the Spirit has been saying as you have prayed "Before, During and After" your meeting times. The ancient spiritual discipline known as "Examen" is a great way of reflecting on the ways God has showed up during your day. It is a practice for discerning God's voice within the flow of a day. In Adele Calhoun's *Spiritual Disciplines Handbook*, she suggests that our Examen questions could include:

- *For what moment today am I most grateful? For what moment am I least grateful?*

- *When today did I have the deepest sense of connection with God, others, and myself? When today did I have the least sense of connection?*

- *Where was I aware of living out of the fruit of the Spirit? Where was there an absence of the fruit of the Spirit?*[175]

Reflect on God's activity in your life today and every day. On a more personal level, I find that my spiritual journal is the best place to interact with God on what he might have been saying to me through my mentor-friends or through various "happenings." I often start my daily entries with "Yesterday." Bill Hybels, in *Honest to God* recommends this practice. He reflects on the people he met, decisions he made, and high and low points of the day.[176] Another journaling practice is to divide a page with a column for requests and one for answers, together with the date. Keep reviewing those pages regularly and record answers as well as items that are unanswered at the moment. Often my prayer requests will relate to the people in whose lives I am "showing up" in that day or that week.

- **Listening and Asking.** Reflect promptly on what you have been hearing from the people God has "given" you. And take time to reflect on whether you are listening attentively, humbly and spiritually. Consider whether you have been more of an answer-giver or a humble-listener. And reflect promptly on which questions best fit your mentor partner or mentor huddle at present. If you keep a journal, reflect on the mentoring meeting as soon as possible after your time together. My best journaling tip is to keep your journal with you. When you meet with your mentor-partners, note down questions you may ask or have asked. And reflect on what the Holy Spirit has been saying in the form of a prayer.

- **Affirming and Admonishing.** Take time to reflect on whether you are affirming repeatedly, significantly and promptly, and whether God has graced you with the wisdom and courage to admonish each other appropriately. If you journal, consider keeping a record of the affirmations and corrections you have engaged in. Then turn them into heartfelt prayers.

Reflect Electronically

A brief text is a powerful way to capture several of the mentoring habits in Chapter Six through Fifteen. A text in the form of a prayer, for example, "Here's what I am praying for you..." or with words of affirmation can be truly life-changing. A while back I stumbled onto the power of making a reflective email one of the to-do's after most mentoring sessions. Now I usually conclude a session this way: "Let's email each other in the next day or so with any things we have learned as we have listened to each other and to what the Holy Spirit might have been saying to us."

Here is an edited example of a reflective email from one of my mentor-friends, Pastor Allan McPherson:

> *Thanks again for meeting with me yesterday. I treasure the time and discernment that came from it. Some reflections from our time:*
>
> 1. *I certainly felt release from functioning in a sense of aimless dissatisfaction.*
>
> 2. *Your discernment affirmed what I'd already been thinking, to function more out of the person God's made me to be. That involves working out ways to carry out the responsibilities and the role I'm called to do out of who I am. I need to pursue more personal/relational interactions with the leaders of ministries that I'm responsible for. I should focus on encouraging and equipping them through meeting with them individually rather than group sessions.*
>
> 3. *As well, I need to seek thru daily prayer the people God wants me to meet with, those who need discipling/ mentoring and pastoral care.*

In *Sacred Companions,* author David Benner devotes a whole chapter to the use of emails in a mentoring friendship. He recognizes the limitations of this medium such as absence of nonverbal contextual cues and the possibility of misunderstanding. Yet, as he reflects:

> ...I have often been surprised at how effective it can be. Sometimes it is the only way people can receive the help they desire. And some people come to feel that the advantages of being able to write whenever they have something to share and read the reply whenever is most convenient for them vastly outweigh any minor disadvantages.[177]

Online platforms for social media and internet video have shrunk the world when it comes to reflective mentoring relationships. A few days ago, from my office in Auckland, New Zealand, I had an online video call with pastors in Dallas, Texas, then Colorado Springs, and later in the day met face to face with another mutual-mentor in a local café in Auckland, New Zealand. When I returned home, a mentor-friend needed to reflect on a recent mentoring interaction and we connected through online messaging. We were able to chat back and forth, exploring in greater depth what the Holy Spirit had been saying to us. What a God-given opportunity to engage in global mentoring!

Reflect Obediently

Just before Jesus was crucified, he left his disciples with a lesson they would never forget. Although he was their Lord, he took the place of a slave and washed their feet, then said, "...I have given you an example that you should also do just as I have done to you."[178] They were to emulate Jesus by taking the lowly place, and unselfishly serving each other. How would this become a life-changing lesson? He said:

> If you know these things, blessed are you if you **do them**.[179]

If our mentoring friendships are to become transformational, we need to go beyond knowing about what we should do to taking steps of obedience. My brokenness shows itself when I settle for merely knowing about what I should do. Typically here is my sequence:

1. I am convinced I should take action.

2. I reflect on the action I should take, maybe even writing out a prayer in my journal.

3. I mistake understanding a truth and reflecting on it for "doing" what I know I should.

To help me move in the direction of life-change through submission to what I know the Holy Spirit is saying to me in my mentoring relationships, I often start by referring back to the reflective emails we have exchanged, with a comment such as: "Let's talk about any steps of obedience we took from our emails." This needs to be done graciously. If small steps of obedience have been taken, we need to celebrate that. Ken Gire's perceptive words in *The Reflective Life* capture the essence of reflective mentoring:

> First, *there must be a sense of anticipation that God wants to speak to us and that He will speak. This anticipation stems from the belief that God is love and it is the nature of love to express itself....*
>
> Second, *there must be a humility of heart, for where we are willing to look and what we are willing to hear will largely determine how many of those moments we will catch. This posture of the heart stems from a belief that words from God characteristically come swaddled in the most lowly of appearances, and that if we're not willing to stoop, we'll likely miss God among the stench of the stable and the sweetness of the straw.*
>
> Third, *there must be a responsiveness to what is heard. A willingness to follow where we are being led, wherever that may be. A readiness to admit where we are wrong, and to align ourselves with what is right and good and true. An eagerness to enter into the joy of the moment. Or in the sorrow of the moment, if that's the case. It is this responsiveness of heart that makes us susceptible to the grace of the moment. And it is what prepares us to receive whatever grace is offered to us in the next.*[180]

The mentoring practices of "Learning" and "Reflecting" belong together. Come to your mentoring partnerships with the heart of a learner, but supplement that with prompt, electronic and obedient reflection. Watch what the Lord of the Church will do.

PROCESSING CHAPTER THIRTEEN

STEP 1: **DEPEND**—SOAK THE PROCESS IN PRAYER

1. Consider this prayer from Ken Gire as you process the skill of reflection:

A Prayer of Grace

Thank You, God,
For those moments in my life
When you opened a window
And offered a word
That nourished the hunger of my soul.
Give me the grace to realize
That these are the words I live by,
Not by bread alone,
Whatever form that bread may take
However satisfying it may seem at the time.
Give me the grace to live not just reflectively but receptively,
That I may not only notice when a window is opened
But also receive what is offered,
Understanding that what is offered
Is my soul's daily bread....[181]

2. Note one or two points from this chapter and reflect on them with a spoken or written prayer:

STEP 2: **MEDITATE**—CONSIDER WHAT THE SCRIPTURES SAY

Psalm 19:14

> [14] *May the words of my mouth and the meditation of my heart be pleasing in your sight, O Lord, my Rock and my Redeemer.*

- Psalm 19 talks about the Book of Creation and the Book of the Law. It's a call to reflect on the wonders of the world and of the Word. Read the whole psalm and consider what it says about the reflective life.

Matthew 17:25-26

> [25] *"Yes, he does," he replied. When Peter came into the house, Jesus was the first to speak. "What do you think, Simon?" he asked. "From whom do the kings of the earth collect duty and taxes—from their own sons or from others?"* [26] *"From others," Peter answered. "Then the sons are exempt," Jesus said to him.*

Matthew 18:12

> [12] *"What do you think? If a man owns a hundred sheep, and one of them wanders away, will he not leave the ninety-nine on the hills and go to look for the one that wandered off?"*

- As you consider your mentoring partnerships, consider how often you encourage each other to reflect on what you have learned?

STEP 3: **RESPOND**—LEARN FROM EACH OTHER AND TAKE ACTION

Reflection and Discussion:

1. Share your thoughts on the Scripture passages above as they relate to spiritual reflection.

2. Discuss Ken Gire's words on reflection: "The fruit of a reflective life should be a changed life. The changes should affect not only who we are but how we live, branching from our soul to our schedule."

3. Why is it important to "reflect promptly"?

4. Share stories of ways you have "reflected electronically."

5. What are some steps of obedience you need to take as a result of processing Chapter Thirteen:

Personally?

As a group?

Mentoring Practices:

1. Find a way of recording what the Holy Spirit has been saying to you through the mentoring time together.

2. Follow up your mentoring session with a reflective email, text or handwritten card.

3. Take action to obey whatever the Holy Spirit might have said to you during your time together.

4. Start your next session by reviewing any steps of obedience you took since last you met.

CHAPTER FOURTEEN

MULTIPLYING

*"You are on this earth to continue the mission
that Jesus left for you: 'Go and make disciples of all nations.'
But you can't do that on your own, nor are you expected to. God
tells us to work together with the Christians He has placed in our
lives to bring his healing and transformation into the life of
the world. His plan of redemption involves the church
working in unity to reach the people around."*[182]
—Francis Chan

*"You have heard me teach many things that have been
confirmed by many reliable witnesses. Teach these great truths to
trustworthy people who are able to pass them on to others."*
—2 Timothy 2:2 (NLT)

How can mutual mentoring catch fire in a church context? One way is the stealth approach. Two people experience life-change as they meet to listen to each other and to what the Holy Spirit is saying. They share their positive experiences with others and form new relationships. In the ideal world it starts with two people, then four, then sixteen until the world is won. I have lived for most of my mentoring life in the hope that an individual-by-individual approach will one day result in a whole church becoming infected with a commitment to invest deeply in others. I'm still committed to investing my life in other individuals, but this approach is simply not enough. It's not enough because we are made for a community of more than us and one other. God places us in communities called local churches. We are a spiritual family, a new community that Paul describes in Ephesians 2:14-22. This is a community where racial, economic, and relational walls have been broken down. We are more than a collection of individuals. Paul says that "…we are fellow citizens with God's people and members of God's household…a holy temple…being built together to become a dwelling in which God lives by his Spirit."[183] As pastor and author Francis Chan puts it:

> *While every* individual *needs to obey Jesus's call to follow, we cannot follow Jesus* as individuals. *The proper context for every disciple maker is the church.*[184]

We are designed to need community. We need to create a mentoring culture within each local church. In part, that will take place as individuals start investing more intentionally in each other. But to become a culture change, rather than sporadic change in individuals here and there, the primary leaders in the church need to lead the way. They need to model it, teach it and promote it while folding it into every small group or ministry team structure.

At one level, "multiplying" doesn't seem to qualify as a mutual mentoring practice. It's not something you do (though God said to our first parents, "Be fruitful and multiply…"[185]) such as some of the other practices like "listening" or "asking." It is however a strategic element in church-based mentoring, and making disciples to the ends of the earth is the mandate of the Master Mentor: the Lord Jesus.

Here are three ways to adopt the practice of multiplying so that it becomes a habit of your life and your church.

Multiply Individually: Disciples Making Disciples

If this book resonates with you, put it into practice with another individual in your relational orbit. Start by praying. Ask God to lead you to one other person that can partner together with you with the goal of spiritual transformation. One of the themes of this book is to avoid the limitation of looking for a spiritual giant. Whom has God placed in your life, whether they are more mature or less mature than you, where you sense there is a God-given connection? Approach that person. Start meeting together. Maybe you could start by reading each chapter in *The Lost Art of Lingering*. As you go, aim to fold the ten practices in Chapter Six to Fifteen into your meetings together, one at a time, or in clusters of two (Praying and Meeting, Listening and Asking, Affirming and Admonishing, Learning and Reflecting, Multiplying and Releasing). Another option is to use the materials supplied in Resource One (20 Warning Lights For Highly Vulnerable Leaders) or Resource Two (Lingering on the Emmaus Road), or other Scripture-Based studies through www.ArtofLingering.org. When you meet to discuss one of those studies, try practicing what you learn from Chapter Six through Fifteen as you go.

As you fold the practice of "Multiplying" into your person-to-person meetings, keep the following strategies in mind:

- Early on in your meeting, discuss the importance of the principle of multiplication—what Francis Chan calls, "disciples making disciples." Talk about the challenges this presents as well as the opportunities.

- Consider putting a time limit on your regular sessions together. For example, meet for three months (or maybe a semester), once a week, then commit to each finding another person to repeat the process with.

- Start praying together that the Holy Spirit will direct you to the next person you could invite into a mutual mentoring partnership. Share some possible names and start praying for them.

Multiply Corporately: Disciples Making Disciples in the Church

My life has been a testimony to the power of one person investing deeply in another (for example my grandmother's investment in me). The bigger quest though is, "Can we find a way to work with the Holy Spirit to create a mutual mentoring culture in our churches?" A way where Paul's words in Ephesians 4:15-16 begin to come to fruition:

> *We are to grow up in every way into him who is the head, into Christ, from whom the whole body, joined and held together by every joint with which it is equipped, when each part is working properly, makes the body grow so that it builds itself up in love.*

Where should we start if the goal is nothing short of every member "working properly"—loving one another, bearing each other's burdens, encouraging one another, teaching and admonishing each other and in the process, growing up into maturity in Christ? We need to start with our leaders modeling the process. In Ephesians 4, Paul says that the Risen Christ has given gifted leaders to the Church: apostles, prophets, evangelists, pastors and teachers, so that they will equip the members for works of service.

Implement *"Lingering"* as a Leadership Team

If you are a church leader and desire to "infect" your whole church with a multiplying mindset, I suggest that you and your primary leadership team consider taking a semester to implement the ideas in *The Lost Art of Lingering* together, before you attempt to develop a church-wide approach to mentoring.

In Part One: More Than Just a Good Idea, a key question rounds out each chapter: "What are the next steps of obedience you need to take—personally and as a group?" Take a few minutes to jot down ideas at the end of each meeting, and begin by sharing any steps you have taken individually and as a group. In Part Two: Practices that May Become Habits, work through the skills and keep referring back to the previous ones as you go.

Implement *"Lingering"* in Your Small Groups

If your primary leadership team is engaged in the mutual mentoring practices, convinced of their importance, and practicing them (however imperfectly), the chances of your whole church becoming a mentoring/disciplemaking culture are probably greater. However, in reality, as long as your leadership has lead out in mentoring, that is the time to roll out *The Lost Art of Lingering* as a resource for your Small Groups.

Implement *"Lingering"* in Targeted "Huddle Groups"

These would be small groups of people that wish to become mentoring communities. Chapter Four contains examples of churches with huddle groups focused on becoming mentoring/disciplemaking communities. The key issue there is for the members to have a multiplication mindset—that they are in the group with a view to one day starting one of their own.

Multiply Globally: Disciples Making Disciples to the Ends of the Earth

As important as it is in a mentoring context to multiply individually by passing on the baton of God's truth to the next generation, and to multiply corporately by redeveloping our churches to become disciplemaking communities, God's plan is much more expansive than that. When God gave the father of the faithful, Abraham, his covenant, he promised to bless him personally, and to make him a blessing to many people, but the scope was even wider than that:

> *I will make you into a great nation, and I will bless you;*
> *I will make your name great, and you will be a blessing.*
> *...and all peoples on earth will be blessed through you.*[186]

The promise came to one man, Abraham, through one nation, Israel, but the blessing was intended for all nations. That's multiplication to the ends of the earth! "Until our vision of the church encompasses the entire globe, we do not have an accurate view of God's church or His plan of redemption."[187] God's plan is global. We must make disciples individually, and through our churches, but our focus also needs to be on the mission of Christ to the whole world. "Therefore go and make disciples of all nations..."[188] is our abiding mandate.

I've had the privilege of ministering in Burma/Myanmar. I received a simple but clear request from a pastor in Mandalay, that I call, "The Man of Myanmar" (my version of Paul's "Man of Macedonia") to help with church-based training. I went there to be a blessing but in the process have been profoundly blessed. The pastor has a small church, a Bible College, and Schools of Evangelism. When his students graduate, their next assignment is to go plant a church. I had the joy of training 35 pastors at a three day conference. I saw something different to the pale version of Christianity I've been part of for years. When I said, "Let's read Matthew 5:1-16," they eagerly found the passage in their Burmese Bibles and all read it out loud, enthusiastically. When I looked across the audience, about a third of them were not even looking at their Bibles, they had memorized it. When the pastor said, "Let's pray!" they all prayed, out loud and passionately. I know that is just a form of prayer, but when I returned to New Zealand and preached in one of our churches, very few looked engaged. Now, I realize that there are cultural factors, and that God alone knows our hearts; but God did something in my heart as I reflected on what he is up to in that needy, poverty stricken land. Allow the Risen Christ to speak to you as you process these words from Francis Chan:

> *God has called your church to play a role in His plan of redemption. And since His plan is a global plan, your church needs to think beyond your city limits. You can't be everywhere at once, and your resources and manpower are limited. But in order to be a part of God's mission on earth, you need to think in global terms.*[189]

The Lost Art of Lingering is not a "city-on-the-hill" type book. I don't have a mega church that you can all flock to see the principles in this book fully implemented. I have written it with the goal of adding to the conversation on how our lives personally can be multiplied as we linger intentionally with people God connects us to, how our churches can become disciplemaking/mentoring cultures, and ultimately communities that have the nations on our hearts. Through www.ArtofLingering.org, I invite you to share stories of multiplication—personal, corporate and global.

PROCESSING CHAPTER FOURTEEN

STEP 1: **DEPEND**—SOAK THE PROCESS IN PRAYER

1. Consider this prayer by Teri Lynne Underwood as you process Chapter Fourteen:

> Lord, may we be devoted to seeking opportunities
>   to share of Your great love...
> Give us eyes that see those in need around us
>   and hearts that long to share truth, freedom,
>   mercy and grace.
> Use us, Lord,
>   in our homes, in our schools, in our workplaces, in the
>   grocery store, at the park.
> AND AS WE GO
>   cause us to be disciple-makers,
>   always prepared to give an account of
>   the great gift of salvation
>   through Jesus Christ our Lord,
>   Amen.[190]

2. Note one or two points from this chapter and reflect on them with a spoken or written prayer:

STEP 2: **MEDITATE**—CONSIDER WHAT THE SCRIPTURES SAY

Matthew 28:18-20

> [18] Then Jesus came to them and said, "All authority in heaven and on earth has been given to me. [19] Therefore go and make disciples of all nations, baptizing them in the name of the Father and of the Son and of the Holy Spirit, [20] and teaching them to obey everything I have commanded you. And surely I am with you always, to the very end of the age."

2 Timothy 2:1-2

> [1] You then, my son, be strong in the grace that is in Christ Jesus. [2] And the things you have heard me say in the presence of many witnesses entrust to reliable men who will also be qualified to teach others.

- How do these two Scriptures reflect the principle of multiplication outlined in this chapter?

Romans 15:19-22

> [19] ...So from Jerusalem all the way around to Illyricum, I have fully proclaimed the gospel of Christ. [20] It has always been my ambition to preach the gospel where Christ was not known, so that I would not be building on someone else's foundation. [21] Rather, as it is written: "Those who were not told about him will see, and those who have not heard will understand." [22] This is why I have often been hindered from coming to you.

- How do these words from the Apostle Paul reflect God's plan of redemption to reach all of humanity?

STEP 3: **RESPOND**—
LEARN FROM EACH OTHER AND TAKE ACTION

Reflection and Discussion:

1. How do you think mutual mentoring could catch fire in your church?

2. Why do you think many of our mentoring relationships become ends in themselves?

3. How can we ensure that our mutual mentoring partnerships embody the principle of multiplication?

4. What do you think is the best way to encourage multiplication throughout your church?

5. Discuss the quote from Francis Chan in this chapter: "God has called your church to play a role in His plan of redemption. And since His plan is a global plan, your church needs to think beyond your city limits. You can't be everywhere at once, and your resources and manpower are limited. But in order to be a part of God's mission on earth, you need to think in global terms."[191]

Mentoring Practices:

1. Take this as an opportunity to review the first four pairs of mutual mentoring skills:

- Praying and Meeting
- Listening and Asking
- Affirming and Admonishing
- Learning and Reflecting

2. Decide on ways that you will incorporate the principle of multiplication into your one-on-one mentoring partnerships.

3. If you are in a leadership role, outline steps that need to be taken to fold the practice of multiplication into your small groups, ministry teams and global initiatives.

CHAPTER FIFTEEN

RELEASING

*I am the vine; you are the branches. Whoever abides in me
and I in him, he it is that bears much fruit,
for apart from me you can do nothing.*
—John 15:5 (ESV)

*Jesus is God active in the life of the world,
in our personal lives and in ministry at every turn.
The issue is not* How does Jesus get in on our ministries?
Instead, because he is the living and reigning Lord, the issue is now
What is he up to, and how do I hitch a ride on
whatever he is up to?[192]
—Andrew Purves

There comes a stage in every mentoring relationship when it is time to move on. And a philosophy of multiplication requires that we do. We need to find a way to release each other to God, to recognize that spiritual transformation is God's work not ours, to hold our God-given mentoring relationships with an open hand, and to look for other people that the Lord of the Church has put into our orbit.

Humanly, it is common to settle in to a long-term mentoring relationship, and be unaware of possessive attitudes. In *The Leadership Baton* I described three guidelines to ensure that our mentor-friendships don't become toxic:

1. Beware of anyone who talks about "my disciple."

2. Be open to times of intensive learning, but let the relationship be more fluid than possessive.

3. Adopt a team approach to mentoring.[193]

We need to adopt the lifelong practice of releasing each other to God—to release spiritually, openhandedly and generously.

Release Spiritually: This is Christ's Ministry, Not Yours

We need to relinquish our grip on each other and realize that our focus needs to be on Christ not on ourselves. In his profound book, *The Crucifixion of Ministry*, Andrew Purves puts it this way:

> ...our ministries must be displaced by the ministry of Jesus. Displacement is more than relinquishment. Displacement is not an invitation to let Jesus take over by letting him in on our territory. Rather, we must be bumped aside firmly, perhaps mortifyingly. Otherwise we will not let go of our grip on our ministries. We are too attached to them and to their payoff, even if at times the payoff is negative.[194]

During our mutual mentoring times together, and as we eventually move on from each other, we need to depend totally on the Lord Jesus. Apart from him we amount to nothing and achieve nothing. Release any unhealthy grip we have on each other, and in Purves' words, ask "How do I hitch a ride on whatever he (Jesus, *Ed*.) is up to?"[195]

Release Openhandedly: They Don't Belong to You

We all have our limits in terms of the number of meaningful mentoring relationships we can sustain. Ever since I read Paul Stanley and Robert Clinton's seminal book on mentoring, *Connecting: Mentoring Relationships You Need to Succeed in Life*, I've adopted three of their categories on effective mentoring:

1. **Intensive.** There is a time and need for very regular and intentional input into each other.

2. **Occasional.** Often after an extended "intensive" period in my mentoring relationships, we slip into an occasional, as-needed routine. The beauty of this is that it leaves us with open hands for others.

3. **Lifelong.** I have a few friends that have been with me for life. We have mentored each other in-depth for long stretches, we have moved on, but most importantly we always know we are there for each other.[196]

In addition to using these, I add a fourth:

4. **As needed**. If you choose to adopt the framework, based loosely on how Jesus mentored people, "Who are the 70 people God has placed in my relational network?" "Who are the 12?" "Who are the 3?" "Who is the one?" it's unlikely that you can care equally for all of them (unless you have unusual capacity). You could minister in-depth to 1, 3 or maybe even 12. I find the "as needed" category, releases me from overload. The people that I am no longer working intensively with know that if something happens that calls for more regular input, then we are there for each other.

I love the metaphor for the Christian life of people on inflatable tire tubes, flowing down a mighty river. From time to time some of the tubes cluster together in threes or fours, sometimes up to twenty or thirty. Then people flow on and link up with other groups. The objective is not who has the biggest flotilla. Rather, it is all about the interchange between the people for as long as they are linked, and allowing the life of Christ to flow from one to the other. And, in the case of mentoring, the links are made by the Lord of the Church, through his Spirit.

Release Generously: Introduce Them to Others

In this life stage I sometimes jokingly refer to myself as a spiritual broker (unpaid!). I have the huge privilege of making connections for people in ministry—helping them access other mentors that will take them much further than I can.

In his autobiography, guru of leadership studies, Warren Bennis describes his relationship with Doug McGregor, President of Antioch College:

> *The term* mentor *doesn't do justice to what a great one does. I've written about mentoring before—about the reciprocal nature of the relationship, for example—but I don't think I've adequately acknowledged the generosity a mentor shows. A mentor does so much more than share his or her wisdom with the mentored. The mentor allows the protégé to share in his or her achievement, an extraordinary gift. Moreover, the mentor puts his or her reputation on the line with every good word dropped about the mentored people in power, every recommendation made. In that sense, mentoring is an act of faith. Every time you recommend someone, you put yourself at risk.... When I look back, I am stunned by the faith Doug McGregor had in me, so much more faith than I had in myself. A half-century after it happened, I still wonder what my life would have been like if Doug had not decided I needed to go to MIT and made sure I was accepted. Being Doug's protégé was the next role that would shape my life. I had to grow to become the person Doug vouched for again and again. And by example he showed me how.*[197]

This final mutual mentoring skill, "Releasing," is in a way, letting go, releasing our grip on each other and allowing the Lord of the Church to take over. As we pray, then meet, we realize that this is Jesus' ministry—he has gone ahead of us, and he is there with us as we meet. And as we do, like the Emmaus Road mutual mentors, our hearts burn with love for him. When we do meet to listen and question each other, we relinquish the reins; we freely admit that we simply cannot do the work of transformation. We lay our mentoring ministry down at the foot of the cross, and in doing so it has a new basis, described by Purves:

> *Our new basis for ministry is a sharing in the continuing ministry of Jesus, for the church and her ministry can only be found where Jesus has already showed up. He has to carry the load and do the job of saving people, for I am no longer capable or available. I have discovered a terrible limiting truth about myself. I am not the Messiah. I don't do salvation any more. I am being crucified; I am gone from the center of the picture.*[198]

I subscribe to what Joey O'Connor calls "broken wholeness."[199] We are all in various stages of brokenness and wholeness. There are periods in our lives when we don't have it all together. This brings us to the end of ourselves. There are other seasons when God puts the broken pieces together and we live into all we were meant to be in Christ. Learning to become a transformational mutual mentor is not a tidy experience.

Take, for example the very first practice mentioned: **Praying**—Pray before, during and after. Which of us would claim to have graduated from the School of Prayer? Not me anyway. Sometimes God graces me with a dependent spirit for several days in a row. Other times it's almost as if I have never learned—I carry on in my own strength. I take great comfort in the thought that our Heavenly Father is like the "prodigal son's" father.[200] When he sees me take even a few steps in the right direction, he comes running with open arms.

Sometimes I **meet** wholly to **listen** and learn from my fellow mentor(s); sometimes I'm rather distracted. I have learned that as long as my mentor-partners know that my heart is toward them, they will be patient with me. There are mentoring sessions when the questions I **ask** have a touch of divine wisdom about them, at other times I feel like a slow learner in the art of questioning.

At times I remember to **affirm**, affirm, then affirm some more. But I occasionally retreat into a more self-centered approach to life, and forget to encourage the people in my mentoring network. There are times when my attempts at **admonishing** and teaching have a sense of divine timing about them, on other occasions they are a bit clumsy.

From time to time God graces the mentoring partnerships I'm in with a nice rhythm of **learning and reflecting**. At others, learning can become an end in itself with little reflection. I wish I could say that I always get it right in terms of the **multiplying and releasing** practice. Thankfully God knows that this is the desire of my heart.

The ten mentoring practices presented in this book are not a linear exercise where you complete one then move to the next, they are more like interlocking circles. As you fold these skills into your life, or into the fabric of your mentoring huddle, or your whole church, prayerfully they will become second nature to you—more like lifelong habits than a list of skills you need to check off.

As I said in the Preface, *The Lost Art of Lingering* is written for women and men who want to invest more deeply in the lives of other individuals by forming intentional spiritual friendships. I pray that this goal has been reached—that you are informed, inspired and motivated to take the next step. It is also written for church leaders who long to see Spirit-orchestrated mentoring friendships become the norm throughout their church. Individual-to-individual as well as church-wide mentoring both require intentionality—a passion and a plan.

I had the privilege of teaching mutual mentoring to 35 students at Shiloh Bible College in Mandalay, Myanmar (Burma). Their response was enthusiastic and humbling. These 20 to 30 year old men and women made commitments to form mutual mentoring relationships with fellow students. It was the response of their lecturers though that most caught my attention. They said, "This gives us a completely different view of our role as teachers here at Shiloh. We now see ourselves as mentor-teachers." It inspired me to glimpse the Lord of the Church using these mentoring principles in the Developing World.

I'm working with a church in Wanganui, on the east coast of the North Island of New Zealand. The goal of the primary leaders is "to watch God produce a disciplemaking, mutual mentoring culture" in their church by the end of this year. They are intentional! All of the leaders and their spouses (30% of the church) have committed to three one-day seminars based on this book, with the aim of implementing the ten mentoring practices in the three months between each seminar. I love their aim: to see God at work, producing a culture where the biblical one-anothers become the norm.

Join in and see what God will do, individually or collectively, as we mutually mentor each other and then watch the Spirit transform us to become more like the Lord Jesus.

PROCESSING CHAPTER FIFTEEN

STEP 1: **DEPEND**—SOAK THE PROCESS IN PRAYER

1. Consider this prayer by Katie Barclay Wilkinson as you process Chapter Fifteen:

> May the mind of Christ my Savior
> > Live in me from day to day,
> > By His love and power controlling
> > All I do and say.
>
> May the Word of God dwell richly
> > In my heart from hour to hour,
> > So that all may see I triumph
> > Only through His power.
>
> May the peace of God my Father
> > Rule my life in everything,
> > That I may be calm to comfort
> > Sick and sorrowing.
>
> May the love of Jesus fill me
> > As the waters fill the sea;
> > Him exalting, self-abasing,
> > This is victory.[201]

2. Note one or two points from this chapter and reflect on them with a spoken or written prayer:

STEP 2: **MEDITATE**—CONSIDER WHAT THE SCRIPTURES SAY

John 5:19-23

> [19] *Jesus gave them [the Jews Ed.] this answer: "I tell you the truth, the Son can do nothing by himself; he can do only what he sees his Father doing, because whatever the Father does the Son also does.* [20] *For the Father loves the Son and shows him all he does. Yes, to your amazement he will show him even greater things than these.* [21] *For just as the Father raises the dead and gives them life, even so the Son gives life to whom he is pleased to give it.* [22] *Moreover, the Father judges no one, but has entrusted all judgment to the Son,* [23] *that all may honor the Son just as they honor the Father. He who does not honor the Son does not honor the Father, who sent him."*

- In what ways does the relationship between the Son and his Father relate to the need to submit ourselves fully to the leading of the Spirit in our mentoring relationships?

John 15:5-12

> [5] *"I am the vine; you are the branches. If a man remains in me and I in him, he will bear much fruit; apart from me you can do nothing.* [6] *If anyone does not remain in me, he is like a branch that is thrown away and withers; such branches are picked up, thrown into the fire and burned.* [7] *If you remain in me and my words remain in you, ask whatever you wish, and it will be given you.* [8] *This is to my Father's glory, that you bear much fruit, showing yourselves to be my disciples.* [9] *As the Father has loved me, so have I loved you. Now remain in my love.* [10] *If you obey my commands, you will remain in my love, just as I have obeyed my Father's commands and remain in his love.* [11] *I have told you this so that my joy may be in you and that your joy may be complete.* [12] *My command is this: Love each other as I have loved you."*

- Based on this passage, what are the main elements in life transformation?

STEP 3: **RESPOND**—
LEARN FROM EACH OTHER AND TAKE ACTION

Reflection and Discussion:

1. What are the signals in a mentoring relationship that it is time to move on?

2. What are some guidelines to ensure that you "move on" well from an intensive mentoring relationship?

3. How can we avoid a possessive attitude in our mentoring relationships?

4. What does Andrew Purves mean by "displacement" in his quote in this chapter?

5. Describe any intensive, occasional and lifelong mentoring relationships that God has given you.

6. As a result of reading this chapter, what steps of obedience do you need to take:

Personally?

As a group?

Mentoring Practices:

1. Take this as an opportunity to review the ten mentoring skills:

    - Praying and Meeting
    - Listening and Asking
    - Affirming and Admonishing
    - Learning and Reflecting
    - Coaching and Releasing

2. Which of these skills do you need to focus on to improve? Why?

3. Review all of your current mentoring relationships in the light of the need to be:

    - Releasing Spiritually
    - Releasing Openhandedly
    - Releasing Generously

PART THREE
Mentoring Resources

These resources give you the opportunity to practice what you have learned in Part One and Two. They provide the opportunity to inject more intentionality into your mentoring meetings. Each resource comes with the conviction that God's Word, when we approach it meditatively and obediently, has the power to effect life transformation.

Resource One, "20 Warning Lights for Highly Vulnerable Leaders" allows you to sit at Jesus' feet and learn from his Sermon on the Mount. You have the option of working through the whole sermon, paragraph by paragraph, or choosing particular lights that may be flashing on your spiritual dashboard. Note that in Resource One, Two and Three, there are mentoring questions that will enable you or your group to process some of the life implications of the passage you study.

Resource Two, "Lingering on the Emmaus Road" gives you the chance to accompany Jesus on the Emmaus Road.

Resource Three, "Holy Discontent" looks at 2 Peter 1:3-11 to help you become all God wants you to be as one of his devoted followers.

More Scripture-based resources such as these first three will be provided on www.ArtofLingering.org.

Resource Four, "The Art and Craft of Great Questions" introduces you to a collection of questions that you can fold into your mentoring sessions. Learning how to ask questions rather than provide answers is at the heart of mutual mentoring for life change.

Resource Five, "Mentoring and Discipleship Books" provides a list of titles on mentoring and disciplemaking, as well as others you may find helpful if you adopt the suggestion of "coffee, goals and a book" in your mentoring get-togethers.

Resource Six, "The Biblical One-Anothers" is a reasonably comprehensive list of the biblical one-anothers, on the understanding that this is one of the strongest arguments for mutual mentoring.

Resource Seven, "Lingering Together Wisely" offers a review of The WISDOM Process™ which is one of the best ways I know to encourage participatory, reflecting learning in your mentoring relationships.

RESOURCE ONE

20 WARNING LIGHTS FOR HIGHLY VULNERABLE LEADERS
Matthew 5-7

I'm no auto-mechanic, but I do take note of the lights on my dash. I'm mildly concerned if the "out of gas" light starts flashing; I become even more attentive if the "over-heating" gauge swings to the red zone, or if the "oil is low" symbol appears. When these lights flash, I become anxious about my passengers, my own safety and my car.

Are any lights blinking on your spiritual dashboard?

Which of these following 20 "Warning Lights" are flashing on your spiritual dashboard? Please read the Sermon on the Mount (Matthew 5-7) through at one sitting first to get an overall view of the kind of leaders Jesus was calling his disciples to be. Then look at the paragraphs that relate to the warning lights more closely.

When you meet with your mentor-friend, consider which of these 20 Warning Lights are "green" (not a particular concern to you at the moment), which ones may be "amber" (a smaller worry) and any that are "red" (issues that need to be attended to). This mentoring commentary on the Sermon on the Mount can be used in at least two ways:

1. Work consecutively through the "Warning Lights." The advantage of this is that you will allow the Spirit to address issues in your life that you may not necessarily look at if the choice was left to you. Sometimes in your mentoring sessions you will just discuss one "light"—other times you might look at two of them.

2. Each person in your mentoring pair (or huddle) chooses one flashing warning light to discuss and work through until all the items flashing on the spiritual dashboards have been addressed.

The following "mentoring commentary" is written to help you push into some of the main things that Jesus was teaching in his sermon. If you wish to have a more in-depth commentary that still has a very practical flavor, I suggest that you read William Klein's book, *Become What You Are*.

1. PRIDE: Have you become too big for your boots?

**Aim to be a humble leader
who lives before an Audience of One.**

Matthew 5:3

[3] *"Blessed are the poor in spirit, for theirs is the kingdom of heaven."*

Matthew 6:1

[1] *"Be careful not to do your 'acts of righteousness' before men, to be seen by them. If you do, you will have no reward from your Father in heaven."*

Over breakfast once, a friend jolted me with the challenge to live my life before an Audience of One, God himself. Now if God's approval is the only thing that really matters, then what is God really looking for? Is the Lord concerned about our actions? Most definitely! Yet according to the Sermon on the Mount the main thing that interests God is our attitude toward himself, toward ourselves and toward fellow sinners.

"**Blessed**," said the Lord Jesus to his followers, "**are the poor in spirit**."[202] The original word used in this verse for *poor* is the word for absolute, grinding poverty. For this person, every day is a rainy day. Notice that Jesus said "poor in spirit." He did not say, "Blessed are the poor spirited," or "Blessed are the wimps." To be "poor in spirit" means to be utterly dependent on God for everything. It is the attitude of spiritual brokenness.

Now right from the start of Jesus' sermon you realize this notion of spiritual poverty is countercultural. The Pharisees would have said something like, "Blessed are the confident and proud" (see Luke 18:9-12). In our day, people would likely say, "Blessed are the self-assertive, blessed are the independent, or blessed are the rich in spirit." Mike Mason, in his insightful book on the experience of Job, says:

> We Christians do not like to think about being absolutely helpless in the hands of our God. With all of our faith, and with all of his grace, we still prefer to maintain some semblance of control over our lives. When difficulties arise, we like to think that there are certain steps we can take…to alleviate our anguish and be happy.[203]

I can identify with Mike Mason. I prefer to be always in control. "Blessed are the poor in spirit" prompts me to ask the question: "Will I be depending on God today?" I find it helpful to list the main activities of the day each morning in my prayer journal, and to tell God I am completely dependent on his Spirit if the tasks of the day are going to amount to anything worthwhile.

Psalm 127 is one passage that haunts and inspires me. Verse one begins, "Unless the LORD builds the house, its builders labor in vain." Too often I find myself building the house. I am trying to be both builder and architect. The attitude Jesus is encouraging in his disciples is reliance on the Builder. One of the attitudes of the virtuous, says the Lord Jesus, is that of brokenness, of spiritual bankruptcy.

Mentoring Questions:

- What do you think Jesus meant when he said, "Blessed are the poor in spirit…"?

- To what extent do you live for the applause of people or of God? (Matt. 6:1)

- How would you know that you were becoming prideful? What would be the signs that you would notice or others might see in you?

- Who do you have in your life that is empowered to let you know if you are becoming prideful?

Extra Readings: *1 Peter 5:5-11.*

Notes:

2. JOYLESSNESS: Has the joy been drained out of your ministry?

Aim to be a joyful leader who meets with God's approval.

Matthew 5:3-10

> ³ "Blessed are the poor in spirit for theirs is the kingdom of heaven.
> ⁴ Blessed are those who mourn, for they will be comforted.
> ⁵ Blessed are the meek, for they will inherit the earth.
> ⁶ Blessed are they who hunger and thirst for righteousness, for they will be filled.
> ⁷ Blessed are the merciful, for they will be shown mercy.
> ⁸ Blessed are the pure in heart, for they will see God.
> ⁹ Blessed are the peacemakers, for they will be called sons of God.
> ¹⁰ Blessed are those who are persecuted because of righteousness, for theirs is the kingdom of heaven."

Obviously the most repeated word in the Beatitudes is the word *blessed*. Some would say Jesus is spelling out a prescription for happiness or that *blessed* is little more than another word for happy. While I am sure that happiness is a by-product of the blessed life, I think Charles Swindoll, in his book *Simple Faith*, captures more of the meaning when he says,

> *By repeating the same word to his band of simple-hearted, loyal followers, he reassured them that enviable qualities such as delight, contentment, fulfillment, and deeply entrenched joy were theirs to claim. In other words, he promised that by tossing aside all the extra baggage that accompanies religious hypocrisy and a performance-oriented lifestyle, we will travel the road that leads to inner peace. In doing so we become "blessed."*[204]

In other words, if you want to put yourself in the place to be blessed by God, you need to be a person who adopts the attitudes described in the Beatitudes.

Mentoring Questions:

- What did Jesus mean when he repeatedly said, "**Blessed** are…" in Matthew 5:3-12? Was he saying, "Happy are…," "Joyful are…," "To be congratulated are…," "Those who experience God's blessing are…," or something else?

- What does it mean to be truly "bless-ed" as a Christian?

- How do you see the relationship between being happy and being joyful?

- How would you describe your "joy quotient" at the moment?

- What are some things that make you really happy?

- How does this relate to Jesus' list in v. 3-12?

Extra Readings: *Philippians 4:4-7.*

Notes:

3. INWARD FOCUS: Are you being who you are meant to be—salt in a decaying world and light in a dark world?

Aim to be an outwardly-focused leader who brings glory to God.

Matthew 5:13-16

[13] "You are the salt of the earth. But if the salt loses its saltiness, how can it be made salty again? It is no longer good for anything, except to be thrown out and trampled by men. [14] You are the light of the world. A city on a hill cannot be hidden. [15] Neither do people light a lamp to put it under a bowl. Instead they put it on its stand, and it gives light to everyone in the house. [16] In the same way, let your light shine before men, that they may see your good deeds and praise your Father in heaven."

I like the title of William Klein's excellent book on Christ's "Sermon on the Mount," *Become What You Are*. If someone you regard highly says, "You are the salt of the earth," you should take it as a huge compliment. When Jesus said to his disciples, "You are the salt of the earth," and "You are the light of the world," he wasn't just saying "you *should be* salty," or "you *should be* light." He was probably saying, "This is how I see you. You in my eyes are the salt of the earth, now go and be salty!" and "You are the light of the world, now go shine!"

In the world of Jesus' day, salt was for preserving, purifying and was intensely valuable. Jesus is essentially saying, "Keep being who you are—salty people in a decaying world." Light functions in dark places. Hiding light defeats its purpose. So most likely Jesus is saying, "You are the light of the world, now go and enlighten it."

Individually we need to hear these affirming words from the Lord Jesus and corporately as local churches, we need to take them to heart. Saltiness and light are best experienced as believers in a community who bless this dark and decaying world.

Mentoring Questions:

- What do you think Jesus meant by his word pictures of "salt" and "light"?

- How would you rate your level of "saltiness" at the moment? Why?

- To what extent are you really letting your light shine or hiding your light so that people hardly know you belong to Christ? Why?

Extra Readings: *Matthew 28:19-20.*

Notes:

4. ANGER: Are there issues of unresolved anger in your life?

Aim to be a leader who reconciles quickly.

Matthew 5:21-26

[21] "You have heard that it was said to the people long ago, 'Do not murder, and anyone who murders will be subject to judgment.' [22] But I tell you that anyone who is angry with his brother will be subject to judgment. Again, anyone who says to his brother, 'Raca,' is answerable to the Sanhedrin. But anyone who says, 'You fool!' will be in danger of the fire of hell.

[23] Therefore, if you are offering your gift at the altar and there remember that your brother has something against you, [24] leave your gift there in front of the altar. First go and be reconciled to your brother; then come and offer your gift. [25] Settle matters quickly with your adversary who is taking you to court. Do it while you are still with him on the way, or he may hand you over to the judge, and the judge may hand you to the officer, and you may be thrown into prison. [26] I tell you the truth, you will not get out until you have paid the last penny."

Jesus raises the issue of physical murder to a much higher level. He says that unchecked anger is as much disobedience to the Law of God as murder. It's so possible to be guilty of injurious thoughts and appear so clean on the outside. The call of the Lord to his disciples is to avoid letting anger build up until we explode with stupid statements.

If Jesus is really saying, "become what you are," his call here is to remember how we have been forgiven by God's great grace then we need to go and forgive others. Greatly forgiven sinners forgive greatly. When we nurse our anger we can become prisoners to the person who has hurt us. Instead we need to reconcile quickly with those who have harmed us.

An experience in a small church in Vienna, Austria is etched on my mind. The worship leader came to the part of the service when we were about to take communion. He stopped and tapped a young woman on the shoulder. They went out the door for a few minutes, came in, hugged and together we remembered Christ in the bread and the cup. I found out later that the young woman was his daughter. They had exchanged angry words on the way to the church. And they put Jesus' words into practice—expressing their brokenness and experiencing the joy of forgiveness.

Mentoring Questions:

- What are some things (or people) that make you angry?

- How do you typically deal with anger?

- How should we deal with anger according to Jesus' teaching in this section?

- Share some stories of how you have tried to reconcile with people who have something against you?

Extra Readings: *Ephesians 4:25-28.*

Notes:

5. IMPURITY: How are you coping with lustful thoughts?
Aim to be a leader who maintains purity in mind and body.

Matthew 5:27-30

[27] "You have heard that it was said, 'Do not commit adultery.' [28] But I tell you that anyone who looks at a woman lustfully has already committed adultery with her in his heart. [29] If your right eye causes you to sin, gouge it out and throw it away. It is better for you to lose part of your body than for your whole body to be thrown into hell. [30] And if your right hand causes you to sin, cut it off and throw it away. It is better for you to lose one part of your body than for your whole body to go into hell."

Like Jesus' words on murder and anger, he here raises the standard from physical adultery to heart adultery. It's possible to be committed to maintain physical purity and be riddled with impurity at the heart level. As William Klein says,

*"A sexually unfaithful heart is not a righteous heart,
even if the physical act is never consummated."*[205]

The solution is radical—nothing short of surgery will do! Metaphorically, our eyes need to be plucked out and our hands need be lopped off. The Lord is calling his disciples to take whatever steps are necessary to remove the cancer of lust. We need to take drastic steps to remove the familiar sequence: looking, desiring, planning and acting. Again, Klein's words are powerful:

*"Unless stopped somewhere along the way,
the train of a lustful look will arrive at the station of adultery."*[206]

Mentoring Questions:

- How well are you dealing with issues relating to lust?

- What are your greatest vulnerabilities in the area of sexual lust?

- What are some of the radical steps (that equate to plucking out our eye and cutting off our hand) we can take to deal with the sin of lust?

- How would your friends know if you were dying on the inside morally?

Extra Readings: *1 Corinthians 6:12-20.*

Notes:

6. INSENSITIVITY: Are you neglecting those closest to you?

Aim to be a leader who upholds the marriage covenant.

Matthew 5:31-32

[31] "It has been said, 'Anyone who divorces his wife must give her a certificate of divorce.' [32] But I tell you that anyone who divorces his wife, except for marital unfaithfulness, causes her to become an adulteress, and anyone who marries the divorced woman commits adultery."

Jesus was underlining what the prophet Malachi said in Chapter 2 verse 16—that God intends marriages to be permanent and never dissolved. God's mercy according to these words of Jesus allows for divorce in the case of sexual unfaithfulness. Jesus is not saying that adultery must terminate marriage but that it is a valid ground for divorce.

The bigger issue here is to maintain faithfulness in our marriages. We need to work at our marriages and maintain purity in the way that Jesus outlined in verses 27-30. I believe that leaders are walking targets for the arrows of the Evil One when it comes to marital faithfulness. It's possible to be successes in the church yet failures at home—to be sensitive to those we serve in the church but insensitive to our spouses and children.

Mentoring Questions:

- What are some ways that marriage is under attack in our culture?

- What would your spouse say about your relationship with him/her if they knew you wouldn't get defensive?

- What steps could you take to demonstrate commitment to your spouse?

- Why do some leaders care more for God's family than their own family?

Extra Readings: *1 Timothy 3:1-5.*

Notes:

7. UNRELIABILITY: Can your word be depended on?
Aim to be a leader who tells the truth at all times.

Matthew 5:33-37

[33] *"Again, you have heard that it was said to the people long ago, 'Do not break your oath, but keep the oaths you have made to the Lord.'* [34] *But I tell you, Do not swear at all: either by heaven, for it is God's throne;* [35] *or by the earth, for it is his footstool; or by Jerusalem, for it is the city of the Great King.* [36] *And do not swear by your head, for you cannot make even one hair white or black.* [37] *Simply let your 'Yes,' be 'Yes,' and your 'No,' 'No'; anything beyond this comes from the evil one."*

"In a time of universal deceit, telling the truth is a revolutionary act." If those words of George Orwell were true in his day, they are doubly accurate in ours. Actually this quote harmonizes with the whole Sermon on the Mount—true disciples of Jesus are radically different, they are revolutionaries in the best sense of the word. They stand out in a crowd. Their word is their bond. When they say "Yes," they really mean "Yes" and when they say "No," they are telling you the truth. In the Old Testament, oath-swearing (not using God's name) was allowed.

As with the examples of murder and adultery, here Jesus raises the bar for his disciples. His call is to say a simple "no" or "yes" and really mean it. This is not an argument to refuse to take an oath in courts in our day, rather to be known by truth-telling. The call is to become what you are, "a truth-teller" made in the image of God who is himself truth.

Mentoring Questions:

- When you recount an experience do you typically embellish the truth? Why?

- Why do we want to look good in the eyes of others?

- Why is it so difficult to tell the complete truth about something?

- How good are you at keeping your promises?

Extra Readings: *Ephesians 4:25-32.*

Notes:

8. HALF-HEARTEDNESS: Do you go the extra mile or just do enough to help?

Aim to be a leader who is generous to a fault.

Matthew 5:38-42

³⁸ "You have heard that it was said, 'Eye for eye, and tooth for tooth.' ³⁹ But I tell you, Do not resist an evil person. If someone strikes you on the right cheek, turn to him the other also. ⁴⁰ And if someone wants to sue you and take your tunic, let him have your cloak as well. ⁴¹ If someone forces you to go one mile, go with him two miles. ⁴² Give to the one who asks you, and do not turn away from the one who wants to borrow from you."

Jesus firstly calls his disciples to go way beyond the pay-back system implied in the Law of the Old Testament (Exodus 21:23-25; Deuteronomy 19:21) and be who they are as redeemed sinners, so overwhelmed by God's generosity in Christ that they go the extra mile.

When people insult us (implied in the hand slap on the face) we don't need to retaliate. Instead, in effect, we turn the other cheek. When people want to sue us and "take our tunic" (an inner garment), we give them much more—our cloak (an outer garment) as well. Again we simply refuse to retaliate. Instead we treat fellow-sinners with grace—we treat them much better than they deserve. In Jesus' day, soldiers would sometimes force a citizen to carry their pack for a mile. What should they do? Retaliate? Refuse? No, says Jesus, his disciples are radically different, and they are generous to a fault. They go way beyond the expected standards of the day. How could you apply the spirit of Jesus' words in our day?

Mentoring Questions:

- How would you rate yourself on a generosity scale (1=Stingy and 7=Very generous)?

- When someone insults you, what would it look like to "turn the other cheek"?

- When someone asks you for a favor, what would it look like to "go the extra mile"?

- When someone asks you for money, what would it look like to practice Jesus' words: "Give to the one who asks you"?

Extra Readings: Romans 12:9-16.

Notes:

9. HARSHNESS: How do you treat those who irritate you?
Aim to be a leader who treats others better than they deserve.

Matthew 5:43-48

[43] "You have heard that it was said, 'Love your neighbor, and hate your enemy.' [44] But I tell you: Love your enemies and pray for those who persecute you, [45] that you may be sons of your Father in heaven. He causes his sun to rise on the evil and the good, and sends rain on the righteous and the unrighteous. [46] If you love those who love you, what reward will you get? Are not even the tax collectors doing that? [47] And if you greet only your brothers, what are you doing more than others? Do not even pagans do that? [48] Be perfect, therefore, as your heavenly Father is perfect."

To love our friends and despise our enemies summarizes the prevailing standard of Jesus' day and ours. Most societies operate on this premise. Jesus reversed the standard: instead of retaliating they should bless. Instead of looking for ways of getting even, they should look for ways to help their enemies.

Note the final words in this paragraph of the Sermon—"be perfect as your Father in heaven is perfect." In other words, "Be generous like Your heavenly Father." As his children, treat fellow sinners with great grace. Having experienced God's forgiveness, go out and lavishly forgive others.

As with all of the sections on anger, lust, faithfulness and truthfulness, these words of Jesus make us cry out, "I simply can't do this! I am not adequate!" These radical teachings drive us to our knees. They call us to practice the very first Beatitude: "Blessed are the poor in spirit." We depend on God to do through us what we simply cannot do through our own strength.

Mentoring Questions:

- What are some of the kind things you've done lately? Have any of those acts of kindness been for someone who has offended you?

- What would it look like to do things for people you don't really know or for people you have difficulty relating to?

- Do you have enemies (past or present)? How have you dealt with these people?

- What would it look like to really love your enemies?

Extra Readings: *Romans 12:17-21.*

Notes:

10. SHOWYNESS: Do you draw attention to your good deeds?

Aim to be a leader who is characterized by acts of secret goodness.

Matthew 6:1

¹ "Be careful not to do your 'acts of righteousness' before men, to be seen by them. If you do, you will have no reward from your Father in heaven."

In Matthew Chapter 6 Jesus warns about the danger of showy righteousness. The Pharisees performed their good deeds "to be admired by others." They lived to be noticed by people—"hypocrites" was the word Jesus used of them. Their good works were opportunities to prance on the stage and to gain the praise of others. In contrast Jesus called his disciples, as he calls us today, to live before an Audience of One—for God's approval alone.

It's so easy to parade our goodness before people—to be saying in effect, "Look at me. Notice how spiritual I am. I practice the spiritual disciplines!" In his excellent book, *Holy Fools,* Mathew Woodley says,

> *Theatrical righteousness* (look at me, notice me, pay attention to me) *leads to bondage. When the applause doesn't come, or when others give it sporadically or imperfectly, how do we respond? At our best, we're disappointed. At our worst, we demand it.*[207]

The call of this passage is to pray and fast and give, but without drawing attention to ourselves. We need to practice secret goodness.

Mentoring Questions:

- In this verse, Jesus features the possibility of doing our good deeds or spiritual disciplines to impress others. What are some ways we could do this in subtle ways in our day?

- Why do we so often tell people about good things we have done?

- How could you help each other truly live before an Audience of One, God Himself?

Extra Readings: *Luke 21:1-4.*

Notes:

11. SELFISHNESS: How generous are you to those who are needy?

Aim to be a leader who is quietly generous.

Matthew 6:2-4

[2] "So when you give to the needy, do not announce it with trumpets, as the hypocrites do in the synagogues and on the streets to be honored by men. I tell you the truth, they have received their reward in full. [3] But when you give to the needy, do not let your left hand know what your right hand is doing, [4] so that your giving may be in secret. Then your Father, who sees what is done in secret, will reward you."

Notice that Jesus said, "When you give alms," not "If you give alms." He expects his disciples to give alms—that is to contribute to the poor and needy. But the emphasis here is not on giving to the poor but on the motive behind our generosity. If a religious person gives to the needy out of a desire to be noticed, their reward is on this earth only.

However, when we give to the needy and the poor we need to do it incognito. The call is to become what we are: generous people because our Heavenly Father has been generous to us. Proverbs 19:17 says, "He who is kind to the poor lends to the LORD, and he will reward him for what he has done." Note that the emphasis in this proverb is on giving with God alone as our audience. Sure, we give because the poor need our gifts, but our focus is on giving to God, not merely to people.

Mentoring Questions:

- Would you describe yourself as a happy generous giver or someone who needs to improve in this area? Why?

- Think back to the last time you gave to the poor or to a charitable organization. What was your motive?

- What are some of the principles that guide you when you decide who to give your money to?

- How much of our Christian giving should go to the poor and needy? Why?

Extra Readings: *2 Corinthians 8:1-5.*

Notes

12. PRAYERLESS: Are you too busy to pray?

Aim to be a leader whose life cannot be explained apart from the Holy Spirit in answer to prayer.

Matthew 6:5-8

[5] "And when you pray, do not be like the hypocrites, for they love to pray standing in the synagogues and on the street corners to be seen by men. I tell you the truth, they have received their reward in full. [6] But when you pray, go into your room, close the door and pray to your Father, who is unseen. Then your Father, who sees what is done in secret, will reward you. [7] And when you pray, do not keep on babbling like the pagans, for they think they will be heard because of their many words. [8] Do not be like them, for your Father knows what you need before you ask him."

Again, Jesus says, "When you pray," not "If you pray." His focus in Chapter 6:5-8 is on the "hypocrites" who engage in theatrical righteousness. They pray to be noticed. There is a more subtle hypocrisy when we are too busy serving God (even making up sermons on prayer or talking a lot about our prayers) to spend time on our knees.

Think how the Disciples' Prayer (what we call The Lord's Prayer)[208] answers your tendency to be prayerless and helps us to overcome the tendency to merely say our prayers:

- It is incredibly brief. God isn't impressed by our lengthy and theatrical prayers. He loves simplicity and honesty.

- It is focused on God, his Person, His Kingdom, His will, before we mention our needs.

- We should pray for basic material needs, forgiveness, deliverance from temptation and rescue from the Evil One.

We can become more prayerful by praying with others. William Klein, in *Become What You Are* says,

> *We must not miss the corporate language that structures the entire Lord's Prayer. God is our Father who gives us our daily bread, who forgives us our debts as we have forgiven others....*

Klein continues,

> *In view of Jesus' words here, how will you change your praying? Let it sink in that God is your Father, your "Dad" who loves you beyond measure, and at the same time is the omnipotent King of the universe. So, will you pray more often? Will you use different words? Will your public prayers take on a different character?*[209]

Mentoring Questions:

- How would you describe the quality of your prayer life in the last month?

- To what extent is your prayer life a sporadic exercise or a way-of-life?

- If your prayer life desperately needs an upgrade, what steps will you take?

Extra Readings: Matthew 7:7-11; *Colossians 4:2-6.*

Notes:

13. LACKING DISCIPLINE: When did you last engage in fasting of any kind?

Aim to be a leader who earnestly seeks God in secret prayer and fasting.

Matthew 6:16-18

[16] "When you fast, do not look somber as the hypocrites do, for they disfigure their faces to show men they are fasting. I tell you the truth, they have received their reward in full. [17] But when you fast, put oil on your head and wash your face, [18] so that it will not be obvious to men that you are fasting, but only to your Father, who is unseen; and your Father, who sees what is done in secret, will reward you."

Again, Jesus doesn't say, "If you happen to fast sometime…." Instead he presumes that his followers will fast. In verse 16, he says that when we fast we shouldn't look dismal. The hypocrites do that! They parade the spiritual discipline of fasting to show off. They want people to be impressed about how spiritual they are.

Fasting is a time-honored spiritual practice to express our earnestness of soul before God. It accompanies prayer. Dallas Willard suggests that the disciplines of abstinence (like fasting) open a channel for the disciplines of engagement (like prayer) to flow. Adele Calhoun, in the *Spiritual Disciplines Handbook* says that fasting means "to let go of an appetite in order to seek God on matters of deep concern for others, myself and the world." She defines fasting as "…the self denial of normal necessities in order to intentionally attend to God in prayer."[210]

This raises the bigger question of how disciplined you really are. When did you intentionally give up food, drink, shopping, TV, music, the internet, or other things to intentionally be with God? None of these things are a magical way to get into favor with God. Rather they should be responses to God's grace. He has treated us so extravagantly that we gladly exercise the spiritual disciplines for the purpose of godliness.

Stop and take stock of the bigger question of whether you are lacking in self-discipline or are exercising grace-filled discipline in order to become more like Jesus.

Mentoring Questions:

- Why would a person want to fast?

- Why do so few Christians fast?

- What has been your experience with fasting to this point in your life?

- According to this passage, what is the danger with a spiritual discipline like fasting?

- What are some of your greatest burdens? Consider together how you might engage in prayer and fasting relating to one of these burdens.

Extra Readings: *Acts 13:1-3; 14:23.*

Notes:

14. EARTH-BOUND: Are you primarily investing in earth or heaven?

Aim to be a leader who lives for lasting treasure.

Matthew 6:19-24

[19] "Do not store up for yourselves treasures on earth, where moth and rust destroy, and where thieves break in and steal. [20] But store up for yourselves treasures in heaven, where moth and rust do not destroy, and where thieves do not break in and steal. [21] For where your treasure is, there your heart will be also. [22] The eye is the lamp of the body. If your eyes are good, your whole body will be full of light. [23] But if your eyes are bad, your whole body will be full of darkness. If then the light within you is darkness, how great is that darkness! [24] No one can serve two masters. Either he will hate the one and love the other, or he will be devoted to the one and despise the other. You cannot serve both God and Money."

The key verse in this paragraph is v. 24—"Where your treasure is, there your heart will be also." It's interesting that Jesus didn't say, "Where your heart is, there your treasure will be also." Sometimes as we give generously to God and to people in need, our hearts respond in even greater generosity. Our hearts follow where our treasure is. Where are you investing your talents, treasure and time?

In his book, *What Jesus Said About Successful Living*, Haddon Robinson says,

> *How can we know if we are mastered by our money? A couple of questions come to mind. First, how did we get the money? Did we sacrifice something eternal to get it? If so, we have become slaves to money. Would we put competitors down and destroy them to be sure we got what was due us? If so, money is determining our priorities. Second, what do we do with our money? Let's put it bluntly. Is the cause of God in the world better off because we have been entrusted with money? Or does God only get our spare change?*[211]

Take a few minutes to audit your life. Are you earth-bound? Are you primarily investing in heaven or earth? What would the Lord Jesus say to you if he wrote a letter to you on this topic?

Mentoring Questions:

- "Money" in this passage could mean currency or material possessions. Talk about your spending patterns—how much is spent on yourself versus the extension of God's kingdom?

- How does your life show clearly that God is your Number One? Consider these categories:

    – Your work.

    – Your leisure.

    – Your daily schedule.

    – Your purchases over the last 3 months.

Extra Readings: *1 Corinthians 3:10-15.*

Notes:

15. ANXIOUS: What does your worry quotient look like?

Aim to be a leader who rests in your Father's tender care and refuses to worry.

Matthew 6:25-34

[25] "Therefore I tell you, do not worry about your life, what you will eat or drink; or about your body, what you will wear. Is not life more important than food, and the body more important than clothes? [26] Look at the birds of the air; they do not sow or reap or store away in barns, and yet your heavenly Father feeds them. Are you not much more valuable than they? [27] Who of you by worrying can add a single hour to his life? [28] And why do you worry about clothes? See how the lilies of the field grow. They do not labor or spin. [29] Yet I tell you that not even Solomon in all his splendor was dressed like one of these. [30] If that is how God clothes the grass of the field, which is here today and tomorrow is thrown into the fire, will he not much more clothe you, O you of little faith? [31] So do not worry, saying, 'What shall we eat?' or 'What shall we drink?' or 'What shall we wear?' [32] For the pagans run after all these things, and your heavenly Father knows that you need them. [33] But seek first his kingdom and his righteousness, and all these things will be given to you as well. [34] Therefore do not worry about tomorrow, for tomorrow will worry about itself. Each day has enough trouble of its own."

Jesus started this section of his sermon with the word, "Therefore...." Humanly, it might heighten our worry quotient if we give generously to God in the way that verses 19-23 talk about. No, says Jesus, the reverse is true. When you give generously to God, he will provide your basic needs. You have no need at all to worry. God provides for birds, flowers and humans. He is our Heavenly Father who tenderly cares for us. He knows that we need things like food, drink and clothes. Haddon Robinson, commenting on this section of the Sermon on the Mount puts it this way:

> *The way we look at life, Jesus said, has a lot to do with how much we worry. If we focus our attention on temporal things, such as bank accounts, careers, and physical appearance, we have reasons to worry...On the other hand, if we focus on that which is eternal—God's kingdom and his work in the world—*

our hearts will be at ease. As we commit ourselves to God, he commits himself to us. And he promises that if our hearts are where his heart is, he will take care of our needs.

Are you a worrier? Allow Jesus words in this section to release you from any unhealthy anxiety.

Mentoring Questions:

- What are some of the bigger anxieties that Jesus would want you to cast off?

- What are some of your smaller worries?

- When are some of these worries legitimate and when do they become a sin?

- Which of your worries are about things that are beyond your control?

- What should we do with our bigger and smaller worries according to this passage?

- How will you hold each other accountable in these areas?

Extra Readings: *Philippians 4:4-8.*

Notes:

16. JUDGEMENTAL: Are you an accepting or a judgmental person?

Aim to be a leader who removes the speck out of your own eye first.

Matthew 7:1-5

¹ "Do not judge, or you too will be judged. ² For in the same way you judge others, you will be judged, and with the measure you use, it will be measured to you. ³ Why do you look at the speck of sawdust in your brother's eye and pay no attention to the plank in your own eye? ⁴ How can you say to your brother, 'Let me take the speck out of your eye,' when all the time there is a plank in your own eye? ⁵ You hypocrite, first take the plank out of your own eye, and then you will see clearly to remove the speck from your brother's eye."

Throughout this Sermon, the big idea is found in this verse:

> *For I tell you that unless your righteousness surpasses that of the Pharisees and the teachers of the law, you will certainly not enter the kingdom of heaven.*[212]

Again and again Jesus is concerned about the possibility of hypocrisy. That's true with this section as well. Humorously Jesus describes someone that is trying to take a speck out of another person's eye (as a Carpenter he would have known about specks), while ignoring the massive plank in their own.

Jesus is not concerned with the need we all have to make sound judgments. Rather his concern is with a judgmental attitude. In *Become What You Are,* William Klein says,

> *Disciples...always try to avoid a critical spirit. How we treat others betrays whether or not we have genuinely experienced God's mercy. If we treat others with a critical, judgmental spirit, we reveal that we have never truly understood God's grace in our lives.*[213]

The way I would put it is that greatly forgiven sinners forgive greatly. So often I've found myself being critical of someone and then doing the very same thing the next day. For example recently I was mad at someone who cut me off when I was driving towards a traffic light, only to do much the same the next day. This passage releases me from a judgmental attitude and draws me toward a life of holiness. The answer to my critical attitude toward my fellow driver is to:

1. Clean up my own tendency to cut into lanes of traffic when I am in a hurry.
2. To remember this log in my eye.
3. To allow my fellow driver to get into line and give him a kindly wave!

Mentoring Questions:

- What are some of the areas where you have caught yourself being critical of others recently?

- What are the sins in others that bother you the most?

- Jesus talks about taking the speck out of our eye first. How could you do that? What steps would you take?

- How do you know when is the right time (or inappropriate time) to try to help others deal with sins in their lives?

Extra Readings: *Romans 14:1-18.*

Notes:

17. HYPOCRITICAL: Do you fail to do to others what you like people to do for you?

Aim to be a leader who practices the "Golden Rule."

Matthew 7:12

[12] "So in everything, do to others what you would have them do to you, for this sums up the Law and the Prophets."

In this timeless principle that we call the "Golden Rule", Jesus says, "In everything do to others as you would have them to do you; for this is the law and the prophets." This is a summary of the Law—it amounts to showing that we love God by really loving our neighbor as ourselves.

The surrounding cultures apparently stated this principle in a negative way: "If you don't want to be treated badly, don't treat others badly." Jesus' statement is positive by saying—do really good things to others, don't just avoid doing bad things to them. This is for every situation in life and the standard is really high. In effect it amounts to Jesus' followers "becoming what they are"—people who reflect how gracious God has been to them. We are not to sit on the sidelines, trying to avoid doing to others what we would not like them to do to us, but we should seek out opportunities to treat people better than they deserve. Take positive steps to bring love into the lives of the people around you.

Mentoring Questions:

- What are some of the things you really like people to do for you (e.g. giving affirming comments)?

- Why would we fail to practice Christ's "Golden Rule": "In everything, do to others as you would have them do to you…"?

- Christ is calling us to positively do good things for others. What are some of the things you might do for others this week?

Extra Readings: *Romans 12:17-21.*

Notes:

18. PEOPLE PLEASING: Do you tend to follow the crowd or take a stand?

Aim to be a leader who takes the narrow road.

Matthew 7:13-14

[13] "Enter through the narrow gate. For wide is the gate and broad is the road that leads to destruction, and many enter through it. [14] But small is the gate and narrow the road that leads to life, and only a few find it."

Jesus called his disciples to take a stand. Rather than being passive, they were to "Enter through the narrow gate...." The description of the destinations is vivid. There are eternal consequences when we choose the narrow road over the much traveled road. The gate is wide and the road is easy for people who are lurching on to destruction. The gate is restricted and the road is winding and difficult for the people who are on their way to life.

Essentially those on the wide road seek the approval of people rather than God. Those on the narrow road, live before an Audience of One—God himself. They live for his approval.

In our culture, to be broad and open-minded is one of the highest values. It has great appeal. The main problem is its outcome—destruction.

William Klein invites the readers of his book, *Become What You Are* to imagine themselves on the slopes of the hill overlooking the lake. He says,

> *For you the issue is to become what you are. Do not turn back on your profession. Do not tire of the journey. Do not give in to the enemy's temptation to take an easier way. Do not choose popularity over conviction. Do not elect comfort over commitment. Push wholeheartedly through the narrow gate, and persist on the hard (or difficult) way, following Jesus himself.*[214]

Mentoring Questions:

- How bold are you as a witness to Christ? Why?

- Have there been times in your life when you have been more courageous in your witness? Why was that?

- What does the "narrow door" look like in your life?

- Why does the broad way look so attractive?

- How does the narrow gate and the broad way relate to the whole of the Sermon on the Mount?

Extra Readings: *2 Timothy 1:6-8.*

Notes:

19. UNDISCERNING: Can you tell the difference between true and false teaching?

Aim to be a leader who can discern the difference between truth and error.

Matthew 7:15-20

[15] "Watch out for false prophets. They come to you in sheep's clothing, but inwardly they are ferocious wolves. [16] By their fruit you will recognize them. Do people pick grapes from thornbushes, or figs from thistles? [17] Likewise every good tree bears good fruit, but a bad tree bears bad fruit. [18] A good tree cannot bear bad fruit, and a bad tree cannot bear good fruit. [19] Every tree that does not bear good fruit is cut down and thrown into the fire. [20] Thus, by their fruit you will recognize them."

In this part of his sermon, Jesus points out that we need to be very discerning in selecting human teachers we listen to. How would you know the difference between a false teacher and a true one? In Acts 17:11 we read of a group of Christians in Berea. They were "more noble" than those in Thessalonica—they eagerly searched the Scriptures to see whether the things Paul and Silas were teaching agreed. That is what we need to do in our day. Rather than accept everything we hear, we need to evaluate it in light of the clear teachings of the Scriptures. We need to look at what various parts of the Bible say about a particular teaching and determine whether this person is really speaking from God.

In 1 Timothy 4:16, Paul calls his young apprentice Timothy to watch over his life and his doctrine, to persevere in them, because in that way he will avoid slipping into error. That is timeless advice. Keep sharp in your understanding of the Bible and theology and keep guarding your own character as well. Consider these questions:

- Does the discipline of study have a place in your life…?

- Are you spending as much time studying and reading solid Christian materials as you are "studying" the mass media…?

- If you have a good "handle" on the truth yourself, have you considered ways to share your knowledge with others? Can you become a teacher of others?[215]

Mentoring Questions:

- Do you feel capable of discerning between a true teacher from a false teacher? Why or why not?

- What would it take to make you more proficient in this area?

- What are some of the steps you could take?

Extra Readings: *1 Timothy 4:15-16.*

Notes:

20. DISOBEDIENT: Do you intend to obey what Christ has said, but seldom get around to it?

Aim to be a leader who puts Christ's words into practice, without delay.

Matthew 7:21-27

[21] *"Not everyone who says to me, 'Lord, Lord,' will enter the kingdom of heaven, but only he who does the will of my Father who is in heaven.* [22] *Many will say to me on that day, 'Lord, Lord, did we not prophesy in your name, and in your name drive out demons and perform many miracles?'* [23] *Then I will tell them plainly, 'I never knew you. Away from me, you evildoers!'* [24] *Therefore everyone who hears these words of mine and puts them into practice is like a wise man who built his house on the rock.* [25] *The rain came down, the streams rose, and the winds blew and beat against that house; yet it did not fall, because it had its foundation on the rock.* [26] *But everyone who hears these words of mine and does not put them into practice is like a foolish man who built his house on sand.* [27] *The rain came down, the streams rose, and the winds blew and beat against that house, and it fell with a great crash."*

The clear point of Jesus' illustration of the wise and foolish men is that we must not just think about his words, we must do them. We must put his words into practice. We need to include:

- The principles of the Beatitudes.
- Being what we are—salt in a decaying world and light in a dark world.
- A reconciling attitude with people who hurt us.
- Heart purity as well as physical purity.
- Faithfulness in marriage.
- Speaking the truth.
- Going the extra mile.
- Loving our enemies.
- Giving to the poor without drawing attention to ourselves.
- Praying in secret.
- Practicing spiritual disciplines, like fasting, in a non-showy way.

- Investing our treasures in heaven not earth.
- A worry-free life.
- A non-judgmental attitude.
- Taking a stand for Christ even when it is not popular.
- Discerning between false teachers from true teachers.

The great omission of the Great Commission[216] is when it is quoted in this way: "Go and make disciples of all nations, baptizing them in the name of the Father and the Son and of the Holy Spirit, teaching them everything I have commanded you...." It's the great omission because it leaves out the word **obey**. Jesus said, "...teaching them to **obey** everything I have commanded you."[217]

Mentoring Questions:

- Review the whole sermon. Which of these "Warning Lights" do you need to pay most attention to?

- What steps have you taken to obey what God was saying to you as you thought about any flashing lights?

Extra Readings: *Matthew 28:19-20.*

Notes:

RESOURCE TWO

LINGERING ON THE EMMAUS ROAD

Luke 24:13-35

How would it change the way that you live, and the way that you linger with others in a mentoring partnership, if you knew that the Lord Jesus was right there with you? Luke gives us an insight into what that might look like in his account of two people processing major life-challenges. When we meet them they are on a journey to Jerusalem with heavy hearts, and at the end of the story they are journeying back to Jerusalem, with hearts aflame with love for Christ.

If I could go back in time, and choose one biblical event that captures the essence of mentoring for life-change, this Emmaus Road encounter is it. As you process this brief mentoring commentary, pray that you will encounter the Risen Christ, as he walks with you daily, and that in the process you will implement key lessons you have learned in *The Lost Art of Lingering*. Here are some suggestions on how to use this chapter:

- Read all of Luke 24 so you can interact with the context of the Emmaus Road encounter with the Lord.

- Read Luke 24:13-35 through slowly, and meditatively, imagining that you are on that road with the two disciples and Jesus.

- Reflect on each section of the biblical text below, and the brief mentoring commentary.

- Take a few minutes to jot down your possible answers to the mentoring questions.

- Meet together in your mentoring pair or huddle, and discuss your answers to the various questions.

- Record any action steps you need to take.

Luke 24:13-16

> *[13] Now that same day two of them were going to a village called Emmaus, about seven miles from Jerusalem. [14] They were talking with each other about everything that had happened. [15] As they talked and discussed these things with each other, Jesus himself came up and walked along with them; [16] but they were kept from recognizing him.*

Only a bit more than a week before, crowds of onlookers and Jesus' followers acclaimed Jesus as their King. They threw down their cloaks, waved palm branches and shouted, "Hosanna."[218] Now, two of those people, on the same day Jesus appeared to some women, decided to leave town. Everything had crumbled. Their hopes of deliverance from Roman oppression by an all-conquering Messiah were dashed. Later in the story, Luke identifies one of them as Cleopas. Who was the other person? Is this the person called Clopas mentioned in John 19:25? If so, then we know his wife was Mary. Whether they were two male friends, or a married couple, Luke tells us they were kept from recognizing Jesus. That may mean that God prevented them from recognizing Jesus, or that there were other factors such as intense grief, or unbelief that made them so blind to their heavenly guest.

Whatever the reason, they don't have an ability to sense the companionship of Christ with them on their own. Reflect on the number of times in any given day when you talk to others about your concerns and joys, but are unaware of the presence of the Lord Jesus. He is with us. Consider the number of occasions that you have talked to others, but not to your Lord.

Notice that Luke says, "...Jesus himself came up and walked along with them...." He took the initiative. They were not pursuing him, he was pursuing them. Stop and thank the Lord Jesus for his pursuing love. He will not let you go.

Mentoring Questions:

1. What are some of the things that prevent us from recognizing the very real presence of Christ with us?

2. What practical steps could you take to be more aware of the presence of the Lord Jesus in your mentoring relationships?

Luke 24:17-19

> [17] *He asked them, "What are you discussing together as you walk along?" They stood still, their faces downcast.* [18] *One of them named Cleopas, asked him, "Are you only a visitor to Jerusalem and do not know the things that have happened there in these days?"*
>
> [19] *"What things?" he asked.*

Jesus joined the discussion with a general question: "What are you discussing together (Luke uses the verb 'discussing' for throwing an idea back and forth) as you walk along?" The disillusioned and sad disciples stopped, and Cleopas asked a question that would have made First Century audiences laugh: *Are you the only one unaware of what has just happened in Jerusalem?* If anyone knew what had just happened, it was Jesus. In his commentary on the gospel of Luke, Philip Graham Ryken captures the irony of that question:

> *In truth, Cleopas was the one who did not know what was happening in Jerusalem! Jesus knew it all, better than anyone, for it had happened to him! ...Instead of being the only person*

who did not know what was happening, Jesus was the only person who did! But rather than acting like a know-it-all, he took the time to help these disciples see their salvation. "What things?" he said ...inviting them to tell him what they understood.[219]

As you meditate on Jesus' artful and respectful questions, review what you learned in Chapter Eight: "Listening," and Chapter Nine: "Asking."

Luke 24:19-24

> [19] *"About Jesus of Nazareth," they replied. "He was a prophet, powerful in word and deed before God and all the people.* [20] *The chief priests and our rulers handed him over to be sentenced to death, and they crucified him;* [21] *but we had hoped that he was the one who was going to redeem Israel. And what is more, it is the third day since all this took place.* [22] *In addition, some of our women amazed us. They went to the tomb early this morning* [23] *but didn't find his body. They came and told us that they had seen a vision of angels, who said he was alive.* [24] *Then some of our companions went to the tomb and found it just as the women had said, but him they did not see."*

Jesus' probing questions exposed the ignorance of the two friends, about the true identity of Jesus. They saw him as a mighty prophet like Moses, but they either didn't know, or couldn't remember Jesus' predictions about his suffering, death and resurrection. They knew about his crucifixion, but were unconvinced about his resurrection. Philip Ryken remarks,

> *...the Gospel according to Cleopas really was no gospel at all. The word "gospel" means "good news," but there is no good news unless Jesus has risen from the grave.... This explains why Cleopas and his friend were so sad. They did not know for sure that Jesus was alive.*

Instead, they were focused on Jesus as the redeemer of Israel—the one who could deliver them from Roman oppression.

Mentoring Questions:

3. What can we learn about the art of questioning from this account of Jesus with the two friends on the Emmaus Road?

4. The two friends on this Emmaus Road were processing what was probably one of the most tragic events in their lives. What are some of the major and minor challenges you are facing at the moment? How is your response similar to or differ from these two people?

Luke 24:25-27

[25] He said to them, "How foolish you are, and how slow of heart to believe all that the prophets have spoken! [26] Did not the Christ have to suffer these things and enter his glory?" [27] And beginning with Moses and all the Prophets, he explained to them what was said in all the Scriptures concerning himself.

Jesus admonishes them—not suggesting that they are mentally slow, but that they have missed the main point of the mission of the coming Messiah. Although his question, "Did not the Christ have to suffer these things and enter his glory?" definitely implies an affirmative answer, it was the last thing these disciples would ever have imagined. That the Messiah would suffer, rise again, and be glorified is the key to understanding all of Scripture. The Risen Lord then takes them on a journey through Moses (the first five books of the Old Testament) and all the prophets, and interprets them in light of his suffering for the sins of the world and his ultimate glory. Ultimately, Cleopas and his friend will have their eyes opened. Here they have the Scriptures opened to them and their hearts burned.

In our mentoring relationships, this is a reminder of the power of Scripture to affect life change, and it is a call to Christ-centered, Scripture-based discipling.

Mentoring Questions:

5. Jesus' interaction with these two people showed how little they really knew the message of the Old Testament.

- How well do you know the Scriptures about Christ's suffering and glory? Which ones would you turn to?

- How well do you know what is in each book of the Old Testament?[220]

- What do you plan to do about that?

6. What part does Scripture play in a transformational mentoring relationship? How is this reflected in your current mentoring practices?

Luke 24:28-29

[28] As they approached the village to which they were going, Jesus acted as if he were going farther. [29] But they urged him strongly, "Stay with us, for it is nearly evening; the day is almost over." So he went in to stay with them.

Near-Eastern rules of hospitality required "strangers" to stay the night. In fact, the biblical word for hospitality means, "love of strangers." In essence the two disciples were saying, "stay a little bit longer, linger with us." Jesus accepted their offer. Interestingly, the disciples still didn't realize who they were talking to. Before you judge these followers of Jesus, consider again the number of times in a given day that the Lord is at work in your life, but you fail to acknowledge it.

Luke 24:30-35

> [30] When he was at the table with them, he took bread, gave thanks, broke it and began to give it to them. [31] Then their eyes were opened and they recognized him, and he disappeared from their sight. [32] They asked each other, "Were not our hearts burning within us while he talked with us on the road and opened the Scriptures to us?"
>
> [33] They got up and returned at once to Jerusalem. There they found the Eleven and those with them, assembled together [34] and saying, "It is true! The Lord has risen and has appeared to Simon." [35] Then the two told what had happened on the way, and how Jesus was recognized by them when he broke the bread.

The roles are reversed here. Jesus was the guest, but now he is the host who takes the bread, blesses it, breaks it and gives it to them. It almost reads as if this is the Lord's Supper or Communion. That's unlikely because Luke tells us that only the apostles were present at the Last Supper (Luke 22:14), and there is no mention of the cup here. In these times, blessing and breaking bread was common with every meal.[221] What we do have though is an essential ingredient in any transformative mentoring experience: table fellowship. Darrell Bock puts it this way:

> ...it is no accident that Jesus is revealed as he sits having table fellowship with the two disciples. The table was the place for fellowship in the ancient world. Here family and friends gathered to share time with each other. Luke has underscored the importance of meal scenes throughout his gospel. The table was a place where Jesus was heard and where his presence came across most intimately. This fact suggests that Jesus

reveals himself in the midst of the basic moments of life. He is at home in the midst of our everyday activity.[222]

It was as Jesus broke the bread that their eyes were opened. They connected the dots. They suddenly realized that Jesus was the promised Messiah, the suffering Servant, and glorious Lord. Their hearts were slow initially (v. 25), then they burned (v. 32) as Jesus opened the Scriptures to them. Their eyes were blinded initially (v. 16), now they were wide open. In some ways this still happens today. Chuck Swindoll puts it this way:

> *Some of our Lord's best visits are those we do not expect. And they come at those lowest times, when a mate has walked away, when a loved one has died, when we're released from work, when the lessons of life seem unintelligible, when a sudden twist sends life in a different direction, when "good-bye" takes a friend far away. Those are the times God Himself seems far away, when in fact He's closer than ever…and we're closer to learning something about Him.*[223]

The main point of this story is that Jesus Christ is the Risen Lord, who continues to reveal himself to his followers, through the Scriptures, as the ever available Friend. Consider the main moves in the narrative:

Confused and disappointed disciples:

- Fellowshipping together about life's "happenings."

- Unaware of the Presence of Christ and his vital interest in them.

- Experiencing a spiritual uplift as Christ reveals himself through the Scriptures.

The Living Lord:

- Coming alongside his followers and allowing them to process life.

- Opening the Scriptures to them.

- Revealing himself as they have table fellowship.

Our Christian lives amount to a long walk of obedience with the Risen Christ. He knows all about us. Psalm 139:2-4 puts it this way: "You know when I sit and when I rise; you perceive my thoughts from afar. You discern my going out and my lying down; you are familiar with all my ways." The wisest, kindest, most powerful person in the universe is right there with you. Take a walk with him. Linger with him. He knows when you are upbeat, and when you are broken. Tell him about everything. And do this in the company of your mentor-friends.

Mentoring Questions:

7. What does this section about Jesus accepting hospitality and experiencing table fellowship with the two friends relate to your mutual mentoring relationships?

8. What are some contemporary ways of showing table fellowship?

9. In the quote above, Swindoll says, "Some of our Lord's best visits are those we do not expect." What are some ways that the Risen Lord Jesus has visited you recently?

10. In what ways are you like (or unlike) the confused and disappointed disciples in Luke 24:13-35?

Steps of Obedience:

Review your answers to the mentoring questions above. What do you plan to do about the things you have written?

RESOURCE THREE

HOLY DISCONTENT
2 Peter 1:3-11

How would you describe your Christian life at the moment? Using the terms Peter describes in 2 Peter 1:3-11, where would you place yourself on this continuum:

- Pure or Impure?
- Effective or ineffective?
- Productive or unproductive?

As you consider your answers, are you contented or somewhat discontented? In Philippians 4:11, the Apostle Paul said, "…I have learned to be content whatever the circumstances." Contentment is so important, but it's also essential to experience what I'm calling, "Holy Discontent." Many Christ-followers are contented with Christ and their circumstances, yet at times discontented with their lack of spiritual growth. How about you? Every now and then, when I take stock of my Christian walk, I come back to a few key Bible passages. 2 Peter 1:3-11 is one of them.

Here are a few suggestions on how you might fold this life-changing passage into your mentoring partnership or mentoring huddle:

- Read all of 2 Peter through to get the context of the passage we are studying.

- Read 2 Peter 1:3-11 through slowly, and meditatively, keeping in mind what you know about the author—the Apostle Peter.

- Reflect on each section of the biblical passage below, and the brief mentoring commentary.

- Take a few minutes to jot down your possible answers to the mentoring questions.

- Meet together in your mentoring pair or huddle, and discuss your answers to the various questions.

- Record any action steps you need to take.

2 Peter 1:3-4

> [3] *His divine power has given us everything we need for life and godliness through our knowledge of him who called us by his own glory and goodness.* [4] *Through these he has given us his very great and precious promises, so that through them you may participate in the divine nature and escape the corruption in the world caused by evil desires.*

These verses remind us that if we are mildly or majorly discontented with our walk with Christ, the problem is not with God, it is with us. From his side he has supplied everything we need to be all he wants us to be. His divine power is available for all we need to live a godly life. Peter says that the source of that power is our experiential knowledge of the One who called us. When we are discontented, we need to come back to all we know through the promises in Scripture about God's glory and goodness. That's how we can become all God wants us to be and escape the "corruption in the world" all around us. To put it simply, we need to plug in daily to his power source. It's available to us right now.

Mentoring Questions:

1. Where would you place yourself on the three aspects of the continuum described above?

- Pure_____Impure
- Effective_____Ineffective
- Productive_____Unproductive

2. How frequently or infrequently do you plug into God's power supply? Practically, how do you do that?

3. Peter talks about God's great and precious promises. How connected to God's Word have you been in the last month?

Compare these two translations:

2 Peter 1:5-7 (NIV)

> [5] *For this very reason, make every effort to add to your faith goodness; and to goodness, knowledge;* [6] *and to knowledge, self-control; and to self-control, perseverance; and to perseverance, godliness;* [7] *and to godliness, brotherly kindness; and to brotherly kindness, love.*

2 Peter 1:5-7 (ESV)

> [5] *For this very reason, make every effort to supplement your faith with virtue, and virtue with knowledge,* [6] *and knowledge with self-control, and self-control with steadfastness, and steadfastness with godliness,* [7] *and godliness with brotherly affection, and brotherly affection with love.*

At first glance the eight godly virtues in this paragraph look sequential. You have faith then you add on goodness and so on. The original word for "add" in verses 5-7 above had an interesting background. In the days when this was written, it was used to describe what happened when a chorus master would put on a Greek play. Greek plays could be very expensive, so out of his own pocket he would add to, or *supplement* what the State had put up for the show. Tod Bolsinger's paraphrase of these verses captures the meaning of "add":

> *From your faith, produce virtue that is commendable by the world's best standards.*

> *From your virtue, produce a wisdom that can apply that virtue in real-world situations.*
> *From your wisdom, produce a self-control that can enjoy freedom in Christ while knowing safe limits.*
>
> *From that inner strength, produce endurance to face whatever challenge arises before you.*
> *Let this constancy of character reveal integrity of actions and beliefs, both in worship and in life, and especially in the Community of Faith, through loving vulnerability and generous mercy.*
> *Last, let all that is produced through your faith lavishly and consistently overflow in redemptive love to everyone in your life.*[224]

On his part, God has provided us with the power to live godly lives. Our responsibility is to "make every effort"[225] to live out these eight Christian virtues. We need to apply ourselves diligently to these virtues.

Faith

Our first faith step is placing our trust in Christ for the forgiveness of our sins, and every step of the way after that is by faith. Peter's call here is to put our faith in the power of God and in the amazing promises of God, and keep growing in faith. A life that pleases God is by faith from start to finish.

Goodness

The word for "goodness" (note that the ESV translates it "virtue") means moral excellence. It's not just about *doing* good, but *being* good. How is goodness achieved? By faith! We supplement our faith with goodness. When I think of goodness expressed in sheer generosity, my mind goes to a story about Earnest Shackelton who led an expedition to the South Pole:

> *Early in his career, Shackelton became known as a leader who put his men first. This inspired unshakeable confidence in his decisions, as well as tenacious loyalty. During the march back from 88° south, one of Shackelton's three companions, Frank Wild, who had not begun the expedition as a great admirer of Shackelton, recorded in his diary an incident that changed*

> *his mind forever. Following an inadequate meal of pemmican and pony meat on the night of January 31, 1909, Shackelton had privately forced upon Wild one of his own biscuits from the four that he, like the others, was rationed daily: "I do not suppose that anyone else in the world can thoroughly realize how much generosity and sympathy was shown by this," Wild wrote, underlining his words. "I DO by GOD I shall never forget it. Thousands of pounds would not have bought that one biscuit."*[226]

Are you cutting corners morally, or are you supplementing your faith with goodness. And more importantly are you growing in a goodness that is demonstrated in loyalty and generosity?

Knowledge

Peter is talking about the kind of knowledge we acquire as Christians when we read, and think and discuss things together. The primary source of this knowledge is God's Word. That's where our minds learn about God, his character and love for us, which will lead us to know more about his will. Allow your goodness, your moral excellence, to drive you to know more of God, his Word and to pursue knowledge. Christians are to be lifelong learners. We need to stretch our minds by continually increasing in knowledge. Is that true of you?

Self-Control

In his book, *Honest to God*, Bill Hybels captures the meaning of self-control in four words, "delayed gratification," and "advanced decision-making." When we are not in control of ourselves, we gratify ourselves immediately. We are self-indulgent rather than self-controlled. Delayed gratification is a process of dealing with present pain for the joy of future pleasure. We say "No" now for greater gain later. This applies to so many areas of life like our sexuality and weight control. Hybels says the way he does that is through advanced decision-making. He doesn't debate, "Shall I do this, shall I not." He has already decided beforehand.[227] Are you a person who shows self-control? And are you increasing in this quality?

Perseverance

We are to supplement our self-control with perseverance, or steadfastness. The people Peter was writing to had many reasons to quit. They lived like refugees. Peter says they were scattered all over the world.[228] They were suffering all kinds of trials,[229] and they were being unjustly accused of all sorts of things.[230] The self-control Peter is talking about isn't a flash in the pan, it perseveres and becomes a consistent habit of life.

Godliness

Godliness is the goal to which our faith and goodness, and self-control, and perseverance leads. Godliness is an inward quality of a heart that is set apart for God, what John Piper calls, "the Godward life." As we make every effort to persevere, there flows out a godly life, a life lived for God's glory, not our own.

Brotherly Kindness

The kind of godliness that Peter is talking about isn't hard line, legalistic piety. It produces mutual affect for those around us. The original word Peter uses here is a family expression, it is warm and kind. Are you growing in sisterly or brotherly kindness? Or have you become somewhat harsh lately in your relationships?

Love

We must supplement our mutual affection with love. Peter had experienced unending love from Jesus. G.K. Chesterton often used fairy tales to make his point about unconditional love. One of his most treasured is *Beauty and the Beast*. Chesterton said the chief lesson of that story is this: "Unlovely things must be deeply loved, before they become loveable." Unlovely Peter had been transformed by the love of Christ. This is *agape* love, the kind of love that keeps on loving even when there is resistance.

If you have come to the end of this list of Christian virtues and feel inadequate, then come back to the first one: faith. The only way to live the Christian life is by daily dependence on God.

Mentoring Questions:

4. If you were to choose three of the eight Christian virtues that need attention at the moment, which ones would they be? Why?

5. What are some specific ways to begin improving in those areas?

2 Peter 1:8-11

> ⁸ *For if you possess these qualities in increasing measure, they will keep you from being ineffective and unproductive in your knowledge of our Lord Jesus Christ.* ⁹ *But if anyone does not have them, he is nearsighted and blind, and has forgotten that he has been cleansed from his past sins.* ¹⁰ *Therefore, my brothers, be all the more eager to make your calling and election sure. For if you do these things, you will never fall,* ¹¹ *and you will receive a rich welcome into the eternal kingdom of our Lord and Savior Jesus Christ.*

What will happen if we don't keep growing in these eight qualities? Peter says we will experience spiritual blindness ("nearsighted and blind"), and spiritual dementia (not remembering how greatly our sins have been forgiven).

What takes place if we do increase in these virtues? We will be effective, productive, will never fall, and will receive an enthusiastic welcome into the eternal kingdom. How motivating!

Have you experienced a holy discontent as you have studied this passage? Consider these words from Douglas Moo's commentary on 2 Peter and make every effort to change:

> *The way in which Peter begins his list of virtues might suggest that he thinks his readers at this point only possess faith and that they have to add all the others. But Peter goes on to show*

that this is not the case. In verse 8 he implies that they already "possess" these virtues.... No, the issue is not one of having them or not having them; the issue is one of growing in the degree to which the Christian exhibits them. We must not be content, Peer suggests, with a B- in "goodness" or "knowledge" or "self-control" or "godliness" or "brotherly kindness" or "love." We should not be content until we have an A+ in each one.

Now this is a goal that I don't think any of us will achieve in this life. But Peter's point is that we need to be constantly on the way toward this goal, getting closer to it all the time. For it is only as we move along in this way that we will be able to avoid being "ineffective and unproductive" in our Christian walk.[231]

Mentoring Questions:

6. How do you relate to Douglas Moo's comments?

7. What action steps do you need to take as a result of meditating on this passage?

RESOURCE FOUR

THE ART AND CRAFT OF GREAT QUESTIONS

A good question can be more powerful than a good answer. It invariably surfaces matters that need attention in our lives. Jesus' disciples found that out. Here is a small sample of the questions he asked his followers:

- "*You of little faith, why are you so afraid?*" (Matthew 8:26)
- "*Why do you worry...?*" (Matthew 6:28)
- "*Can you drink the cup I am going to drink?*" (Matthew 20:22)
- "*Who do you say that I am?*" (Luke 9:20)
- "*Which of these three do you think was a neighbor...?*" (Luke 10:36)
- "*Were not all ten cleansed? Where are the other nine?*" (Luke 17:17)
- "*What do you want me to do for you?*" (Luke 18:41)
- "*Do you want to get well?*" (John 5:6)
- "*Simon son of John, do you truly love me more than these?*" (John 21:15)

A friend once asked Isidor I. Rabi, a Nobel prize winner in science, how he became a scientist. Rabi replied that every day after school his mother would talk to him about his school day. She wasn't so much interested in what he had learned that day, but she always inquired, "Did you ask a good question today?" "Asking good questions," according to Isidor Rabi, "made me a scientist."[232] Based on the example of the Lord Jesus with his Twelve, asking good question nudges us toward true discipleship.

SUGGESTIONS FOR USING THESE QUESTIONS

Based on the example of Jesus with his disciples, our long-term goal should be to grow in the ability to ask wise questions. On the way towards that goal, it may help to use sets of questions to hone your question-making skills.

Every now and then, our mentoring partnerships may get into a rut. Consider injecting the character questions or one of the collections of questions to your times together.

- **CHARACTER QUESTIONS (Arranged in alphabetical order)**

  – Read through these questions and have each person pick one category that they would agree to be asked about.

  – Discuss the questions in those categories when you meet.

  – Note any action steps you need to take.

- **COLLECTIONS OF GREAT QUESTIONS (from various sources)**

  – Choose one of the sets of questions.

  – Pick one or two questions each you would like to be asked about.

  – Note any action steps.

CHARACTER QUESTIONS
APPROVAL

- To what extent are you living for the approval of other people and to what extent are you living for "an Audience of One"—God himself?
- Why do we often crave the approval of others over the Lord's approval?
- What are some practical steps you can take if you find yourself too focused on the approval of other people?

CONTENTMENT

- To what extent are you contented or discontented at present? Why?
- To what extent are Paul's words in Philippians 4:11— "I have learned to be content whatever the circumstances" true of you?

DEPENDABILITY

- How dependable are you?
- To what extent can your word be relied upon?
- When was the last time you broke your word? Missed a commitment? Showed up late?

ENERGY LEVELS

- Are you serving Christ energetically or "running on empty"? Why?
- Do you wake up excited about the day or with dread? Why?
- Which activities create energy and excitement for you? What are some of the things that drain your energy?

EVANGELISM and COMPASSION

- What is your relationship with lost people at present?
- Would you ever be accused of being too friendly with sinners? Or would you be accused of being aloof from sinners? (See Luke 15:1-2)

- To what extent do you show compassion and concern to the sick, the poor and the lonely?

FAMILY

- To what degree are you caring for God's family more than your own family? Why?
- How would your spouse or your children describe your relationship with them if they knew you wouldn't get defensive?
- Would any of them be exasperated by you? Who and why?

FATIGUE

- What are the warning signs that you might be approaching overload or burnout?
- What are some of the masks that you wear to cover up any signs of overload or burnout?
- Whom have you empowered to speak truth into your life regarding overload?

FINANCES

- To what extent would you describe yourself as a generous person?
- How do you determine how much to give to the Lord? What is your view on tithing?
- Do you have major debts? How are you dealing with them?

FITNESS

- How would you describe your level of your physical fitness at present?
- How could you increase your level of fitness?
- To maintain wellness, what should you be attending to?

GRACE and TRUTH

- To what extent are you a grace-giver (treating people much better than they deserve)?

- To what extent are you a loving truth-teller (telling the truth in love even when it may not be received well)?
- Who are the people that you allow to speak grace and truth into your life? Have you given these people permission to do so? When they do that, are you defensive?

HUMILITY

- To what extent are you humbly serving Christ and living for his approval?
- How would you know that you were becoming prideful? What would be the signs in you?
- Who do you have in your life that is empowered to let you know if you are becoming prideful?

JOYFULNESS

- What is your level of joy in your work?
- Has joy been drained out of your life and ministry? Why?
- What are some things that make you really joyful? What are the joy-killers in your life?

JUDGMENTALISM

- How judgmental are you? How often do you find yourself criticizing other people (openly or secretly)?
- To what extent do sinful or less mature people feel attracted by you or repelled by you? Why?
- Do people come to you for prayer and counsel? Why or why not?

LIFE RHYTHMS[233]

- What are some of your life rhythms? Daily? Weekly? Monthly? Quarterly? Annually?
- To what extent are you observing a Sabbath time and Sabbath attitude in your life and ministry?

LIFELONG LEARNING

- How often are you engaged in the discipline of reading good books?
- What have you been reading to help you be a student of culture?
- What have you been reading lately to keep you on the cutting edge of leadership or ministry?

LUST

- How well are you dealing with the lustful thoughts in your life?
- Where are your greatest vulnerabilities?
- What are some of the ways you cultivate purity in mind and deed?
- How would your friends know if you were dying on the inside morally?

MARRIAGE

- What would your spouse say about the quality of your marriage?
- To what extent does your spouse receive the "first fruits" of your attention and energy?
- How would you (and your spouse) describe the level of your sexual intimacy in marriage?
- How would you (and your spouse) describe the level of spiritual intimacy in your marriage?

OVERSENSITIVITY

- Why do some people tend to be defensive when they are criticized?
- How do we determine when criticism should be listened to and when it should be ignored?
- What are some ways you have learned to deal well with criticism?

SABBATH[234]

- How does your life reflect God's desire for us to have a Sabbath rhythm (work and rest) in your life?
- Why do many Christ-followers neglect to fold in a Sabbath day and Sabbath principle in their lives?
- What are the essential elements in a Sabbath way of life?

SELF-CONTROL

- Which areas of life are you exercising good self-discipline over and which ones need attention?
- To what degree are you self-controlled in your eating and drinking habits, or sleep patterns?
- To what extent is your life controlling you or are you allowing the Holy Spirit to control your life?

SILENCE and SOLITUDE

- When did you last sit in God's presence in silence, just to be with him and listen to him?
- How often do you plan times of prayer and fasting? Why?

SPIRITUAL FRIENDSHIPS

- Who are the sacred companions (close soul friends that you are leaning on and helping to become like Christ) in your life?
- Who is like a spiritual father or mother to you?
- Who are you investing your life in at present?

SPIRITUALITY

- How would you describe the state of your connectedness to Christ in the last month? Are you aware of his presence? Are you distracted by much serving? Are you sitting at Jesus' feet?
- What is your level of love for Jesus at present?
- Is prayer a sporadic exercise or a way-of-life for you? Why?

TIME MANAGEMENT

- To what extent do you manage your time wisely and well?
- What are some guidelines you use to organize your time?
- What are some time wasters in your life?

WEAKNESSES and STRENGTHS

- To what degree are you ministering out of a sense of brokenness and weakness?
- Do you mask your weaknesses? What are they?
- What are your greatest strengths in leadership or ministry?
- To what level are you ministering out of who you are or are you operating more out of what people want you to be?

WORRY

- What are the major burdens in your life at present?
- What are the smaller worries you have?
- How are you dealing with your anxieties?

COLLECTIONS OF GREAT QUESTIONS

CLARIFYING QUESTIONS[235]
(Ele Parrott)

- Would you like to tell me more? (This is always good to ask before making the assumption that the mentee is finished sharing.)
- How does [fill in the blank] make you feel? (Succinctly restate what you thought you just heard.)
- What are your opinions in this situation?
- How do you find yourself praying about this?
- What do you think Jesus is teaching you through this?
- How can you glorify God in this situation? (This, by far, is a very valuable question to ask. It takes away the "why" of the situation, and replaces it with a "how." This is exactly what the Holy Spirit would like us to choose to do.)

GOSPEL-CENTERED QUESTIONS[236]
(Jonathan K. Dodson)

- What do you desire more than anything else?
- Where have you made much of yourself and little of God?
- Is technology interrupting your communion with God? Why?
- Is work a source of significance? How?
- What fears keep you from resting in Christ?
- What consumes your thoughts when you have alone time?
- When people see how you spend money, do they conclude that God is a priceless treasure, exceedingly valuable above all worldly goods?

GREAT QUESTIONS
(Various Sources)

- If you knew you only had six months to live, what would you abandon, and what would you give yourself to? (Peter Drucker Foundation)
- What are you trusting God to change in your life? Why? (Christopher Cass)

- What has become clear to you since last we met? (C.S. Lewis with J.R.R. Tolkien)
- When you die, what will be your greatest legacy? (Fred Smith)
- Do you see your best years behind you or ahead of you? Why? (Ken Blanchard)
- What are one or two recurring themes that have satisfied you most in your life stages? (Ken Blanchard)

MENTORING QUESTIONS[237]
(Keith Farmer)

- **Spirituality:** How are you and God doing?
- **Relationships:** How are you doing with those closest to you?
- **Emotions:** How are you emotionally?
- **Rhythms:** What rhythms have you established that will help you live well?
- **Vulnerabilities:** If Satan was going to take you out of ministry, from your experience, how would he be likely to do it?

TEN REFLECTIVE QUESTIONS[238]
(Henry Rogers)

1. If you could hit rewind on your life, what would you do differently? Why?
2. How has your thinking changed over the last five years?
3. If you could ask God one question today and get a verbal response, what would it be?
4. Which human being has been the greatest influence in your life?
5. What is the best advice you ever received? Who gave it to you?
6. What is one character trait or quality you wish you had? Why?
7. What is one piece of advice you would give to a person in transition (such as entering high school)?

8. What is one thing you would tell a person getting married?
9. If you could meet one person today, who would you want to meet, and what would you say to them?
10. What has life's pain taught you?

X-RAY QUESTIONS[239]
(David Powlison)

1. Who do you love? Hate?
2. What do you want, desire, crave, lust, and wish for?
3. What do you seek, aim for, and pursue? What are your goals and expectations?
4. Where do you bank your hopes?
5. What do you fear? What do you not want? What do you tend to worry about?
6. What do you think you need? What are your felt needs?
7. What are your plans, agendas, strategies, and intentions designed to accomplish?
8. What makes you tick? What lights up your world?
9. Where do you find refuge, safety, comfort, escape, pleasure, security?
10. What or whom do you trust?
11. Whom must you please? Whose opinion of you counts?
12. On your deathbed, what would sum up your life as worthwhile?
13. How do you define and weigh success or failure, right or wrong, desirable or undesirable, in any particular situation?
14. What would make you feel rich, secure, prosperous?
15. What would bring you the greatest pleasure, happiness, and delight? The greatest pain and misery?
16. What do you see as your rights? What do you feel entitled to?
17. In what situations do you feel pressured or tense? Confident and relaxed?
18. What do you pray for?

19. What do you think about most often? What preoccupies or obsesses you?
20. What do you talk about? What is most important to you?
21. Where do you find your identity? How do you define who you are?

RESOURCE FIVE

MENTORING and DISCIPLESHIP BOOKS TO LINGER OVER

This Resource (listed in alphabetical order by title) is included because one goal of writing *The Lost Art of Lingering*, is to contribute to an ongoing conversation on how our churches can become Christ-exalting, gospel-centered, discipling/mentoring cultures. Please consider using these books to further your study of mentoring and discipleship. I've given you some observations and comments for each book. While I recommend these books overall, I don't agree with everything in them.

A Generous Presence
By Rochelle Melander
The Alban Institute, Herndon, VA, 2006.

This is a very readable account of what the author calls, "Coaching." The strong relational feel of this book sounds much more like spiritual mentoring to me. Part 2 of Melander's book is very complementary to the Ten Mentoring Practices identified in Part Two of *The Lost Art of Lingering*. In particular her description of being a "fierce presence" and the power of affirmation will help you grow as a listener and encourager.

As Iron Sharpens Iron
By Howard and William Hendricks
Moody Press, Chicago, IL, 1995.

Howard Hendricks, or "Prof" as we called him, had few peers when it came to the art of mentoring. With his son, William, he provided a practical guide to mentoring relationships for men. They show how to build character in a mentoring relationship, as well as some of the practical steps such as how to find a mentor along with learning and growing together.

Building a Discipling Culture
By Mike Breen and Steve Cockram
3 Dimensions Ministries, Pawley's Island, SC, 2011.

This book is a call, not just to add disciplemaking as a focus, but to see God bring about a disciplemaking culture. Part 1: *Understanding Discipleship* and Part 3: *Using Huddles to Disciple People*, add a great deal to the conversation on how to fold a mentoring/discipling culture into your church.

Building Up One Another
By Gene A. Getz
David C. Cook, Colorado Springs, CO, 2002.

In this seminal and intensely practical book, Gene Getz discusses twelve of the primary biblical one-anothers. It is a call to slow down long enough to honor, serve, accept, encourage, and build up one another. If you wish to explore the mutuality commands of Scripture in greater depth after reading Chapter Five: "Linger with One Another," *Building Up One Another* is a great place to start.

Built to Last: Towards a Disciplemaking Church
By Edmund Chan
Covenant Resource Centre, Singapore, 2001.

Built to Last describes how, disciplemaking has been folded into the Covenant Evangelical Free Church in Singapore. It provides an excellent, simple introduction on how local churches can implement a disciplemaking process. Chan's five essentials for this are: 1. World Class Internship; 2. Word and Spirit Church; 3. Life Transforming Ministries; 4. Holistic Disciplemaking; and 5. An Unreached Peoples' Advocate.[240]

Coaching for Christian Leaders
By Linda J. Miller and Chad Hall
Chalice Press, St. Louis, MO, 2007.

There is a great deal of overlap from what Miller and Hall call "Christian Coaching" and what I'm referring to as spiritual mentoring. Chapter 2 and 3 have outstanding sections on core, essential, and supporting skills in coaching. Their section on the skills of listening will enhance your discipling relationships whether you call yourself a mentor or a coach.

Connecting
By Paul D. Stanley and J. Robert Clinton
NavPress, Colorado Springs, CO, 1992.

This seminal book on mentoring has shaped so much of my thinking and practice. Stanley and Clinton define mentoring as "…a relational experience through which one person empowers another by sharing God-given resources."[241] Their concept of a continuum of "Intensive" Mentors (disciple, spiritual guide, coach), "Occasional" Mentors (counselor, teachers, sponsor), and "Passive" Mentors (contemporary figures, historical heroes), is incredibly freeing.

Gospel-Centered Discipleship
By Jonathan K. Dodson
Crossway, Wheaton, IL, 2012.

Dodson calls the church to a comprehensive view of the gospel. So many understand that the gospel saves but doesn't sanctify. In his Foreword, Matt Chandler describes this book as a "Spirit-led, gospel-centered, organically relational, and authentic book."[242] It is all that and more. His chapter entitled, "Gospel Power," on the essential role of the Holy Spirit, should be read again and again by those who long to have a Spirit-led mentoring experience. The chapter on a "Gospel-Centered Culture" is another worthwhile contribution in the quest to mature and multiply disciples in each local church.

Leader Mentoring: Find, Inspire and Cultivate Great Leaders
By Michael H. Shenkman,
Career Press, Franklin Lakes, NJ, 2008.

The sub-title of this book: "Find, Inspire, and Cultivate Great Leaders" is true to its contents. Written from a secular business context, Shenkman talks about how to choose, and invest in mentors who become leaders. He maintains, "No mentors, no leaders!"[243]

Leadership Coaching
By Tony Stoltzfus
Tony Stoltzfus, Virginia Beach, VA, 2005.

Leadership Coaching and Stoltzfus' companion handbook, *Christian Life Coaching*, contain invaluable help if you want to hone your skills of listening and questioning.

Life Together
By Dietrich Bonhoeffer
SCM Press, London, England, 1954 (e-Book).

This book, which flowed out of a unique experience of community in an underground seminary in the Nazi years, captures the essence of true Christian community. Of particular note is his call (Chapter 1: "Community") to be non-manipulative in our relationships. *Life Together* is a highly recommended classic, especially if you wish to explore deeper community in your life together.

Love One Another
By Gerald L. Sittser
InterVarsity Press, Downers Grove, IL, 2008.

Love One Another presents one of the strongest biblical arguments for mutual mentoring (although that term is not used in this book). Flowing out of Jesus' command to love one another, Sittser provides an in-depth, but very readable exposition of how that one-another can be worked out through welcoming, forgiving, serving, encouraging, comforting, and admonishing one another.

Mentor and Friend
By Timothy K. Jones
Lion Publishing, Batavia, IL, 1991.

One of the great contributions of this small book is its emphasis on how to build a spiritual friendship. Timothy Jones describes what our expectations should be of spiritual companions as well as how to develop the God-given relationships. Chapter 8: *When Mentoring Becomes Mutual* is in many ways parallel to some of what I have shared in *The Lost Art of Lingering*. Jones says, "The further the 'disciple' progresses, …the more the 'master' must withdraw from the center of attention, must become, not a 'master' but a 'companion' and even a 'disciple' himself."[244]

Mentor Like Jesus
By Regi Campbell
B&H Publishing Group, Nashville, TN, 2009.

Regi Campbell writes as a practitioner. This is the story of how he has mentored eight groups of men, the way Jesus did. Regi prays, then selects eight men each time, and invests in them holistically. *Mentor Like Jesus* contains practical suggestions on how spend more time with fewer people to make greater kingdom impact. "Graduates" have become elders and leaders in churches.

Mentoring
By Walter C. Wright
Paternoster Press, Bucks, UK, 2006.

Using the analogy of mountaineering, Walter Wright contributes powerfully to the link between mentoring and leadership. He presents mentoring as a strategy for leadership development and personal leadership renewal. It fits within the larger context of relational leadership. Wright says, "Mentors encourage leaders to reflect on who they are (pace), what is important (journey), and how they are shaping the culture of their organization (relationships)."[245]

Mentoring for Mission
By Günter Krallmann
Jensco Ltd., Hong Kong, 1992, 1994.

Krallman focuses on how Jesus imparted his life to others. It is a scholarly, but not stuffy account of the "with-ness" (meaning companionship through close relational ties) principle that Jesus employed as he discipled his Twelve. While being trained to follow, they were being developed as leaders. *Mentoring for Mission* presents a comprehensive approach to discipling that is focused on the purpose of mission.

Mentoring Matters
By Rick Lewis
Monarch Books, Oxford, England, 2009.

This book addresses who you are as a mentor before what you do as a mentor. Lewis' approach is based on the belief that God is up to something good in every person's life. He says, "...good Christian mentoring is after what God is after, and it goes after it in ways that are consistent with the character and nature of God as revealed in Jesus Christ."[246] One of the best contributions of this book is the call to avoid cookie-cutter approaches to mentoring and instead, use methods that harmonize with the uniqueness of each individual.

Mentoring to Develop Disciples and Leaders
By John Mallison
Scripture Union, Lidcombe, NSW, Australia, 1998.

One of the main contributions of this book is the connection Mallison makes between mentoring, discipleship and leadership development. Mentoring is presented as a dynamic system, where the mentor and mentoree are constantly receiving, sharing and giving. John Mallison was a highly esteemed Australian mentor and author. In this book he gave seasoned and practical help on how to fold mentoring into your church culture, including how to conduct a mentoring session and mentor a ministry team.

Multiply
By Francis Chan
David C. Cook, Colorado Springs, CO, 2012.

With the conviction that every Christian is called to make disciples, Francis Chan designed this book to help individuals and churches to begin making disciples. *Multiply* is both a book and a course. His conviction is that we need to teach what we learn and to share life, not just information. This book explores how to live as a disciplemaker, life in the local church, how to study the Bible, and understanding the Old and New Testaments. Chan says, "Jesus has invited us all to be part of His plan. He has designed all of His people to know His joy as we share His love, spread His Word, and multiply His life among all peoples of the earth."[247]

Organic Disciplemaking
By Dennis McCallum
Touch Publications, Houston, TX, 2006.

Organic Disciplemaking flows out of the life of the author and his experiences in his church, The Xenos Church. McCallum presents a comprehensive approach to making disciples in each local church. He starts with how to make disciples, through friendship building, modeling, studying God's Word, prayer and counseling. Then McCallum offers a section on how to coach people who are in the process of making disciples for God's glory.

Practicing Affirmation
By Sam Crabtree
Crossway, Wheaton, IL, 2011.

This book is about the importance of God-centered affirmation. We are created to affirm God the Father, Son and Holy Spirit, and as his image bearers, need to affirm things in others that are God-like. When we see a God-like quality in others (such as truthfulness, kindness, or creativity) we should affirm that. Crabtree's treatment of the affirmation—correction continuum is particularly helpful.

Real-Life Discipleship
By Jim Putman
NavPress, Colorado Springs, CO, 2010.

Real-Life Discipleship presents a clear, uncomplicated way to train disciples to make disciples. It presents discipleship as an intentional, relational and strategic process of making more disciples for Christ. The heart of the book is the description of the process the Real Life Church has implemented: Share, Connect, Minister and Disciple. It also includes a discipleship curriculum for small groups.

Release Your Potential
By Elizabeth Inrig
Moody Press, Chicago, IL, 2001.

This book explores the significance of women ministering to women in each local church. Elizabeth Inrig explains the biblical mandate for woman-to-woman mentoring and provides practical help on how to implement this in your church. She sees mentoring as a transitional process (involving extended time together), a diverse relationship (we need a variety of mentors), a demanding relationship (requiring spiritual maturity), and a vibrant relationship (growing out of the needs and questions of the person being mentored).[248]

Reverse Mentoring
By Earl Creps
Jossey-Bass, San Francisco, CA, 2008.

This book describes the power of reverse mentoring, involving the humility that invites a younger person to tutor an older person. Creps shows how this can transform our churches by activating young leaders rather than neglecting them. We can easily slip into what this book calls, "positional blindness"—allowing our leadership roles to blind us to the opportunity to release the huge potential in younger folk.

Right Questions for Church Leaders
By Lovett Weems
Lovett H. Weems, 2012 (Kindle Edition).

On the premise that leaders don't need answers as much as "right questions," Weems presents a series of well-thought-out questions under various categories such as: "The Church's Purpose," "Reaching New Disciples," and "Making Good Decisions." For example, under the category of good decisions, he identifies three pertinent questions:

1. What is the goal of the decision?
2. What information do we need before deciding?
3. How will we get this information?

This material harmonizes well with Chapter 9: "Asking" in *The Lost Art of Lingering*.

Sacred Companions
By David G. Benner
InterVarsity Press, Downers Grove, IL, 2002.

This book contributes hugely to the topic of how to cultivate spiritual friendships for the purpose of spiritual transformation. Part One: "Spiritual Friendship", describes the transformational journey we are on; the essentials of sacred companionship: hospitality, presence and dialogue; and the ideals of spiritual friendship. Of particular note in the conversation about mutual mentoring is Benner's Chapter 8: "Spiritual Accompaniment in Small Groups." If you want to fold spiritual mentoring into all of your small groups, this is a chapter to start with.

Spiritual Mentoring
By Keith R. Anderson and Randy D. Reese
InterVarsity Press, Downers Grove, IL, 1999.

The core conviction of Anderson and Reese is "…that spiritual formation is nurtured most profoundly when disciples are 'apprencticed' to a spiritual mentor, who will partner with God's

Holy Spirit toward spiritual development."[249] This is a "why-to" and "what-to" book rather than one that emphasizes the "how-to's." The authors base their conclusions on the way Jesus trained his Twelve, and introduce the reader to men and women from church history that exemplified what it means to be spiritual mentors. One of the strongest emphases of this book is on the relationship of the Holy Spirit to our mentoring partnerships.

The Disciple: Following the True Mentor
By James M. Houston
David C. Cook, Colorado Springs, CO, 2007.

James Houston provides a profound philosophy of discipleship in this book. On the premise that to be Jesus' disciple was to be with him and learn to be like him, *The Disciple* adds greatly to the conversation on the relationship between discipleship and spiritual mentoring. The author unpacks how mentoring fits with our modern and postmodern world. One of his strongest contributions is his description of the purpose of discipling/mentoring. He says we are discipled to be persons in Christ; we are discipled by God's Word; and we are discipled for worship in Christian community.

The Divine Mentor
By Wayne Cordeiro
Bethany House Publishers, South Bloomington, MN, 2007.

The Divine Mentor introduces us to a range of biblical mentors. Rather than merely depending on everyday mentors around us, Wayne Cordeiro describes how various characters in the Bible provide the mentoring that he needs daily. He invites the reader to be mentored by Abraham on faith, by Samson on sexual self-control, and Daniel on how to influence your community.

The Elements of Mentoring
By W. Brad Johnson and Charles R. Ridley
Palgrave MacMillan, New York, NY, 2004.

Johnson and Ridley provide their list of the primary elements of mentoring. Written from a business context, the authors outline what excellent mentors do (matters of skill), traits of excellent mentors (matters of style and personality), as well as knowing ourselves as mentors (matters of integrity). Chapter 16: "Accept Increasing Friendship and Mutuality" synchronizes well with parts of *The Lost Art of Lingering*.

The Heart of Mentoring
By David A. Stoddard
NavPress, Colorado Springs, CO, 2003.

David Stoddard provides ten proven principles for developing people to their fullest potential. This is a must-read book for church-based mentors as well as Christians in the workplace. Here is a sample of the ten principles: "Mentoring is a journey that provides perseverance," "Mentoring includes helping mentoring partners to determine their priorities, uncover their passions, and honestly address their pain," and "Mentoring concentrates on the needs of the one being mentored, not the agenda of the mentor."[250]

The Leadership Baton
By Rowland Forman, Jeff Jones and Bruce Miller
Zondervan, Grand Rapids, MI, 2004.

This book is an argument for a holistic approach to church-based training. Readers are invited to consider strategic goals (whole-life development of "Head," "Heart," and "Hands,") strategic components (Courses, Community and Mentoring), and apply this to three groups of people (governing boards, staff and emerging leaders). The chapter on mentoring identifies five phases in the mentoring process: 1. Identification, 2. Imitation, 3. Instruction, 4. Involvement, and 5. Release. *The Leadership Baton* is another book that complements *The Lost Art of Lingering*.

The Making of a Mentor
By Ted W. Engstrom and Ron Jenson
Authentic Media, Milton Keynes, Bucks, UK, 2005.

Rather than presenting a "how-to" book on mentoring, the authors invite the readers to consider nine character traits of mentors including encouragement, honesty, and servanthood. The opening sentence in the Introduction, "Jesus ministered to many, but he focused on a few," is worth the price of the book. Engstrom and Jenson ask "Why did Jesus and his disciples narrow their attention to small groups of people," and answer, "Because they understood the secret of living forward—spiritual multiplication through intentionally influencing a few people at a time."[251]

The Measure of a Man
By Gene A. Getz
Regal Books, Ventura, CA, 2004

Dr. Getz unpacks the 20 qualities of a godly leader from Paul's lists in 1 Timothy 3 and Titus 1. This classic book encourages fathers, husbands and mentors-to-men to examine the character qualities that God is looking for in the home, in the church, and in the world. Each chapter is a call to honestly evaluate strengths and challenges in your character. The Measure of a Man is more than a mere study, it is a call to mutually mentor each other and take incremental steps toward spiritual health.

The Mentor's Guide
By Lois J. Zachary
Jossey-Bass, San Francisco, CA, 2000.

This book describes mutual mentoring in an educational setting. A key principle in this book is that mentor-partners are both learners together, committed to lifelong learning. Zachary presents mentoring as a learning partnership, where the mentor's role has moved from what she calls a "sage on the stage," to a "guide on the side."[252] The book is a practical guide, with multiple exercises to help mutual mentors hone their skills.

The Trellis and the Vine
By Colin Marshall and Tony Payne
Matthias Media, Kingsford, NSW, Australia, 2009.

According to Marshall and Payne, all Christians are to be disciple-making disciples and pastors are to be trainers. Using the metaphor of a trellis (ministry structures and maintaining institutional matters) and the vine (believers growing into maturity in Christ and multiplying), the authors maintain that both need constant attention, but trellis work looks more impressive because it is visible. What we must do is to attend to vine life—to focus on growing the vine, through making disciple-makers.

Transforming Discipleship
By Greg Ogden
InterVarsity Press, Downers Grove, IL, 2003.

The sub-title of this book captures it's essence: "Making Disciples a Few at a Time." As with several of the books above, Ogden emphasizes Jesus' method of investing in a few rather than many. One of the author's great contributions to church-based mentoring is his description, in Part 3, of multiplying reproducing discipleship groups. He suggests that the greatest transformation he has observed in his church is through "triads," or small reproducible discipleship groups. Greg Ogden's chapter on "Transformation" is worth reading several times and seeking to practice. He offers three ingredients: 1. Transparent Trust, 2. The Truth of God's Word, and 3. Mutual Accountability.

Transforming Together
By Ele Parrott
Moody Publishers, Chicago, IL, 2009.

Ele Parrott describes in her Introduction how this book has grown over time. She has learned that spiritual mentors are formed by the "stuff" of life, and also by being led by the Holy Spirit through the ebb and flow of life to become more like Jesus. Included in the book are inspiring stories of how Parrott has mentored various women and been blessed immeasurably in the process. Her chapter on "Learning to be an Active Listener" is central in the quest to become an authentic spiritual mentor.

Woman to Woman Mentoring
By Janet Thompson
LifeWay Press, Nashville, TN, 2000.

This is a ministry coordinator's guide that is full of practical advice on how to implement a woman-to-woman mentoring ministry in your church. Janet Thompson has produced this helpful resource based on years of experience in Saddleback Community Church.

RESOURCE SIX

THE BIBLICAL ONE-ANOTHERS

In Romans 1:11-12, Paul expresses his deep longing to see the believers in the church at Rome:

I long to see you so that I may impart to you some spiritual gift to make you strong—that is, that you and I may be mutually encouraged by each other's faith.

Mutual encouragement! His desire was that he would encourage them and that they would encourage him. Consider the mutuality of each of these biblical one-anothers.

THE OVERARCHING ONE-ANOTHER

John 13:34	"A new command I give you: **Love one another.** As I have loved you, so you must love one another."
John 15:12	"My command is this: **Love each other** as I have loved you."
John 15:17	"This is my command: **Love each other.**"
Romans 13:8	"Let no debt remain outstanding, except the continuing debt to **love one another**, for he who loves his fellowman has fulfilled the law."

Galatians 5:14	"The entire law is summed up in a single command '**Love your neighbor as yourself**.'"
1 Thessalonians 4:9	"Now about brotherly love we do not need to write to you, for you yourselves have been taught by God to **love each other**."
2 Thessalonians 1:3	"We ought always to thank God for you, brothers, and rightly so, because your faith is growing more and more, and **the love every one of you has for each other is increasing**."
Hebrews 13:1	"Keep on **loving each other** as brothers."
1 Peter 1:22	"Now that you have purified yourselves by obeying the truth so that you have sincere love for your brothers, **love one another** deeply, from the heart."
1 Peter 3:8	"Finally, all of you, live in harmony with one another; be sympathetic, **love as brothers**, be compassionate and humble."
1 Peter 4:8	"Above all, **love each other** deeply, because love covers over a multitude of sins."
1 John 3:11	"This is the message you heard from the beginning: **We should love one another**."
1 John 3:23	"And this is his command: to believe in the name of his Son, Jesus Christ, and to **love one another** as he commanded us."
1 John 4:7	"Dear friends, let us **love one another**, for love comes from God...."

1 John 4:11-12	"Dear friends, since God so loved us, we also ought to love one another. ¹² No one has ever seen God; but if we **love one another**, God lives in us and his love is made complete in us."
2 John 1:5	"…I ask that we **love one another**."

MEETING AND GREETING ONE-ANOTHERS

Romans 15:7	"**Accept one another**, then, just as Christ accepted you, in order to bring praise to God."
Romans 16:16	"**Greet one another with a holy kiss.…**"
1 Corinthians 16:20	"…**Greet one another with a holy kiss.**"
2 Corinthians 13:12	"**Greet one another with a holy kiss.**"
1 Peter 5:14	"**Greet one another with a kiss of love.…**"

EVERYDAY ONE-ANOTHERS

Mark 9:50	"…Have salt in yourselves, and **be at peace with each other**."
John 13:14	"Now that I, your Lord and Teacher, have washed your feet, you also should **wash one another's feet**."
Romans 1:12	"…that is, that you and I may be **mutually encouraged by each other's** faith."
Romans 12:10	"**Be devoted to one another** in brotherly love. **Honor one another above yourselves**."

Romans 12:16	"**Live in harmony with one another.**..."
Romans 14:13	"Therefore let us **stop passing judgment on one another.**..."
1 Corinthians 1:10	"I appeal to you, brothers, in the name of our Lord Jesus Christ, that all of you **agree with one another** so that there may be no divisions among you and that you may be perfectly united in mind and thought."
1 Corinthians 12:24-25	"...But God has combined the members of the body and has given greater honor to the parts that lacked it, [25] so that there should be no division in the body, but that its parts should have equal **concern for each other**."
Galatians 5:13	"...But do not use your freedom to indulge the sinful nature; rather, **serve one another in love**."
Galatians 5:26	"Let us not become conceited, **provoking and envying one another**."
Ephesians 5:19	"**Speak to one another** with psalms, hymns and spiritual songs...."
Ephesians 5:21	"**Submit to one another** out of reverence to Christ."
Philippians 2:3	"Do nothing out of selfish ambition or vain conceit, but in humility **consider others better than yourselves**."
Colossians 3:9	"**Do not lie to each other**, since you have taken off your old self with its practices."

Colossians 3:16	"Let the word of Christ dwell in you richly as you **teach and admonish one another** with all wisdom, and as you sing psalms, hymns and spiritual songs with gratitude in your hearts to God."
1 Thessalonians 4:18	"Therefore **encourage one another** with these words."
1 Thessalonians 5:11	"Therefore **encourage one another and build each other up**, just as in fact you are doing."
1 Thessalonians 5:13	"...**Live in peace with each other.**"
1 Thessalonians 5:15	"Make sure that nobody pays back wrong for wrong, but always try to **be kind to each other** and to everyone else."
Hebrews 3:13	"But **encourage one another daily**, as long as it is called Today, so that none of you may be hardened by sin's deceitfulness."
Hebrews 10:24-25	"And let us consider how we may **spur one another on toward love and good deeds.** ²⁵ Let us not give up meeting together, as some are in the habit of doing, but let us **encourage one another**—and all the more as you see the Day approaching."
James 4:11	"Brothers, **do not slander one another**...."
James 5:9	"**Don't grumble against each other**, brothers and sisters, or you will be judged...."

James 5:16	"Therefore confess your sins to each other, and **pray for each other** so that you will be healed...."
1 Peter 4:9	"**Offer hospitality to one another** without grumbling."
1 Peter 5:5	"...All of you, **clothe yourselves with humility toward one another,** because, 'God opposes the proud but gives grace to the humble.'"

"GOING DEEPER" ONE-ANOTHERS

Galatians 6:2	"**Carry each other's burdens**, and in this way you will fulfill the law of Christ."
Ephesians 4:2	"Be completely humble and gentle; be patient, **bearing with one another in love**."
Ephesians 4:32	"**Be kind and compassionate to one another, forgiving each other**, just as in Christ God forgave you."
Colossians 3:13	"**Bear with each other and forgive whatever grievances you may have against one other**...."
James 5:16	"Therefore **confess your sins to each other**, and **pray for each other** so that you may be healed...."

RESOURCE SEVEN

LINGERING TOGETHER WISELY

One of the key practices in mutual mentoring as described in this book is learning for the purpose of life transformation. We need to learn humbly (submitting to God and each other), intentionally (injecting resources that will facilitate true learning), and interactively (engaging fully in dialogue and action). As mentioned in Chapter Twelve, The WISDOM Process™ is a powerful tool to encourage genuine learning and to resolve tough issues. Consider folding this process into your mentoring experience.

THE WISDOM PROCESS™
By Bruce B. Miller

As children of God living in a hostile world, we need to learn how to think like Christ. We need to learn how to think biblically, how to use godly wisdom in life. Tested by thousands of people and hundreds of teams, The WISDOM Process™ offers a surprisingly simple and profoundly powerful way to think. Today we are drowning in data and starving for wisdom. We "Google" for information on any topic, but we cannot find wisdom for life's complex challenges. This simple process can guide you to wisdom.

Role of Prayer

We access the guidance of God's Spirit through prayer and the Word of God. God wants us to use our minds to study His Word to gain His revealed life direction. The Bible tells us, *"If any of you lacks wisdom, he should ask God, who gives generously to all without finding fault, and it will be given to him,"* James 1:5. Bible Study should be covered with prayer. Paul prayed like this for the Colossians, *"For this reason, since the day we heard about you, we have not stopped praying for you and asking God to fill you with the knowledge of his will through all spiritual wisdom and understanding,"* Colossians 1:9 (see also James 1:1-5; Ephesians 1:15-17). In answer to your prayers, the Spirit will shape your desires. Then you will have the mind of Christ. Rather than prayer being a specific step in The WISDOM Process™ it should be threaded throughout the process of your study.

The WISDOM Process™

Work the issue: *What's really at stake here?*

Prepare your heart and mind before engaging God's Word. Take a moment to pray about the issues in your life and the issues arising from the Scripture for each day. Consider how the Lord may want to impact you. Bring your questions to the study of God's Word.

Investigate Scripture: *What does God say?*

God's Word is our authority for life. It is our guide for belief and behavior. Our lives must be grounded in the Word of God. It is our only source of absolute, divine truth. We have no other source that we can look to with complete trust and confidence. Spend time prayerfully and carefully considering what the biblical text is saying.

Seek counsel: *What do wise people say?*

After studying the Scripture for ourselves, it is wise to seek the counsel of others. In Proverbs Solomon says there is wisdom in a multitude of counselors. Wise people listen to advice (Prov. 12:15; 13:10; 19:20). We provide you with biblical research to help you understand God's Word better, but of course, this counsel itself must be judged by the Word of God.

Develop your response: *What do I think?*

We learn best when we actively engage. Write down answers to questions which challenge you to respond to God's Word. Bring your answers to the group discussion to share with others.

Openly discuss: *What do we think together?*

Life transformation is increased when we sharpen each other in dynamic discussion. Our hope is that you will faithfully attend your Life Group where you can apply God's Word together with other believers. In a group, you encourage and challenge each other to understand and obey God's Word. Together, prepared believers led by the Holy Spirit will often generate a synergism in which ideas and wisdom multiply beyond what any individual could produce.

Move to action: *What will I/we do?*

Christ calls us to obey all He commands (Matthew 28:20). The point of Bible study is not simply knowledge, but obedience. We are studying God's Word to be more and more conformed to the image of Jesus Christ, to grow to maturity. The Bible tells us that hearing the word without acting on it is like building a house on sand, while acting on the truth is like building a house on rock (Matthew 7:24-27; James 1:22-25). We are in the business of building houses on rock! Our study should lead us to move to action in the Spirit's power.

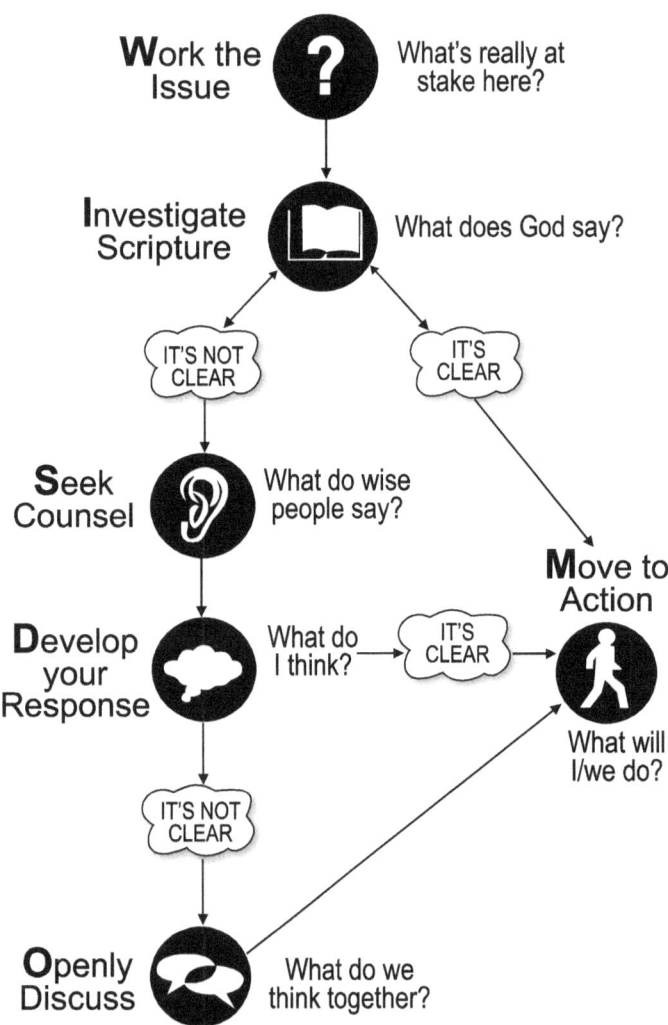

GRATITUDES

When I think about the rich tapestry of people that have contributed to this book, I'm so grateful:

- To Don Overton who introduced me to the power of two-way street mentoring.

- To Gabrielle and Terry Bugg, who embody the outdoor wall hanging they gave us, that epitomizes much of what this book is about: "Sit Long; Talk Much; Laugh Often."

- To Harataki Manihera, who taught me all I know about cross-cultural mentoring and what a deep spiritual lifelong friendship looks like.

- To Andrew Bawi Ceu in Mandalay, Myanmar, who has been teaching me how to be a spiritual father, globally.

- To James Roberts, who showed me how to mentor others on my knees.

- To the amazing team at Columbus Café in Botany Town Center who plied me with some of the best coffee in the world as I sweated over sections of this book.

- To Warren Henderson who taught me the power of a biblical passage in the form of a well-timed text.

- To Bella-Jane Miller who still inspires me to apply these mentoring practices to my role as a granddad to our seven wonderful grandkids: Harrison, Logan, Jaden, Luka, Oscar, Pero and Macy.

- To my daughter Rochelle, who has shown me how to faithfully mentor others while in the crucible of suffering.
- To my much loved sons, Mark and Dave, for their constant encouragement and support.
- To Norm Hitzges, my friend of many years who taught me how to express loyal love and what it means to be Jesus to homeless people.
- To my sister Hazel and her husband David Jackson who generously allowed me to use their beach house to write most of this book.
- To Brian Holmes who inspired me to fold Sabbath rhythms into my mentoring relationships.
- To Allan McPherson who introduced me to the power of reflective emails in a mentoring relationship.
- To Greg and Tina Joseph who taught me the significance of mutual mentoring in a business context.
- To Jason Williams, who in his visit to New Zealand helped me see the huge potential of mentoring one another in the context of a Life Group.
- To Nick Field for his clarion call to radical discipleship in the context of Life Groups.
- To Miles Davison from whom I am constantly learning the power of honesty to build trust in a mentoring relationship.
- To Robert Murchison, who taught me the power of a God-inspired high-trust mentoring friendship.
- To Stu Henderson, who showed me the art of walking with Jesus as we mentored each other.
- To Fred King, who walked across the room when I was a shy fifteen year old and told me he believed in me.

- To Jeff Jones who gave me the opportunity to be a mentor to his very young pastoral staff. Story after story in this book would not have happened if he had not believed in me.

- To Henry Rogers, whose unrelenting encouragement has inspired me to be a mentor to people who look as if they don't need one.

- To Steve Rose, who showed me how networking is integral to effective mentoring.

- To Rick Murphy who catalyzed me toward transparency in mutual mentoring.

- To Bruce Miller who taught me how to admonish lovingly and wisely.

- To Steve Burgason who demonstrated what mentoring those who are not yet Christ-followers looks like.

- To Linda Maikowski who is a constant encouragement and John Maikowski who taught me the importance of being real and gently disruptive in my mentoring relationships.

- To Kevin Harney who taught me how to inject fun into my mentoring partnerships.

- To Gene Getz who showed me how to approach a mentoring relationship with the attitude of an eager learner.

- To Chuck Hendricks who inspires me to gaze on the glory of Christ and in the process experience spiritual transformation.

- To Shellene Garofalakis, my Manager at Living Stones who has been a tireless servant helping me in this writing process.

- To Brad Carr, my pastor and son-in-law, to whom I gave permission to hold me accountable to the spiritual disciplines of Sabbath and slowing. I'm eternally grateful.

- To Jack Warren who has taught me the skill of expressing words of affirmation and well-chosen, loving admonition.

- To Glen Brechner, my mentor-friend, whom I have watched become a mentor-extraordinaire.

- To Earl Lindgren, fellow journaler, who epitomizes what it means to be a loving spiritual mentor-father.

- To Joan and Paul Havala who taught me the power of sharing our life stories in a mentoring relationship.

- To Gordon MacDonald, whose writings have 'found' me, mentored me, and encouraged me more than he will ever know.

- To countless others who have enriched my life beyond measure.

I'm so thankful to Angie Donelson who provided big picture edits, and to the insightful comments from the volunteer readers: Bruce Miller, Iva Morelli, Phil Sorensen, Henry Rogers, Gabrielle Bugg and Dee Ann Rainwater. Many thanks also to Judy Buckert and Laura Parker for their creative work in layout and design.

Thank you Lisa Marcheschi, my wonderful editor, for your servant-heart, great skills, and pure spiritual friendship. Lastly, my sincere thanks to Dave Buckert for founding Confia Publishers to provide effective church-based training resources for churches worldwide.

Soli Deo Gloria!

Rowland Forman
Auckland, New Zealand

NOTES

1. David G. Benner, *Sacred Companions* (Downers Grove, IL: InterVarsity Press, 2002), p. 27.
2. Gordon MacDonald, *A Resilient Life* (Nashville, TN: Thomas Nelson, 2004), pp. 67-68.
3. Lois J. Zachary, *The Mentor's Guide* (San Francisco, CA: Jossey-Bass, 2000), p. 3.
4. Elizabeth Inrig, *Release Your Potential* (Chicago, IL: Moody Press, 2001), pp. 78-79.
5. David G. Benner, *Sacred Companions*, p. 27.
6. Gordon MacDonald, *A Resilient Life*, p. 210. MacDonald's use of the phrase "the happy few" is taken from Shakespeare's The Life of King Henry V. MacDonald uses the expression to describe a group of people that is like an extended family "…where there would be a deep commitment to meet with one another regularly, to share life and its challenges, and to help each other find out what God was saying to us" (p. 206).
7. *WordBook English Dictionary and Thesaurus* (TranCreative Software, 2012), iPhone version 4.4.1.
8. John Ortberg, *The Life You've Always Wanted* (Grand Rapids, MI: Zondervan, 2002), p. 77.
9. David Platt, *Radical* (Colorado Springs, CO: Multnomah Books, 2010), p. 104.
10. Lois J. Zachary, *The Mentor's Guide*, p. xx.
11. Harvard Business Essentials, *Coaching and Mentoring* (Boston, MA: Harvard Business School Press, 2004), p. 147.
12. Earl Creps, *Reverse Mentoring* (San Francisco, CA: Jossey-Bass, 2008), p. xxi.
13. Matthew 4:19.
14. I prefer the term "mentor partner" to "mentor and mentoree."
15. Keith R. Anderson and Randy D. Reese, *Spiritual Mentoring: A Guide for Seeking and Giving Direction* (Downers Grove, IL: InterVarsity Press, 1999), p. 12.
16. John 15:13-15.
17. Matthew 11:28-30.
18. 1 Timothy 3:6-7.
19. John Mallison, *Mentoring to Develop Disciples and Leaders* (Adelaide, Australia: Openbook Publishers, 1998), p. 23.
20. Greg Ogden, *Transforming Discipleship* (Downers Grove, IL: InterVarsity Press, 2003), p. 124.

21. James M. Houston, *The Disciple: Following the True Mentor* (Colorado Springs, CO: David C. Cook, 2007), p. 9.

22. Dennis McCallum, *Organic Disciplemaking* (Houston, TX: Touch Publications, 2006), pp. 33-34. Dennis McCallum points out that "During the late 60's and 70's the idea of discipleship was discredited in America by the so-called 'shepherding movement.' This movement advanced a mistaken, hyper-controlling discipleship theory, rather than a facilitating theory. They argued that learning to obey a human authority is a good way to learn how to obey God. In this movement, your discipler, or 'shepherd' would be encouraged to oversee almost anything, including your personal finances, dating choices, and every other significant decision in your life."

23. Matthew 16:22.

24. Matthew 16:23.

25. John 21:15-19.

26. *WordBook English Dictionary and Thesaurus.*

27. Anderson and Reese, *Spiritual Mentoring*, p. 45.

28. Günter Krallmann, *Mentoring for Mission* (Hong Kong: Jensco, Ltd., 1992), pp. 13-14.

29. Matthew 8:23-27.

30. Luke 9:57-10:4.

31. Regi Campbell, *Mentor Like Jesus* (Nashville, TN: B&H Publishing Group, 2009), p. 4.

32. Teri Lynne Underwood, *Prayers from the Pews: The Power of Praying For Your Church* (Kindle e-book, 2012), p. 85.

33. Mark Batterson, *Soulprint* (Colorado Springs, CO: Multnomah Books, 2011), p. 2.

34. Mathew Woodley, *Holy Fools: Following Jesus with Reckless Abandon* (Carol Stream, IL: Tyndale House Publishers, Inc., 2008), p. 171.

35. Genesis 12:1, paraphrased.

36. Genesis 12:10-20; 20:1-18.

37. Genesis 13:5-18; 22:1-19.

38. Ruth 1:20.

39. Ruth 4:16.

40. 2 Timothy 3:10-11.

41. Malcolm Muggeridge, *A Twentieth Century Testimony* (London, UK: Collins, 1979), pp. 17-18.

42. Alan Andrews, Ed., *The Kingdom Life* (Colorado Springs, CO: NavPress, 2010), p. 186.

43. Charles. R. Swindoll, *Quest for Character* (Portland, OR: Multnomah Press, 1987), p. 52.

44. Arthur Bennett, Ed., *The Valley of Vision: A Collection of Puritan Prayers & Devotions* (Edinburgh, UK: The Banner of Truth Trust, 2005), pp. 134-135.

45. Ted Loder, *Guerrillas of Grace* (Minneapolis, MN: Augsburg Fortress, 1981), p. 102.

46. David Benner, *Sacred Companions*, p. 205.

47. Alan Andrews, Ed., *The Kingdom Life*, p. 225.

48. John 17:6.

49. John 5:19-20.

50. Jeremiah 10:21.
51. Darrell L. Bock, *The NIV Application Commentary: Luke* (Grand Rapids, MI: Zondervan Publishing House, 1996), p. 616.
52. Lance Witt, *Replenish* (Grand Rapids, MI: Baker Books, 2011), pp. 83-84.
53. Alan Andrews, Ed., *The Kingdom Life*, p. 241.
54. C. S. Lewis, *The Weight of Glory and Other Addresses* (New York, NY: HarperOne, 1949, 1976 [revised]), p. 176.
55. Brian G. Hedges, *Christ Formed in You* (Wapwallopen, PA: Shepherd Press, 2010), pp. 258-259.
56. A. W. Tozer, *The Pursuit of God* (Camp Hill, PA: Christian Publications, 1993), pp. 19-20.
57. Owen Collins, Ed., *Classic Christian Prayers* (New York, NY: Random House, 1999), p. 282.
58. Olivia Warburton, Ed., *Hear our Prayer: An Anthology of Classic Prayers* (Oxford, England: Lion Hudson, 2005), p. 12.
59. David G. Benner, *Sacred Companions*, p. 19.
60. James Emery White, *Rethinking the Church* (Grand Rapids, MI: Baker Books, 1997), p. 111.
61. Acts 2:42-47.
62. Teri Lynne Underwood, *Prayers from the Pews*, p. 26.
63. Ibid., p. 28.
64. 1 Corinthians 11:1.
65. Janet Thompson, *Woman to Woman Mentoring* (Wheaton, IL: Tyndale House, 2000).
66. Greg Ogden, *Transforming Discipleship*, pp. 176-177.
67. Dennis McCallum, *Organic Disciplemaking*, pp. 19-20.
68. Ibid., p. 61.
69. Mike Breen and Steve Cockram, *Building a Discipling Culture* (Pawley's Island, SC: 3 Dimension Ministries, 2011), Chapter Four: Bulding a Discipling Culture, Kindle edition.
70. Matthew 28:19-20.
71. David Platt, *Radical*, pp. 103-104.
72. Bruce Miller, "The Glory of the Church," *The Church*, Issue 1, (McKinney, TX: Centers of Church Based Training, 2005), pg. 7.
73. Timothy Jones, *The Art of Prayer* (Colorado Springs, CO: Waterbrook Press, 2005), p. 170.
74. Titus 2:3-5.
75. Tremper Longman III, *Proverbs* (Grand Rapids, MI: Baker Academic, 2006), p. 481.
76. "My soul yearns for you in the night; in the morning my spirit longs for you," *Quotations*, 2012, http://coolessay.org/docs/index-49887.html.
77. John 13:34-35.
78. Gerald L. Sittser, *Love One Another: Becoming the Church Jesus Longs For* (Downers Grove, IL: InterVarsity Press, 2008), p. 38.
79. Ibid., p. 37.

80. Charles R. Swindoll, *Swindoll's New Testament Insights: Insights on Romans* (Grand Rapids, MI: Zondervan, 2010), p. 258.
81. Rowland Forman, Jeff Jones and Bruce Miller, *The Leadership Baton* (Grand Rapids, MI: Zondervan, 2004), p. 106.
82. B. F. Westcott, *Classic Christian Prayers*, p. 115.
83. Jonathan K. Dodson, *Gospel-Centered Discipleship* (Wheaton, IL: Crossway Books, 2012), p. 92.
84. Greg Ogden, *Transforming Discipleship*, p. 154.
85. Nehemiah 2:1-5.
86. Eugene Peterson, *The Unbusy Pastor* (Grand Rapids, MI: William B. Eerdmans, 1989), p. 19.
87. James 5:16.
88. Gerald L. Sittser, *Love One Another*, p. 96.
89. Greg Ogden, *Transforming Discipleship*, p. 154.
90. Colossians 1:9-10.
91. Galatians 3:3.
92. James Montgomery (1771-1854), "The Simplest Form of Speech," *Christian Worship*, (Exeter, England: The Paternoster Press, 1976), p. 535.
93. Rochelle Melander, *A Generous Presence* (Herndon, VA: The Alban Institute, 2006), p. 78.
94. Ibid., p. xi.
95. Philippians 2:4.
96. *American Heritage Talking Dictionary* (The Learning Company, Inc., 1997). All rights reserved.
97. Rochelle Melander, *A Generous Presence*, p. 78.
98. Ibid., pp. 79-80.
99. John Maikowski, used with permission.
100. Edward L. Smither, *Augustine as Mentor: A Model for Preparing Spiritual Leaders* (Nashville, TN: B&H Academic, 2008), p. 157.
101. Ibid., p. 160.
102. Owen Collins, Ed., *Classic Christian Prayers*, p. 160.
103. Anderson and Reese, *Spiritual Mentoring*, p. 28.
104. Rochelle Melander, *A Generous Presence*, p. 97.
105. Michael H. Shenkman, *Leader Mentoring* (Franklin Lakes, NJ: Career Press, 2008), pp. 109-110.
106. Tony Stoltzfus, *Leadership Coaching* (Virginia Beach, VA: Tony Stoltzfus, 2005), p. 149.
107. Ecclesiastes 5:1-2.
108. Anderson and Reese, *Spiritual Mentoring*, p. 28.
109. Revelation 2:7, 11, 17, 29; 3:6, 13, 22.
110. James 4:2.
111. 1 Samuel 3:9.

112. Richard Foster, *Celebration of Discipline* (San Francisco, CA: Harper and Row, 1978), p. 150.
113. Ted Loder, *Guerillas of Grace*, p. 35.
114. "Speak Lord in the Stillness," *Hymns of Faith* (London, England: Scripture Union, 1964), Hymn 85.
115. Mark Buchanan, *The Rest of God: Restoring Your Soul by Restoring Sabbath* (Nashville, TN: W Publishing Group, 2006), p. 191.
116. Matthew 22:18-20.
117. Matthew 8:26.
118. Matthew 6:28.
119. Matthew 20:22.
120. Luke 9:20.
121. Luke 10:36.
122. Luke 17:17.
123. Luke 18:41.
124. John 5:6.
125. John 21:15.
126. Michael Marquardt, *Leading with Questions: How Leaders Find the Right Solutions by Knowing What to Ask* (San Francisco, CA: Jossey-Bass, 2005), p. 65.
127. Luke 24:17-19.
128. John 21:15-17.
129. John 13:36-38.
130. Rick Lewis, *Mentoring Matters*, "Appendix 1: Surprised by Pain" by Keith Farmer (Oxford, England: Monarch Books, 2009), pp. 223-240.
131. Tony Stoltzfus, *Leadership Coaching*, p. 223.
132. Parker J. Palmer, *Let Your Life Speak* (San Francisco, CA: Jossey-Bass, 2000), p. 45.
133. Linda J. Miller and Chad W. Hall, *Coaching for Christian Leaders* (St. Louis, MO: Chalice Press, 2007), p. 33.
134. Owen Collins, Ed., *Classic Christian Prayers*, pp. 96-97.
135. W. Brad Johnson and Charles R. Ridley, *The Elements of Mentoring* (New York, NY: Palgrave MacMillan, 2004), pp. 9-11.
136. Sam Crabtree, *Practicing Affirmation* (Wheaton, IL: Crossway, 2011), pp. 19-20.
137. Ibid., p. 52.
138. *Holy Bible, New International Version*®, NIV®. Copyright © 1973, 1978, 1984, 2011 by Biblica, Inc.™ Used by permission of Zondervan. All rights reserved worldwide.
139. Sam Crabtree, *Practicing Affirmation*, p. 67.
140. John Maxwell, *Mentoring 101* (Nashville, TN: Thomas Nelson, 2004), p. 56.
141. Sam Crabtree, *Practicing Affirmation*, p. 160.
142. Owen Collins, Ed., *Classic Christian Prayers*, p. 161.

143. Bill Hybels, *Who You Are (When No One's Looking)* (Downers Grove, IL: InterVarsity Press, 1987), pp. 73-74.
144. Gerald L. Sittser, *Love One Another*, p. 161.
145. Not his actual name.
146. "Children Learn What They Live: A Memorial," 2005, accessed February 8, 2013, http://www.sixwise.com/newsletters/05/11/30/children-learn-what-they-live-a-memorial.htm.
147. Gerald L. Sittser, *Love One Another*, p. 162.
148. 2 Samuel 7:1-3.
149. Charles R. Swindoll, *David: A Man of Passion and Destiny* (Dallas, TX: Word Publishing, 1997), p. 206.
150. 2 Samuel 12:1-7.
151. John 8:3-11.
152. 2 Timothy 3:16.
153. Gerald L. Sittser, *Love One Another*, p. 169.
154. Galatians 6:1.
155. Owen Collins, Ed., *Classic Christian Prayers*, pp. 45-47.
156. Gerald L. Sittser, *Love One Another*, p. 169.
157. David A. Stoddard, *The Heart of Mentoring* (Colorado Springs, CO: NavPress, 2003), p. 26.
158. Howard Hendricks, *Teaching to Change Lives* (Portland, OR: Multnomah Press, 1987), p. 50.
159. Matthew 11:28-30.
160. Luke 24:27.
161. Luke 15:1.
162. Isaiah 42:3.
163. Matthew 12:20.
164. Regi Campbell, *Mentor Like Jesus* (Nashville, TN: B&H Publishing Group, 2009), pp. 88-92.
165. *Discovery Series* (McKinney, TX: Centers of Church Based Training [CCBT], 2002), www.ccbt.org.
166. Howard Hendricks, *Teaching to Change Lives*, p. 70.
167. Ibid., p. 57.
168. *Life Development Planner* (McKinney, TX: Centers of Church Based Training [CCBT], 2002), www.ccbt.org.
169. Matthew 11:28-30, (The Message).
170. Owen Collins, Ed., *Classic Christian Prayers*, p. 171.
171. Ken Gire, *The Reflective Life* (Colorado Springs, CO: Chariot Victor Publishing of Cook Communications, 1998), p. 161.
172. Psalm 1:1-2 (NIV, 2011).

NOTES

173. Warren Wiersbe to *Back to the Bible* mailing list for *Prayer, Praise and Promises Daily Devotional*. "Separated and Saturated," Psalm 1:1-2, http://www.backtothebible.org.
174. Ken Gire, *Windows of the Soul* (Grand Rapids, MI: Zondervan, 1996), p. 39.
175. Adele Ahlberg Calhoun, *Spiritual Disciplines Handbook* (Downers Grove, IL: InterVarsity Press, 2005), p. 53.
176. Bill Hybels, *Honest to God* (Grand Rapids, MI: Zondervan, 1990), p. 19.
177. David G. Benner, *Sacred Companions*, pp. 127-128.
178. John 13:15.
179. John 13:17.
180. Ken Gire, *Reflections on Your Life Journal* (Colorado Springs, CO: Chariot Victor Publishing of Cook Communications, 1998), p. 12.
181. Ken Gire, *Windows of the Soul*, p. 59.
182. Francis Chan, *Multiply* (Colorado Springs, CO: David C. Cook, 2012), p. 65.
183. Ephesians 2:19-22.
184. Francis Chan, *Multiply*, p. 48.
185. Genesis 1:22 (ESV).
186. Genesis 12:2-3.
187. Francis Chan, *Multiply*, p. 77.
188. Matthew 28:19.
189. Francis Chan, *Multiply*, p. 78.
190. Teri Lynne Underwood, *Prayers from the Pews*, p. 102.
191. Francis Chan, *Multiply*, p. 78.
192. Andrew Purves, *The Crucifixion of Ministry* (Downers Grove, IL: IVP Books, 2007), p. 12.
193. Rowland Forman, Jeff Jones and Bruce Miller, *The Leadership Baton*, (Grand Rapids, MI: Zondervan, 2004), p. 111.
194. Andrew Purves, *The Crucifixion of Ministry*, p. 13.
195. Ibid., p. 12.
196. Paul D. Stanley and J. Robert Clinton, *Connecting* (Colorado Springs, CO: NavPress, 1992). See Chapters 3 through 9 and Chapter 12.
197. Warren Bennis, *Still Surprised* (San Francisco, CA: Jossey-Bass, 2010), pp. 41-42.
198. Andrew Purves, *The Crucifixion of Ministry*, p. 24.
199. Joey O'Connor, *The Longing* (Grand Rapids, MI: Revell, 2004). See Chapter 6: "Broken Wholeness."
200. Luke 15:11-24.
201. *The Hymnal for Worship and Celebration* (Waco, TX: Word Music, 1986), Hymn #390.
202. Matthew 5:3.
203. Mike Mason, *The Gospel According to Job* (Wheaton, IL: Crossway Books, 1994), p. ix.
204. Charles R. Swindoll, *Simple Faith* (Dallas, TX: Word Publishing, 1991), p. 24.
205. William W. Klein, *Become What You Are* (Tyrone, GA: Authentic, 2006), p. 99.

206. Ibid., p. 99.
207. Mathew Woodley, *Holy Fools*, p. 149.
208. Matthew 6:9-15.
209. William W. Klein, *Become What You Are*, p. 156.
210. Adele Ahlberg Calhoun, *Spiritual Disciplines Handbook*, p. 218.
211. Haddon W. Robinson, *What Jesus said about Successful Living* (Grand Rapids, MI: Discovery House Publishers, 1991), p. 217.
212. Matthew 5:20.
213. William W. Klein, *Become What You Are*, p. 187.
214. Ibid., p. 212.
215. Ibid., p. 221.
216. Matthew 28:19-20.
217. Matthew 28:20.
218. Mark 11:1-11.
219. Philip Graham Ryken, *Luke, Volume 2, Luke 13-24*, (Phillipsburg, NJ: P&R Publishing, 2009), p. 645.
220. See Appendix 2: "Assessing the Whole Person," (pp. 201-204) in *The Leadership Baton*, by Rowland Forman, Jeff Jones and Bruce Miller (Grand Rapids, MI: Zondervan, 2004) for an inventory that will uncover how well you know the Scriptures.
221. David E. Garland provides other possible reasons why this may not be the Lord's Supper in the *Exegetical Commentary on the New Testament: Luke* (Grand Rapids, MI: Zondervan, 2001), p. 955.
222. Darrell L. Bock, *Luke: The NIV Application Commentary* (Grand Rapids, MI: Zondervan Publishing House, 1996), p. 616.
223. Charles R. Swindoll, *Insights on Luke* (Grand Rapids, MI: Zondervan, 2012), p. 523.
224. Tod Bolsinger, *ShowTime* (Grand Rapids, MI: Baker Books, 2004), pp. 23-24.
225. 2 Peter 1:5.
226. Caroline Alexander, *The Endurance: Shackelton's Legendary Antarctic Expedition* (New York, NY: Alfred A. Knopf, Inc., 1998), p. 13.
227. Bill Hybels, *Honest to God*, pp. 178-179.
228. 1 Peter 1:1.
229. 1 Peter 1:6.
230. 1 Peter 2:12.
231. Douglas Moo, *The NIV Application Commentary: 2 Peter and Jude* (Grand Rapids, MI: Zondervan, 1996), p. 47.
232. David B. Burns, *"Did You Ask A Good Question Today?"* 2009, http://www.sdcity.edu/Portals/0/CMS_Editors/MESA/PDFs/ResearchAcademy/DidYouAskAGoodQuestionToday.pdf.
233. (Periods of work/activity followed by times of rest/recreation/margin). If this is something you need to attend to, consider reading Bruce Miller's book, *Your Life in Rhythm* (Carol Stream, IL: Tyndale House Publishers, 2009).

234. If you wish to explore what it means to practice a Sabbath way-of-life, consider Mark Buchanan's book, *The Rest of God: Restoring Your Soul by Restoring Sabbath* (Nashville, TN: W Publishing Group, 2006).

235. Ele Parrott, *Transforming Together* (Chicago, IL: Moody Publishers, 2009), p. 91.

236. Jonathan K. Dodson, *Gospel-Centered Discipleship*, p. 155.

237. Rick Lewis, *Mentoring Matters*, "Appendix 1: Surprised by Pain" by Keith Farmer, pp. 223-240.

238. These are questions that Henry Rogers, Chaplain of *Interstate Batteries of America*, employs in his mentoring relationships. Used with permission.

239. David Powlison, *Seeing with New Eyes* (Phillipsburg, NJ: P&R Publishing Company, 2003), pp. 132-140. X-Ray Questions. This chapter is a powerful tool for self-evaluation and mutual evaluation with a highly trusted person or group. Powlison provides the biblical basis for each of these x-ray questions in this chapter as well.

240. Edmund Chan, *Built to Last* (Singapore: Covenant Resource Center, 2001), pp. 16-19.

241. Stanley and Clinton, *Connecting*, p. 12.

242. Jonathan K. Dodson, *Gospel-Centered Discipleship*, p. 12.

243. Michael H. Shenkman, *Leader Mentoring*, p. 18.

244. Timothy K. Jones, *Mentor and Friend* (Batavia, IL: Lion Publishing, 1991), p. 96.

245. Walter C. Wright, *Mentoring* (Bucks, UK: Paternoster Press, 2006), p. xxix.

246. Rick Lewis, *Mentoring Matters*, p. 20.

247. Francis Chan, *Multiply*, p. 7.

248. Elizabeth Inrig, *Release Your Potential*, pp. 84-85.

249. Anderson and Reese, *Spiritual Mentoring*, p. 27.

250. David A. Stoddard, *The Heart of Mentoring*, p. 11.

251. Ted W. Engstrom and Ron Jenson, *The Making of a Mentor* (Milton Keynes, Bucks, UK: Authentic Media, 2005), p. 1.

252. Lois J. Zachary, *The Mentor's Guide*, p. 3.

www.ingramcontent.com/pod-product-compliance
Lightning Source LLC
Chambersburg PA
CBHW060514080526
44586CB00012B/476